The Reconnection Agenda

Reuniting Growth and Prosperity

By Jared Bernstein

On The Economy

jaredbernsteinblog.com

To Kate, Ellie, Sarah, and Kay, with whom the connection remains eternally strong.

Table of Contents

Acknowledgments

First, I'd like to thank my family and especially my wife for helping me carve out the time to write the Reconnection Agenda.

Next, deep thanks to Ben Spielberg, my colleague at the Center on Budget and Policy Priorities (CBPP), with whom some of this material was developed, especially the work in Chapter 2 and much of the analysis of the inequality of opportunity.

Ben and Stephanie Landry were absolutely indispensable in editing the manuscript, the graphics, and the tables. I make mistakes; they catch mistakes.

All of my colleagues at CBPP deserve mention as I'm constantly bugging them and they're constantly educating me. In absolutely no order: Chuck Marr, Nick Johnson, Chad Stone, Chye-Ching Huang, Richard Kogan, Kathy Ruffing, Joel Friedman, Paul Van de Water, Bob Greenstein, Isaac Shapiro, Bryann DaSilva, Brandon DeBot, David Reich, Mike Leachman, Mike Mitchell, Sarah Lueck, Ed Bolen, Edwin Park, Judy Solomon, and Liz McNichol . . . to name a few. I truly appreciate your generosity and just because I put a lot of stuff we talk about in here doesn't mean I'm finished bothering you about it.

Thanks to CBPP's Anthony Martinez and Carolyn Jones for help with "comms" and admin.

And thanks to CBPP writ large for supporting my work on everything in here along with www.jaredbernsteinblog.com, where a lot of these ideas were developed.

For literally decades, I've worked with and learned from Larry Mishel and Dean Baker. Their fingerprints are all over the book.

Finally, I thank Alexander Berger and the Open Philanthropy Project for support of CBPP's Full Employment Project, from which much of this work is drawn.

Chapter 1

Introduction

While there are many uniquely positive attributes about the US economy, something is fundamentally wrong and here's what it is: economic growth can no longer be counted on to deliver broadly shared prosperity. Moreover, the policy agenda put forth by those with the power to do something about this fundamental problem has either proven to be inadequate to the task or has been blocked by gridlocked politics.

I do not come to these observations lightly. Allow me to take you down the path by which I got there. Let's start at the beginning, i.e., the beginning of the Obama administration.

December 16, 2008, Chicago, Illinois: On a dark, snowy Chicago afternoon in mid-December, it was my immense privilege to have a seat at an historic table. A few seats away from me sat the president-elect of the United States, the first African American to hold that title, Barack Obama. Next to him sat my new boss, the vice-president elect: Joe Biden. Scattered around the rectangle were some of the top economic and financial policy thinkers in the land: Christy Romer, Larry Summers, Tim Geithner.

Obama's First Economics Team

Yours truly, all the way to your right (of all places!).
Source: *The New Yorker*, Oct. 12, 2009.[1]

If the privilege was immense, so was the anguish. We knew the economy was in deep trouble. But we could not have known precisely how deep. As we sat there in December planning our economic counterattack against what would become known as the Great Recession, employers were cutting 700,000 jobs from their payrolls. The next month, as the new president took office, that number would jump to 800,000—job losses of a magnitude that

---

[1] http://www.newyorker.com/magazine/2009/10/12/inside-the-crisis

none of us had ever seen. Real gross domestic product (GDP), the broadest measure of the value of all the goods and services in the economy, was contracting at an 8 percent rate, which, if you follow these sorts of things, is technically termed a "nightmare."

I vividly recall the president-elect distinctly *not* emoting the attitude of the dog that caught the car it had been chasing ("OK . . . now what are you gonna do with it?"). Like the rest of us, he viewed this in no small part as a technical problem. That's not meant to sound callous. He was well aware of the human costs as well as the political costs of the deep recession. And had he not reflected on the latter (political costs), David Axelrod, his top political advisor, was there to remind him and the rest of us of them.

But economists view the economy as a system, not unlike the human body. Given the right environment, which in today's advanced economies is some version of capitalism, and leavened with various degrees of intervention from the government sector, it will generally flourish. Like the human body, it needs a steady flow of nourishing inputs, including energy, credit, skilled workers, and so on. And as long those flows are robust and the job market is providing adequate, fairly compensated opportunities for people to help convert those inputs into outputs (the goods and service we need and want), then the various sectors (households, businesses, government) will work together to keep the system going and growing.

At least, that's the theory. Around that table, I'd say we were less focused on econ 101 dynamic flow charts and more on the insight of the renowned economist Mike Tyson: "everyone's got a plan, until they get punched."

The US economy had been punched big time by an imploding housing bubble inflated by "innovative finance" and excessive leverage (borrowing), which is the subject of Chapter 7. During the 2000s housing boom, the sharp appreciation of housing values spun off a huge "wealth effect"—literally trillions of dollars of housing wealth—that financed home-equity withdrawals (borrowing against your ever more valuable home) and just a general sense of rising wealth among homeowners.[2] When the bubble popped, the wealth effect shifted into reverse and demand collapsed, disabling the elegant system described above.

Moreover, as Summers and Geithner explained to the newly-minted team, credit flows were shutting down as bank balance sheets were at least partially forced to recognize a bunch of very bad loans. (I say "partially" because I would soon learn a new phrase—"extend and pretend"—where bankers tell themselves non-performing loans will come back to life any day now!). If credit is the blood of the economic system, the veins of the US economy had suddenly become extremely sclerotic.

---

[2] Technically, the wealth effect describes the empirical fact that as someone's wealth appreciates by a dollar, they tend to spend about 3-5 cents of that dollar. Note that this holds even when the newfound wealth is just "on paper," as is the case in an appreciating home value.

So the discussion was all about what it would take to get the system back up and running. Large injections of liquidity would get credit flowing again. But it's one thing to get the blood flowing (to boost the credit supply) and quite another to get the heart beating strongly again (to stimulate demand). For that, we'd need a significant Keynesian stimulus package, and much of the conversation that day focused on the size and content of what would become the Recovery Act (and a big part of my life for the next few years, as VP Biden would be tagged to be its implementer-in-chief).

Credit flows, supply, demand . . . the technical expertise in the room, including my own, believed that our job first and foremost was to get the economic system back to some sort of equilibrium.

I personally was there in part because of a related but different expertise: not just the creation of growth, but the distribution of growth. Obama/Biden ran on a platform that focused not just on getting the economy growing again, but on implementing policies that would steer more of that growth to the middle class.

This was an especially big deal to the new VP. Though I'd met him briefly before, our first of many long conversations had taken place a few weeks prior to the Chicago meeting in his Delaware home. I got there around 10 AM (on Amtrak—when you visit Biden, you travel by his favorite mode of transport), and as he walked me into the kitchen and we passed an impressive new latte/espresso maker, Biden asked me if I wanted a cup of coffee.

"Sure," I replied. So he reached into a cabinet right above the fancy machine and pulled out a jar of instant coffee.

"Really?" I blurted out, pointing at the machine.

"Oh, that's Jill's [his wife]. I've got no idea how to work it. You still want coffee?"

It's a test of my blue collar street cred, I decided, so I said, "of course!" and proceeded to drink about the worst cup of coffee I'd had before or since.

But our conversation was as memorable as the instant coffee was terrible. And as the Obama/Biden era comes to an end, this is an important time to revisit what was said.

Joe Biden gets a lot of flack for . . . probably the best way to put it is: for being Joe Biden. He's a character who can and does talk himself into all kinds of trouble. But there's something genuinely remarkable, or remarkably genuine, about him: after being in the Senate, an otherworldly institution that pretty much erases your connection to normal people (Senator E. Warren: take note!), Biden has somehow maintained a visceral concern for the struggles of the middle class.

As he will remind you, he grew up with those struggles. And more than almost anyone else I've met in government service, he believes that there's a role for government in helping middle-class people meet their economic challenges. That's what he and President Obama campaigned on and it's what Biden and I talked about that morning. He had his own ideas, of course—they'd been intensely campaigning for a year. But he wanted to know what it would take to reconnect economic growth and the prosperity of the middle class.

My response—thinking ahead to the Chicago meeting—was that the first thing it's going to take is economic growth. The last few decades had confirmed beyond a reasonable doubt that growth was not sufficient for middle-class prosperity, but it was obviously necessary. And like I said, we were in the midst of a raging downturn.

But Biden pushed me to think beyond the downturn. With considerable foresight, he pointed out that if the past few recoveries hadn't much reached the middle class, why should we expect the next one to do so? One of the things we discussed—the topic of Chapter 3—was the importance of full employment and what it would take to get there. Seeing the Recovery Act coming, we also talked about using crisis to foment opportunity, particularly as regards building up the nation's deteriorating stock of public goods, aka, infrastructure investment.

Today, I sit well on the other side of those tumultuous days. The Great Recession is far behind us. The measures we took, along with those of the Fed, worked pretty well—in fact, much as we thought they would.[3] I recall a discussion with Larry Summers, an

---

[3] Those who recall a December 2013 paper by Christy Romer and me will reasonably beg to differ regarding my "this worked-out-as-we-expected" assertion. In that paper, Christy and I took our incoming administration's forecast for GDP and unemployment and appended our estimates of the "deltas"—the changes in GDP and unemployment we thought the Recovery Act would induce. Later, post-hoc estimates

economist who's been through enough of these sorts of crises to take the long view, during the early days of our work together, wherein he pointed out the differences between our much deeper interventions than those of the Europeans, suggesting that a bit of a natural experiment was underway. As I write today in April 2015, they're struggling with anemic growth rates and high unemployment while our macroeconomy is relatively strong.

I'm not saying we got everything right by a longshot. We didn't. Our interventions ended too soon and we pivoted to deficit reduction years before we should have. But let me assure you that this book is not going to re-litigate this question; we have other big fish to fry.

Instead, my point is this. Present company excluded, that Chicago meeting room was filled with some of the best economists we've got, men and women with the clearest understanding of the economic system. The measures we started crafting that day, ones that Axelrod, Phil Schiliro, and others helped to somehow cram through an awfully tough Congress, had their expected impact.[4]

And yet, Biden was right. The ensuing recovery has once again largely failed to reach the middle class. What growth we've seen

---

of that question matched our own. In other words, we were wrong about the levels because we underestimated the depth of the recession. But we were in the right ballpark on the changes.

[4] This piece I wrote for the *Washington Post* provides more background on the technocratic aspects of our response to the Great Recession and defends that "expected impact" point: http://www.washingtonpost.com/opinions/technocrats-know-how-to-fix-the-economy-and-they-did/2015/01/23/4d6cf83c-a29e-11e4-903f-9f2faf7cd9fe_story.html

has been concentrated at the top of the economic scale. We are now (in early 2015) more than five years into an economic expansion that began in mid-2009, much to the relief of the folks in that Chicago meeting room. But income and wealth inequality are growing strongly again; corporate profitability has never been higher; the financial markets are again on a tear. Real median household income, on the other hand, is still lower than it was when the recovery began.

And that is why I needed to write this book. The smartest economists I know demonstrably had the expertise to restart the system, even after a major crash. But not to put too fine a point on it, no one knows how to fix the part of the system that's still broken. In fact, no one seems to know the answer to Biden's question: how can we reconnect middle-class prosperity and overall growth?

The Reconnection Agenda

This book aspires to answer that question. I'll spend a few pages explaining the problem as I understand it, but the majority of what follows is less diagnostic and more prescriptive. One of the reasons so many people feel like the country and the economy are "going in the wrong direction" is that they see neither solutions that make sense to them nor policy makers willing to try to help. By the time you finish these pages (if I've done my job), you will see a clear, plausible way forward, a way in which growth once again reaches down and lifts the living standards of the vast majority of households, not just a narrow slice at the top of the wealth scale.

Of course, this immediately raises a pressing question. Assume for a moment that I actually lay out a convincing reconnection agenda. Well, just because you can see the path forward doesn't mean you can start marching down it. What if it's blocked by hostile forces, or today's equivalent of the same: gridlocked politics?

It's a fair question, indeed: What good are great ideas (just assume for the moment that what follows is brimming with them) if no one in power is interested in implementing them? Who wants to be dressed up with nowhere to go?

Despair not. Step one is making a compelling case for the economic policies that our political class should be implementing if they want to reconnect the growing economy with the lives of the many households for whom growth has become little more than a spectator sport. Later steps, as I argue below, grow out of the obvious need for a new policy agenda, a need I believe is recognized by a large majority of the electorate, though of course they have very different ideas about how that need should be met.

In other words, one reason there's no real political pressure to do much about the disconnect between growth and more broadly shared prosperity—what I'll call "the fundamental problem" in the pages that follow—is that it's not at all clear to either the average person or the policy elite what should be done. The choir isn't singing because they lack the music. Once they get the hymnal, if it makes sense to them—that is, us—we will sing. And if we do so loudly enough, we will be heard.

More plainly, there's great demand for real, commonsense, easily understood solutions to the fundamental problem. Supply of such ideas, on the other hand, is lacking. By the way, in the basic economic model, that would imply that this book—again, we're still employing the wholly self-serving assumption that these ideas are "all that and a bag of chips," as we used to say—would be very valuable (high demand, low supply = higher price). And yet, it's free. Thus, our first of many examples of how the basic economic model can lead you astray.

At any rate, for now, suspend your justified lack of faith in our political system and let's start by looking at the lay of the economic landscape, wherein I've uncovered bad news and good news.

We've already discussed the bad news: neither one of our sharply divided political parties has much in their economic policy toolboxes that would fix the fundamental problem of narrowly shared growth. That's the motivation for a reconnection agenda.

And we've already touched upon the good news, as well: when it comes to growth, we in America have a real advantage over those in other advanced economies. We've built a flexible, resilient, resourceful, and innovative economy that, unlike those in Europe, has shaken off the mistakes of the recent past—and we're talking about some really big mistakes with sharply negative consequences—that led to the deep recession at the end of the last decade. As noted above, we're more than five years into a stable recovery, posting decent, if not stellar, growth rates and adding jobs at a solid and reliable clip.

But here's the problem: from the perspective of most working households, that word "recovery" needs air quotes. Adding some numbers to facts stated above, since the current expansion began in the second half of 2009 through the end of 2014, GDP was up 14 percent but the typical household's real income was 1.5 percent below where it was in June of 2009. Corporate profits, on the other hand, recently reached their highest level on record as a share of national income, with the record beginning in 1929!

Statistics like that are not meant to foment "class warfare"—to be honest, I'm not even sure what that political attack phrase even means, though I tend to hear it bandied about by those whose class is the only one doing great (with this, I'm with Warren Buffett: ". . . there's been class warfare going on for the last 20 years, and my class has won"[5]).

But let me be unequivocally clear: I celebrate all that growth and profitability. Without it, we can't even begin to discuss the disconnect that motivates what follows in this book. Early on I said growth is necessary but not sufficient to boost the middle class. Well, it isn't just necessary; it's essential, and it constitutes the good part of the recent story of the US economy, especially compared to others.

---

[5] http://www.washingtonpost.com/blogs/plum-line/post/theres-been-class-warfare-for-the-last-20-years-and-my-class-has-won/2011/03/03/gIQApaFbAL_blog.html

Recovery . . . What Recovery?

This insight regarding the limits of growth alone was brought home for me during a presentation I gave here in Washington DC to an audience of what you might call "policy elites"—people, like myself, whose job it is to try to figure out what's going right and wrong in the economy from the perspective of households across the income spectrum. This was during the run-up to the 2014 midterm elections and this particular group wanted to know why President Obama and the Democrats weren't getting more "love" on the economy from an electorate that was probably most efficiently described as deeply pissed off.

As I was working my way toward the above diagnosis, I kept using the word "recovery," as in, "the economic recovery that's been ongoing since the second half of 2009 just isn't reaching most households." Out of the corner of my eye, I noticed a man I knew to be a prominent pollster unable to suppress his scowl so I stopped the proceedings and asked him what was bothering him.

"If you mention the word 'recovery' to people, they don't know what you're talking about. And they conclude you don't know what they're talking about. It's not just that they feel disconnected from an economy that's supposedly growing. It's that they don't think anyone understands or knows what to do about their situation."

Didn't President Obama and his economic team—a team of which I was once a member—already try to do just that?

The Inadequate Toolbox

The problem is that we're rich with diagnoses but poor with prescriptions. And that's because our economic policy toolbox is woefully undersupplied. Surely, as noted above regarding the actions we took against the Great Recession, we have some of the right tools to fix what's broken in a broad, macroeconomic sense. But there are too few effective tools devoted to reconnection.

That's partly because we've allowed our thinking on the options to become so narrow, so cramped, that while too many families feel like their economic lifeboats are taking on water faster than they can bail, policy makers—and I'm talking about the minority that actually want to help them—are unable to offer them much more than "we see the holes and the water flowing in. Here's a graph of the rate of the inflow!"

Try to think of a policy that's out there in the debate to patch the holes. I'll wait . . .

I suspect some readers thought "what debate?" Checkmate. Others may respond, "raising the minimum wage!" Fair point, for sure, and I give that movement a lot of credit (Chapter 9). It's also a solution that's increasingly widely embraced. In that aforementioned 2014 midterm election, one that was a disaster for Democrats, a number of deeply red states (including South Dakota, Arkansas, and Nebraska) raised their minimum wage levels. But let's keep it real. A higher minimum wage is a good idea and moderate increases in the wage floor have a solid history of accomplishing their goal of boosting the incomes of low-wage workers without many negative side effects.[6] But a higher minimum only addresses a small part of the problem.

Why is the economic policy toolbox so incompletely stocked? Actually, the fact that the minimum wage is one of the few things in there provides a hint. After decades of asserting that wage mandates are a scourge on free market economies, many economists have become comfortable with higher minimum wages.[7] The *New York Times* editorial page—decidedly liberal but not exactly "bally five-year-planners," as PG Wodehouse used to call the commies—and the *Washington Post* editorial board regularly endorse increases. There's been a great deal of high quality research on the issue, and it's solidly disproved the notion that the positive impacts of the policy are swamped by the negative effects that opponents typically raise.

In other words, it has become accepted by many—not all—elites that higher minimum wages do not "disrupt markets," or at least not very much. Unfortunately, very few other policy ideas targeting the great disconnect make that cut.

---

[6] The Congressional Budget Office predicted in early 2014 that a three year phase-in of an increase in the Federal minimum wage from $7.25 to $10.10 would lift the earnings of 24.5 million workers and lead to job losses of 500,000. That's 49 beneficiaries to every one job loser. And some minimum wage scholars think CBO high-balled the predicted job losses. http://jaredbernsteinblog.com/the-minimum-wage-increase-and-the-cbos-job-loss-estimate/

[7] In this poll, 40-50 percent of economists agreed that the benefits to low-skilled workers from raising the minimum wage outweighed the costs: http://www.igmchicago.org/igm-economic-experts-panel/poll-results?SurveyID=SV_br0lEq5a9E77NMV

Market Failures are a Lot More Common than You Think

I'm here to tell you that this litmus test—"does the idea disrupt markets?" (and if it does, get it away from me!)—is decidedly, definitely, unquestionably the wrong test to be running. It's the wrong question and as the novelist Thomas Pynchon's warned, "If they can get you asking the wrong questions, they don't have to worry about answers."

The right question is quite different: is the private market economy failing to provide something important and if so, are there policies that can be efficiently implemented to offset that market failure?

Both parts of the question are important and let's be rigorously bipartisan here: there's market failure and government failure, and while the right tends to deny the former the left mustn't deny the latter. It's not enough to portray the fundamental disconnect, pointing out that some important economic functions are broken (as I'll do in the next chapter). You have to have a solution that both makes sense and has a decent chance of generating the intended outcome in the context of our economy.

Moreover, as noted in passing above but discussed in detail in Chapter 9, there's a relatively new wrinkle regarding government failure. Government's inability to enact and implement useful economic policies in recent years is by no means a sole function of administrative incompetence or feckless bureaucrats. It is a strategy.

When government doesn't work, whether it's a website or a Recovery Act (as noted, the latter worked well, despite stiff opposition), it strengthens the narrative of the YOYOs—the "you're-on-your-own-ers." The YOYOs are the folks calling for less government without regard for the challenges we face, like climate, an aging demographic, and explosive financial markets, all of which require government solutions (the subject of Chapter 8). They're the privatizers, the always-cut-never-increase tax advocates, the "we can't afford social insurance" crowd. Their extreme wing would default on the public debt. They stand against "Obamacare"—very much a government solution to a market failure—as it distinctly embodies the "we're-in-this-together" (WITT) ethic they diametrically oppose.[8]

So while I readily admit government failure—you'd have to be swimming in de'Nile not to see that in contemporary politics—it's essential to recognize that such failure is neither an accident nor an immutable act of nature. It's a tactic that can be reversed.

In fact, it must be reversed if we're going to correct market failures, the most important of which is the long-term failure of the economy to create the quantity and quality of jobs needed to reconnect growth to the living standards of the majority.

---

[8] Progressive economist Dean Baker adds an important nuance to this construct. It's not that many in the YOYO political class disdain economic policy. It's that they use such policy to enrich themselves and their donors as opposed to the broader public, including patent, trade, and anti-union policies. In other words, they're not really enamored of market outcomes, either. http://jaredbernsteinblog.com/loser-liberalism-is-a-winner/

As you'll see in what follows, to correct this fundamental economic problem, we're going to need to directly create jobs for those who need and want to work yet can't find a job. We'll need to take steps to raise the historically low bargaining power of the majority of the workforce by elevating full employment to a national goal (Chapter 3). We're going to need to boost our manufactures by fighting back against international competitors who underprice their exports to us (Chapter 4).

Chapter 5 explains how both monetary policy by the Federal Reserve and fiscal policy of the federal government need to step up and play a stronger role in addressing the fundamental problem. Chapter 6 shows that even getting to full employment isn't enough to reconnect everyone to the growing economy. Part of the agenda must reach out to those who struggle to make ends meet, even when jobs are plentiful, including the long-term unemployed, those displaced from the "old economy," and the millions with criminal records. And once we get to full employment, for the benefits of growth to really reach the people who need it most, we've got to stay there. That means doing away with the "economic shampoo cycle"—bubble, bust, repeat—that's characterized our economy for decades now (Chapter 7).

We're going to have to invest more in public goods, from infrastructure to education to a more buoyant safety net to things that slow environment degradation (Chapter 8). Attacking the market failure of poverty and the class immobility of those who start the race with huge odds stacked against them must also be elevated as a national goal.

Thus, I lay out the reconnection agenda in the form of problem, diagnosis, and prescriptions. But after scribbling away in the business for decades now, I've learned that a reconnection agenda will not develop just because some economist writes down some ideas and plots some data (I know . . . slow learner). There needs to be a social and political context within these ideas that can gain traction, along with a clear-eyed view of the extent of government failure and what must be done to correct it. That's a long game for sure, but I end the book in Chapter 10 with some thoughts about why it's so important and how we can move it forward.

All of which raises this final introductory question:

Who's this "We" You Keep Talking About?

So far, I've told you (in Chapter 2, I'll show you) that the US economy, strong and flexible as it is, is failing in fundamental ways to provide the opportunities its citizens need to claim their fair share of the growth. I've even hinted at necessary actions that can help, to be elaborated in later chapters. But readers who've tracked national politics in recent years have a right to ask: just who do you think is going to undertake to do all of this great stuff? As I said right at the beginning, those with the power to do something about the fundamental disconnect are not doing what needs to be done. What's going to change that?

As already stressed, part of what I'm betting on here is that a large swath of people will respond a lot more positively than you'd think to an agenda of the type for which I'm advocating. Let me reiterate, because I think this is so important: I'm convinced that a significant majority of the American electorate is looking for hope on this fundamental economic problem of disconnected growth and prosperity. They just haven't heard convincing solutions from the left or the right.

The YOYOs run around arguing, unconvincingly to most, that government is the problem, while most Democrats nibble at the edges with YOYO-light, maybe sprinkling in a minimum wage increase. Everyone treats the private market economy like a delicate vase that mustn't be bumped, while almost no one in prominence has the courage to stand up and say the following:

Guess what? The economy's broken. It's still growing and that's great, but the critical market mechanisms that we used to be able to count on to fairly distribute that growth are broken and they're not going to get fixed by ignoring them. Nor will they get fixed by most of the solutions put forth by the left or the right. On the right, cutting taxes and "red tape" and repealing Obamacare won't do anything to increase the quantity and quality of jobs. On the left, providing better educational opportunities, while an essential piece of the longer-term puzzle, won't help parents get better jobs today.[9] While the provision of affordable health care is a tremendously important advance, Obamacare won't solve the

---

[9] And, for the record, even the pay of young, college-educated workers has been flat in real terms for years now. Economist Larry Mishel wrote in early 2015: ". . . since 2002, the bottom 80 percent of wage earners, including both male and female college graduates, have actually seen their wages stagnate or fall."
http://www.nytimes.com/2015/02/23/opinion/even-better-than-a-tax-cut.html

disconnect either. Raising the minimum wage—another venerable policy—won't reach the middle class.

Instead, we've got to make full employment a national goal, boost our manufactures, create the needed jobs if the market won't do it, and stabilize our financial sector so it doesn't blow everything up every few years. Each one of those calls for intervening in markets in ways that most policy makers eschew, but that reticence is why we're stuck where we are today.

A convincing agenda built on that foundation could well create the "we" that I'm talking about.

Even if I'm wrong, however, all is far from lost. As I discuss in Chapter 9, while national politics may well remain broken for years to come, sub-national politics has an urgency that's been lost on the national stage. While Congress muddles about in ideological darkness, governors and mayors have to actually do things. They have real states to run, with university systems, public schools, public safety, and infrastructure to worry about. Of course, they lack the purse strings of Congress and they cannot on their own tackle national problems, like offsetting recessions with countercyclical policy (i.e., policies that switch on when the economy tanks and off when it recovers).[10] But the ideas I put forth could be useful to them as well.

---

[10] The fact that states are not allowed to run budget deficits means they must depend on the federal government, which can run deficits, for countercyclical policies in recessions, like extended Unemployment Insurance.

A Note About this Book (important if you plan to read on)

Though I've printed some copies, I'm thinking of this largely as
an e-book and, as such, I'd like to consider it a "living book," one
that can change and grow and shrink to reflect real time
developments in both data and policy. *The* reconnection agenda is
really, of course, *a* reconnection agenda. There are many ideas
that can help reunite growth and prosperity and future economic
developments will solve some problems and create new ones. The
beauty of an e-book is that I can update the manuscript to reflect
the times.

It is also the case (as I fear you've recognized already) that this is
a largely self-edited volume. As noted in the acknowledgements,
my colleague Ben Spielberg read everything closely and provided
invaluable feedback and edits, but because a) I wanted to get these
ideas out there before the 2016 election debate got too far along,
b) I plan to update the text as necessary, and c) publishers are just
not that enamored of this sort of wonkishness, the flow here is
pretty much right from the kitchen stove to the table, piping hot,
but without enough of a copy-edit.

That's where you come in! I've set up a form
(http://goo.gl/forms/jM4xzUErZA) where you can send
corrections and suggestions. And when I make the fix, I'll add
your name (or "handle") to the acknowledgements, implicating
you too in the goal of reuniting growth and prosperity!

So, with all of that throat clearing out of the way, welcome to the
reconnection agenda! I must be crazy or ridiculously hard-headed

or just plain boring, but after decades of pushing on these sorts of ideas, I continue to find them not just essential but uplifting. That's partly due to the WITT ("we're in this together") philosophy that guides much of what follows, but it's also because I see the potential of the US economy to reach everyone in ways that it used to but hasn't for many years. To not try to realize that potential is unacceptable, and thus, time spent crafting, updating, perfecting and promoting a reconnection agenda is not just time well spent. It's some of the most rewarding work people in my field can undertake, and I thank you, readers everywhere, for giving it a look and elevating the ideas in any and every way you can.

Chapter 2

Growth Without Prosperity

I've written many books and papers on the topics of the fundamental problem of growth without broadly shared prosperity, the absence of full employment, imbalanced trade, political dysfunction, and so on. But too many of these publications were poorly weighted in terms of problem and solution. That is, I've spent at least three-quarters, and often more, of my time explaining the problem, leaving too little room for solutions. That's a common economists' disease, as we often have lots of data and charts on what's wrong and less to say about what to do about it.

But for this book, I wanted to work hard to invert those diagnosis/prescription shares. So to ensure that we don't get bogged down in problem-exposition at the expense of solutions, this chapter will be a brief collection of bullet points, with evidentiary charts and tables relegated to Appendix A. Though you could say I'm cheating by dint of the detailed appendix, I'm actually quite proud to point out that this is the shortest chapter in the book.

To be sure, I am 100 percent wedded to careful and thorough diagnosis. Obviously, to get that wrong would undermine the prescription, i.e., the reconnection agenda. But we are thankfully at a point in the evolution of these debates where the major points are not broadly contested. Of course, you can always find someone who essentially turns your graphs upside-down and says "everything's fine!" But in the real world, the strength of the evidence makes my diagnostic job easier.

The need to reconnect growth and prosperity of course implies that a disconnection occurred at some point in the past. The facts below make this case and importantly tie the inequality of economic outcomes (in wages, incomes, and wealth) to real wage and income stagnation, to the opportunities facing those on the wrong side of the inequality divide, to macroeconomic growth, and even to the political process that's needed to reverse these trends.

[Those who are well aware of these facts and don't feel the need to revisit them can skip to the next chapter without losing the flow of the argument. All figures and tables referenced in the sections that follow can be found in Appendix A.]

The Rise of Inequality

- Figure A1 is aptly entitled "Growing Together, Growing Apart." It shows real family income for low-, middle-, and high-income families from the late 1940s up to 2013. Because real income *levels* are very different, I've indexed them to equal 100 in 1979 so each group's income is expressed as a percentage of its 1979 income. Between 1947 and the late 1970s, the rate of income growth for each group was roughly the same, approximately doubling over this period. However, since the late 1970s the income trends have diverged. Real income for the bottom 20 percent of Americans has stagnated over the past 35 years and median income has grown much more slowly than it did prior to 1980. At the same time, until recently, incomes for the top 5 percent have mostly remained on their pre-1980 trajectory.

- A limitation of the above data is that it leaves out taxes, transfers (e.g., the value of food stamps), the value of publicly- and employer-provided medical care, and capital gains and losses (income from the sale of assets). The addition of the value of these variables is both instructive and important but can also be misleading. For example, given the unique cost distortions in the US health care system, assigning the market value of publicly-provided health care significantly inflates incomes of those who receive such benefits (the fact that drugs and medical services here in the US are overpriced compared to other advanced economies shows up as higher incomes for poor people on Medicaid). Also, top 1 percent income is highly cyclical and sensitive to the boom/bust cycle I analyze in Chapter 7, which is partly due to the fact that much of it is income from capital gains.[11]

That said, Figure A2 shows the sharp increase in inequality of comprehensive income, as income for the top 1 percent grew much more quickly than income for all other groups.

- Some inequality critics/deniers argue that while inequality has gone up, the equalizing impact of progressive taxes and transfers has offset its growth. The data in the next figure belie this claim.

Using the same comprehensive data as the last figure, Figure A3 shows that income inequality grew about the same on a pre-tax/transfer basis as on a post-tax/transfer basis. "Income shares" describe what percentage of total income accrues to each group, and this chart represents the change in income shares between 1979 and 2011 for each quintile, both before and after taxes and transfers are taken into account. As shown in the chart, the share of income held by low- and middle-income people declined by more than a percentage point each between 1979 and

---

[11] Ben Spielberg and I examine these measurement issues here: http://jaredbernsteinblog.com/wp-content/uploads/2014/11/CBO_Data_Report_11_24_14-Final.pdf

2011, a clear symptom of growing inequality. The majority of the substantial increase in income share for the top quintile was due mostly to the increase in income share for the top 1 percent. While analyzing after-tax/transfer income reduces the magnitude of the changes in income shares, this trend of increasing inequality is evident in both sets of bars (pre- and post-tax/transfer); in 2011, households in the first through fourth quintiles lost over $5,000 on average after taxes and transfers relative to a scenario where income shares remained constant at 1979 levels.

- For working families, labor market earnings are the building blocks of their income. Figure A4 and Table A1 show remarkable (and high quality, administratively-sourced) trends comparing the real annual earnings of the bottom 90 percent to the top 1 percent. As with the first income chart, the real earnings for both groups approximately doubled between 1947 and 1979. After 1979, however, the two groups' earnings diverged sharply. Whereas high-income individuals (the top 1 percent) earned in 2012 approximately 250 percent of what they made in 1979, the bottom 90 percent saw an increase of only about 17 percent. As shown in the table, which also provides actual earnings values (in 2012 dollars), this disparity meant that the ratio between the earnings of the two groups, which had remained around

9:1 between 1947 and 1979, jumped to over 20:1 by 2012.

There is a key reconnection agenda point that can be gleaned from Figure A1: to the extent that wages or incomes grew in the post-1979 period for the bottom 90 percent, they largely did so in the full employment period of the late 1990s.

- Sticking with wages, the next three figures (A5, A6, and A7) break the analysis down to the most basic building block: the hourly wage for low-, middle-, and high-wage workers by gender. The dispersion of real wages is evident in all three figures, but important nuances exist by gender. Real wages for middle- and low-wage men have been remarkably stagnant and are actually lower in real terms today than in the late 1970s. Middle-wage women, on the other hand, have done better than their male counterparts, a trend that has been associated with increased labor demand in sectors that favor women, like health care, and vice versa for middle-wage men, who have been hurt by the loss of manufacturing jobs (as discussed in Chapter 5).

However, outside of the full-employment 1990s, low-wage women have not seen much real wage growth, and since 2000 wage growth has been largely flat or falling for middle-wage women as well.

- The next wage figure (A8) is a particularly important one that I reference throughout the book. Another version of the "together/apart" theme, it shows the typical worker's real compensation (wages plus non-wage benefits) plotted against output-per-hour, aka productivity growth.

  The figure shows how the growth of inequality since the late 1970s works like a "wedge" between overall growth and the pay of many of the workers contributing to that growth. The bakers are baking a bigger pie, but they're getting smaller slices in return. In the ensuing pages, I discuss some of the factors driving this wedge and thus informing the corrective/connective policy ideas that follow.

- The next two figures (A9 and A10) show historically large increases in inequality in market incomes and wealth from long time series data assembled by noted inequality expert Thomas Piketty and some of his colleagues. Their results are based on pre-tax income and exclude the additional tax, transfer, and medical care data in the comprehensive series featured earlier (although these Piketty et al. data do include realized capital gains).

  The first figure (A9) plots income shares for the top 1 percent and top 0.5 percent. As seen earlier, since the late 1970s, income concentration has been steadily rising. The top 1 percent income share, after falling to a low of a little over 8 percent in 1976, has by now more than doubled and stands at levels comparable to the late 1920s. Increased income inequality is particularly evident over the last twenty years. Between 1993 and 2012, real incomes for the top 1 percent grew at over 13 times the rate at which real incomes grew for the rest of the population. Most recently, from 2009 to 2012, real incomes for the bottom 99 percent grew by less than 1 percent while real incomes for the top 1 percent grew by over 31 percent.

One critical point from these data is that rising inequality, though still very much evident after accounting for taxes and transfers, is largely driven by market outcomes. Based on that insight, many of the prescriptions that follow in the rest of this book target the pre-tax income distribution. Chapter 8 emphasizes the interdependence between pre- and post-tax distributions, noting a) the impact of top tax rates on the share of income going to the top 1 percent, and b) the long-term, inequality-reducing impact of some safety net programs. But that said, there's no question that a truly robust reconnection agenda must target the distribution of market outcomes. We cannot redistribute our way out of this.

Figure A10 provides data back to the early 1900s on wealth, showing how wealth concentration has also increased steadily since the late 1970s and is still in the process of climbing back to historically high levels. The top 1 percent owned about 23 percent of all wealth in 1978; by 2012, this narrow group owned 42 percent of all wealth. The bottom 90 percent has seen no increase in net wealth during this period. As with increasing income concentration, most of this pattern can be attributed to the wealth of the top 0.5 percent.

Inequality and Opportunity

A key theme of the reconnection agenda is the growing relationship between unequal outcomes and unequal opportunities. While the former is easier to show graphically than the latter, the next four figures demonstrate the connection:

- *Increased residential segregation by income*: In Figure A11, data compiled by Sean Reardon and Kendra Bischoff shows how economic segregation in neighborhoods has increased dramatically over the last 40 years. Over 60 percent of families lived in middle-income neighborhoods in 1970; by 2008, that number had dropped to approximately 40 percent. Children living in high-poverty neighborhoods are exposed to more violence, underfunded public goods, and "toxic stress" (see Chapter 8) than children living in low-poverty neighborhoods. These environmental hazards have negative impacts on cognition, academics, and later life outcomes.

- *Growing disparity of college debt*: Figure A12 (also referenced in Chapter 8) shows how the ratio of education debt to income for the bottom 50 percent of the net worth distribution (net worth equals income plus wealth minus debts) has more than doubled since 1995. This ratio almost doubled for the next 45 percent as well, but it remains both lower and unchanged for the top 5 percent.

In chapter 8, I point out how large amounts of education debt negatively affect later outcomes including college completion (with obvious implications for diminished mobility), earnings, and wealth (e.g., home ownership).

- *Growing inequality of enrichment opportunities*: Figure A13 compares families' abilities to invest in enrichment opportunities for their children, including books, computers, high quality child care, tutoring, sports leagues, summer camps, art lessons, and private schooling. There was already a sizable discrepancy in enrichment spending between the richest 20 percent and poorest 20 percent of families in the early 1970s, but the ratio between the two had jumped from about 4:1 in the '70s to about 7:1 by the mid-2000s. Later I explain how the problem of this shift in child-investment by income class is exacerbated by the disinvestment in public goods in this space. That is, as the ability of low-income families to afford enrichment activities like art and sports has fallen relative to wealthier families, public schools are less likely to provide them.

- *Kids from towns and cities with fewer families in the middle class have less upward mobility*: Economists Bradbury and Triest show that the fraction of the population in a "commuting zone" (mostly towns and cities) with incomes between the 25th and 75th percentiles of the nationwide income distribution is positively correlated with economic mobility (see Figure A14). This mobility measure is defined as how far up the income scale we would expect a teenager who grew up in a low-income family in a given commuting zone to get by the time that teenager was an adult. These same authors show a negative correlation between the Gini coefficient, a measure of inequality in a given region, and this mobility measure. Most likely the mechanisms at work here are similar to those behind Figure A11, underscoring the point that kids who grow up where there's more inequality are less likely to be upwardly mobile.

Those charts give you a good statistical lay of the land we'll be traversing in what follows. But before getting into the agenda, I suspect many readers are reasonably wondering what the heck happened in the last thirty-plus years to cause such a clear break point in incomes, wages, and wealth that were once growing together and are now growing apart. Others may wonder, "OK, I see the problem . . . but why does it matter?"

Both of these questions get treatments in later chapters, but a quick sketch of the answers here sets the context for the reconnection agenda that follows.

Factors Contributing to the Growth in Inequality

- *The decline in worker bargaining power*: The reduction in the bargaining power of most workers has been a major factor driving wage inequality in general and the "wedge" shown in Figure A8. But what explains the loss of bargaining power? The decline in unionization of course explains some of this reduction (see Figure A15, which shows the inverse relationship between the change in union membership and the share of income held by the top 10 percent). But more recently, bargaining power has been hammered by the following developments:

  - *The absence of full employment*: This critical factor is at the heart of the reconnection agenda and is the topic of the next chapter. Chapter 4 emphasizes the failure of fiscal policy to press for full employment; this too is a related cause of higher inequality, particularly in recent years when austerity (contractionary fiscal policy even in the face of weak private sector demand) has become a dominant approach to fiscal policy, especially in Europe.

○ *Globalization*: This is another important part of the explanation and, as such, it too gets its own chapter (Chapter 5). It is well understood and documented that globalization contributes to inequality when a wealthy country like the United States increases trade with lower wage countries.[12] But what is underappreciated and is thus explored in Chapter 5 is the role of our large and persistent trade deficits in driving this outcome. Though one should always be careful to not read too much into a couple of lines on a graph as an explanation for relationships like this with lots of moving parts, Figure A16 plots manufacturing compensation against the trade deficit as a share of GDP. Again, the inverse correlation is very clear, as higher trade deficits are clearly associated with stagnant earnings of factory workers. Chapter 5 argues in some detail that there's a lot more than correlation going on here.

---

[12] http://economics.mit.edu/files/6613

○ *Technological change and the college wage premium*: Over the 1980s and 90s, the wage advantage of college- over non-college-educated workers grew quickly and thus made a significant contribution to growing inequality in those years. This gave rise to the view that skill-biased technological change, or SBTC, is an important explanatory factor. SBTC maintains that as new technologies enter the workplace (largely computerization), employers' skill demands outpace the supply of skilled workers, thus leading employers to bid the wages of college-educated workers up relative to the pay of non-college-educated workers.

Since the mid-1990s, however, the college wage premium, at least for those with four-year degrees, has been relatively flat. It's still remained historically high, and thus still contributes to the level of inequality if not the growth. But my own research finds SBTC is often poorly identified and thus overemphasized. For example, in the 1980s, the minimum wage fell sharply in real terms, a change that would also show up as a higher college wage premium.

Also, over the past decade it's not just the demand for less-educated workers that's been subpar. The same could be said for many college-educated workers, especially recent graduates who have had to take lower quality jobs than they expected. Many have even experienced flat real earnings, a particularly tough outcome when you're stuck servicing high levels of college debt.[13] In other words, even those with college degrees are not inoculated from the decline in bargaining power, the absence of full employment, and the other primary factors driving the growth/income disconnect.

Still, it's important to capture the nuances around these points. While the wage advantage received by college workers hasn't been rising for over a decade now, and thus can't be responsible for pushing up inequality, it's still as high as it has ever been, as noted. In Chapter 8, I stress that part of the reconnection agenda is finding the right policy mix to improve both college access and, equally importantly, college completion.

---

[13] See http://www.nber.org/papers/w18901 on weaker demand for college workers and http://www.epi.org/publication/why-americas-workers-need-faster-wage-growth/ on college wage trends.

o   *The erosion of labor standards*: Chapters 7 and 8 both deal in part with the decline in standards established decades ago to support worker bargaining power through overtime rules, minimum wages, a level playing field for union organizing, and numerous other protections. Their erosion has hurt the bargaining power of tens of millions of workers and thus contributed to the rise in inequality.

- *Financialization*: This factor, explored in Chapter 7, describes the rise in the finance sector and, with it, the growth of income sources like capital gains that are concentrated at the top of the income scale. A central motivation for Chapter 7 is that a damaging side effect of financialization has been the rise of the bubble/bust syndrome that not only hurts macroeconomic growth but has contributed to inequality as well.

Another inequality-inducing factor related to financialization is the weakening of corporate governance that has in turn given rise to the "shareholder primacy" movement. This is the idea that one of the corporate sector's main purposes is to increase the near-term wealth of its shareholders, leading to underinvestment in workers, wages, and even physical capital, all in the interest of maximizing equity share prices, dividend payouts, and stock "buybacks."

- *Changes in tax policy*: Chapters 7 and 8 both discuss changes in tax policies, such as preferential tax treatment for income sources of wealthy households, including capital gains, foreign-earned income, debt-financed investment (the deduction of interest payments is a huge boon for private equity firms, for example), and corporate tax expenditures, that have contributed to after-tax inequality without, it should be noted, doing anything much to promote economic growth.[14]

- *The increased shares of those left behind*: I devote Chapter 6 to another factor driving up inequality: the absence of public policies to address those who are victims of various forms of discrimination, including racial minorities and women, but also the long-term unemployed and, very importantly given their large and growing magnitude, those with criminal records. Full employment, it should be noted, is of disproportionate benefit to minorities (see Figure A17); thus, its long absence is a key inequality-inducing factor in this space.

Why Does Inequality Matter?

In my youth in the biz, I would just present the "what" of inequality—the first set of slides discussed above—and call it a day. Then I realized (duh . . .) audiences wanted to know what

---

[14] http://www.cbpp.org/cms/?fa=view&id=3837

caused it, so I added the section you just read. Now, I see there are those who'd like to know: why is it a problem? I mean, every advanced economy has some degree of inequality, even the Scandinavian countries, which do much more than we do to push back against it. Why is the fact that the distance has grown larger a big national problem worth writing books about? Or, to put not too fine a point on it, why does the evidence presented thus far warrant a reconnection agenda?

There are at least four reasons.

First, as I've shown, high levels of inequality reduce the opportunities of those on the wrong side of the income divide. We Americans are typically pretty comfortable with some degree of inequality of outcomes, but we're a lot less comfortable with inequality of opportunities. True, our history is replete with examples where such inequalities have been embedded in our society and even our laws. But national movements to repeal those laws have gathered deep strength from the conviction that striving for equal opportunity is absolutely consistent with the vision of America many of us share.

Second, as shown in Figure A8, by channeling more growth toward the top of the income scale, inequality mechanically creates a wedge between growth and living standards. It is in this sense that higher inequality is associated with stagnant wage growth for many workers and "stickier" (as in less responsive to growth) poverty rates.

Third, as explained in Chapter 7, there are ways in which high levels of inequality dampen macroeconomic growth (Chapter 5 makes a similar point regarding trade deficits, another big contributor to inequality). Part of this has to do with the problem of income flowing mostly to those who already have a lot of it. In a 70 percent consumption economy, the fact of stagnant incomes for the broad majority of households becomes a growth constraint when they're unable to make ends meet or improve their living standards based on their paychecks.

This dynamic leads to what I call the "economic shampoo cycle"—bubble, bust, repeat—as strapped families have access to under-regulated, cheap credit. This higher leveraging and large wealth effects (higher consumption driven by an appreciating asset, like the value of your home) help to inflate the bubbles that have been wreaking havoc on economic expansions both here and abroad for decades.

Fourth, as I discuss in the last chapter, and this is fundamental if we ever hope to launch a true reconnection agenda, there's a toxic interaction between high levels of wealth concentration and money in politics that undermines our democratic process and blocks virtually all of the solutions you'll see in the rest of the book.

Conclusion

That's the context. We've got high and rising levels of inequality in income, wealth, and wages. The extent of these inequalities is arguably having a negative impact on the opportunities for upward mobility for the majority of households. The causes are many but the good news is that they are amenable to policy.

By that I mean that every causal factor on that list has a straightforward policy response that can help offset its impact on inequality. And—you saw this coming—those policies comprise the reconnection agenda that I elaborate throughout the rest of this book, including (in Chapter 10) ideas about how our politics has morphed in dangerous ways that have allowed these inequality inducers to grow and are blocking the agenda to stop them.

So, without further ado, and with the diagnosis firmly under our belts, let us proceed to the reconnection agenda, beginning with its most important goal: the restoration of full employment as a norm in the American job market.

Chapter 3

Full Employment, the Most Important Missing Piece of the Puzzle

Here's a fact that gets to the heart of the reconnection agenda:

During the years when low, middle, and high incomes grew together—when growth was much more broadly experienced than it is today—the US job market was at full employment 70 percent of the time. Since then, growth has too often failed to reach most middle- and low-income households, and we've been at full employment only 30 percent of the time.

Now, correlation isn't causation, and just because two things happened at the same time doesn't mean one caused the other. But this chapter builds the case that the absence of this thing called full employment, which I'll define in a moment, was and is a main reason for the growth/income disconnect.

Based on that evidence, I conclude that full employment must be elevated as a national economic goal. In fact, I'd go as far as to assert that if a politician or policy maker is talking about solving the middle class squeeze, increasing opportunities for those on the wrong side of the inequality divide, or unsticking our "sticky" poverty rates (so that poverty once again falls when growth is strong) and full employment is *not* at the top of their agenda, they're just nibbling around the edges.

A bold assertion, I know, but I defend it below and in much of what follows, which explains not only what we need to do to get to full employment, but how to stay there once we arrive.

What's this "Full Employment" Thing You Keep Going On About?

Full employment is nothing more than an airtight matchup between the number of people seeking jobs and the number of job openings. That doesn't imply an unemployment rate of zero, by the way. There are always people between jobs—"frictional unemployment" if you want to sound wonky and mildly annoying—and there are also some people who are "legends in their own minds" when it comes to their "reservation wage" (the lowest wage they'll accept)—i.e., they think they're worth more than any reasonable employer would ever pay them, so they remain jobless even when there are jobs available to them.

But those groups are small. This is America, and as one of my bosses said to me in my younger days, "if you don't work, you don't eat" (and no, he wasn't Fidel . . . just a capitalist calling it like it is). Yes, there's a social safety net in America, including food assistance, but my boss was making the point that if you're an able-bodied adult and you want to live above a privation level in this country, you've got to work. Unless you're milking a trust fund or a fat bond portfolio, in the words of Bob Dylan, you've gotta serve someone.

At its peak in the late 1990s—the last time we were at full employment, by the way—the share of the "prime-age" population (ages 25 to 54) at work was 82 percent. So, not everybody works, as in "works in the paid labor market," but most people do.[15]

When the job market is at full employment, the unemployment rate is, of course, low. I just mentioned the late 1990s. Well, in April of 2000, that rate was 3.8 percent. That's full employment (for comparison, the jobless rate hit 10 percent during the great recession).

So is something like 4 percent the goal? In fact, economists do a lot of mental noodling about the unemployment rate consistent with full employment. To be more precise, the way most of us think about it is the lowest unemployment rate consistent with stable inflation. You've maybe heard about the problem of economic "over-heating?" (Actually, you probably haven't heard about that for a long time . . . that's part of the problem.) That's when demand outpaces supply: too few workers are chasing too many jobs or too many consumers chasing too few goods. As you can imagine, that's a recipe for faster price growth, aka inflation.

Makes sense, right? But as is all too often the case in economics, we have a reasonable theory but can't nail down a number.

---

[15] There are lots of parents in that age range engaged in caring for their kids who are, of course, working their butts off, but who are not counted as officially employed.

Economists don't really know what the unemployment rate should be at full employment. Some say it's around 6 percent; some say around 4 percent. And economists are simply unable to reliably say it's one or the other.[16] Moreover, that uncertainty matters, because the difference between those two numbers is about three million jobs.

You may think that reality paints the reconnection agenda into a corner: full employment is key to the agenda, but we can't identify the unemployment rate consistent with it.

Not a problem, or, more accurately, only a problem if we slavishly and mistakenly try to target some phantom number. Instead, we must define full employment from the very perspective of the disconnect we're trying to fix. Conditional on stable inflation, we'll know we're at full employment when real wages are rising across the wage scale, not just at the top.

Let me explain.

The Historical Absence of Full Employment and Why It's So Important

The Congressional Budget Office—composed of highly regarded non-partisan wonks who patrol our fiscal and economic waters—actually provides a measure of the unemployment rate they view as consistent with full employment and stable inflation. Like I

---

[16] See here for details of this challenge of nailing down the full employment unemployment rate: http://www.nytimes.com/2014/11/15/upshot/the-surprisingly-elusive-number-that-suggests-full-employment.html?rref=upshot&_r=0&abt=0002&abg=1.

said, it's got a wide margin-of-error around it, but it's still useful for roughly teasing out the historical record.

Their measure is the source of Figure 1 below. It shows the percent of time that the job market has been tight and loose, divided into the two periods where labor markets were distinctly different on this dimension. It imposes the growth of low, middle, and high incomes on top of the full employment bars, just to whack you over the head with the point here.[17]

FIGURE 1

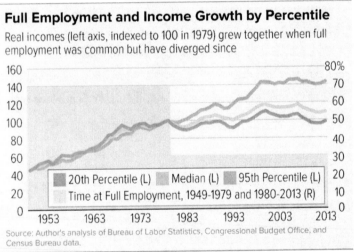

Full Employment and Income Growth by Percentile

Real incomes (left axis, indexed to 100 in 1979) grew together when full employment was common but have diverged since

20th Percentile (L)   Median (L)   95th Percentile (L)
Time at Full Employment, 1949-1979 and 1980-2013 (R)

Source: Author's analysis of Bureau of Labor Statistics, Congressional Budget Office, and Census Bureau data.

THE RECONNECTION AGENDA | JARED BERNSTEIN

---

[17] The family income measures are all indexed to 100 in 1979 so as to be able to plot them on the same scale. They represent the 20th, 50th (median), and 95th percentiles of the income scale. Their values in the last year of the data, 2013, were about $29,000, $64,000, and $217,000, respectively.

This figure raises at least two questions: One, why have job markets been so slack (meaning too many workers chasing too few jobs) post-1979, and two, surely the absence of full employment isn't the only thing driving the evident disconnect in the latter period?

One of the main reasons for the slack in the latter period is the subject of Chapter 5: unbalanced trade, meaning the value of our imports have surpassed that of our exports, which in turn means that we've been exporting a lot of jobs over the weak-job-market period. I'll get back to that soon, but let me be clear from the get-go: to advocate for more balanced trade is not to advocate for less trade. I'm pro-globalization in a big way, and even if I weren't, it wouldn't matter, because it's here to stay. But for now, I'll just point out that when we were at full employment most of the time, the trade balance was about zero (0.5 percent of GDP) and when we weren't, it was about -2.5 percent of GDP.

Economic policy has also been a contributor. Both monetary and fiscal policy—the former being the purview of the Federal Reserve, the latter of the government sector—have at times pushed the wrong way in terms of achieving full employment.

Interestingly, in recent years they've been pushing in opposite directions, with the Fed using their tools to try to lower the unemployment rate and Congress just basically screwing things up, but that too is fodder for the next chapter on the roles we need fiscal and monetary policies to play.

Demographics also play a role as the workforce has gotten older over time and, as older people are pickier about what job they'll take, their spells of unemployment tend to be longer. On the other hand, the labor force actually grew faster over the earlier, full employment period than it did in the latter period, due to both the entry of more women in the labor force and immigration.

The punchline of all of this analysis is a very important one: the primary reason for the very different heights of those two bars in Figure 1 is that labor demand—the quantity of jobs created—has been too weak in the latter period. Since the late 1970s, with just a few exceptions, our economy has failed to generate the necessary quantity and quality of jobs.

The Absence of Full Employment and Its Connection to the Disconnect

But how is it that full employment is so intimately connected to the disconnect between growth and broadly shared prosperity? Simple: absent full employment, the vast majority of workers lack the bargaining power they need to claim part of the growth they're helping to produce. When labor markets are as slack as they've been, employers simply don't need to boost earnings much at all to get and keep the workers they need. On the other hand, when demand is booming, employers often find that they must raise compensation to maintain or expand their workforce. To not do so would be to not meet customer demands and thus to leave potential profits on the table.

I've sometimes found this description of reality to be confusing to people. How could some abstract macroeconomic concept like full employment increase the bargaining clout of average workers? Isn't that what unions do?

It's certainly what they did when they comprised a third of the workforce back in the 1950s. Now they're down to 11 percent overall and 7 percent in the private sector, and while unions' raison d'etre is still to provide collective bargaining power for their members, and as such they play an essential function in a reconnection agenda, they're also kind of busy fighting for their lives.

So, in today's labor market, full employment is one of the best and one of the only friends of people who depend on their paychecks as opposed to their stock portfolios.

Let me show you what I mean based on some research I did with economist Dean Baker.[18] The question we asked ourselves was not: "are tight labor markets a good thing from the perspective of working people?" That's kind of a big "duh." But there are lots of different "working people" out there, from the hedge fund manager to the person who cleans her office. So the question we asked is: "who does full employment help the most?"

And, after a bit a number crunching, the answer we found was: it helps the lowest-wage workers the most, middle-wage workers

---

[18] See our book, *Getting Back to Full Employment*:
http://www.cepr.net/index.php/publications/books/getting-back-to-full-employment-a-better-bargain-for-working-people

somewhat less but still a good bit, and the highest-wage workers not at all. What's striking about that pattern is that it is the opposite of the inequality pattern you see in Figure 1, where the top does better than the middle and the middle better than the bottom. It is for this reason that we judge full employment to be a potent antidote against the forces driving inequality.

In order to crunch the numbers in a revealing way, we took advantage of the fact that both wages and unemployment vary across all 50 states and over time (more observations with more variance yield more revealing statistical analysis). So, using a data series that ran from 1979 to 2011, we generated the results in Figure 2. A 10 percent decline in the unemployment rate, say from 6 percent to 5.4 percent, would raise low wages by 10 percent, middle wages by 4 percent, and high wages by . . . wait for it . . . no percent.

Why doesn't full employment help the wealthy? It's the exception that proves the rule. They're rarely underemployed. High wage earners tend to have very low unemployment rates and since they're already fully employed, lower unemployment doesn't do much for them.

Nor do the reconnection powers of full employment stop there. Figure 2 is derived for hourly wages but incomes are a function of hourly wages, weekly hours worked, and weeks worked per year. By providing both job seekers and the underemployed (say, part-timers who'd rather be working full time) with more opportunities, full employment boosts hours of work as well. For example, back in the late 1990s—the last time the US economy was at full employment—the annual hours of working-age families with kids, which had been relatively flat since the late 1970s, increased by 30 percent, an addition of almost 400 hours per year. That's ten more weeks of full-time work.

FIGURE 2

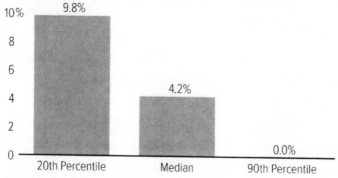

Full Employment Helps Low-Wage Workers Most

Wage growth by wage percentile after a 10 percent decline in the unemployment rate

Source: Bernstein and Baker. *Getting Back to Full Employment*, 2013.

Middle-income annual hours went up a bit over those years, but not much: just by 4 percent, or about 130 hours. The annual hours of high income families hardly budged. But again, that's because their family labor supply is pretty much tapped out.[19]

---

[19] These data were run for me by Arloc Sherman of the Center on Budget and Policy Priorities, using the Census Bureau Annual Social and Economic Supplement data series. The sample includes families with children, headed by someone 25 to 54.

So full employment boosts wages and hours and does so in a way that counters inequality. While inequality steers the benefits of growth to the top of the income scale, full employment grabs the wheel and steers them towards the bottom and middle.

OK, But There's Downside, Right?

Remember how I mentioned "overheating" back there at the beginning of this chapter? Many economists will tell you: "sure, we all love full employment. But how do you like runaway inflation? Because that's what you're courting if you listen to this guy" (that would be me).

They're talking/worrying about something real. There is an inverse relationship between a tighter job market and faster wage and price growth. I mean, I've just been touting that very relationship regarding diminished slack and faster real wage growth, so clearly I believe it. But here again, what matters is the magnitude of that inverse relationship.

When it comes to these sorts of relationships between economic variables, you should never let anyone tell you, "don't move X [where X is good], because you'll get Y [where Y is bad]." Like "don't raise the minimum wage or people will lose jobs." Or "don't provide poor people with some benefit because they'll work less" (somehow these same gum flappers argue that when you give the rich a benefit, like a tax cut, they'll work more, but let's not go there).

What's missing is the extent of the tradeoff. There are studies which find that minimum wage increases can lead to job losses, though the consensus is that for moderate increases, any such losses are diminishingly small relative to the gains. A recent Congressional Budget Office report guesstimated that a proposed increase would benefit 24.5 million workers and lead to the loss of 500,000 jobs. That's a 49:1 beneficiary-to-job-loser ratio and a deal many low-wage workers would quickly accept (and given that there's a lot of churn in the low-wage sector, when those job losers are re-employed, it will be at a better job). The recipients of safety net benefits, like nutritional support or housing vouchers, may work a little less than they would otherwise, but these effects have been found to be quantitatively small relative to the benefits of the programs, which (as I show in Chapter 8) are now being found to produce positive impacts over the life-cycle of children who received such benefits.[20]

So it is with the inverse relationship between unemployment and inflation. The correlation exists, but for numerous reasons, it's not a serious threat. First, it's not of a scary magnitude. Economists' definition of full employment is an unemployment rate consistent with stable inflation, so at least by that definition, there's nothing to worry about until the unemployment rate falls too far. What's

---

[20] On the minimum wage, see here:
http://www.cbo.gov/sites/default/files/cbofiles/attachments/44995-MinimumWage.pdf. On the safety net and work disincentives, see here:
http://www.cbpp.org/cms/?fa=view&id=3795.

too far? It's when inflation starts rising. So it's all pretty circuitous.

Even then, conventional estimates are that if the jobless rate goes below the full employment rate by one percentage point, inflation will increase by less than half a percent, about 0.3 percent according to some recent work.[21] As I've stressed, a lot of good economic things happen to people when the job market gets that tight, and we're talking about people who haven't had much good economic news for a while. A little faster inflation might be worth it, or slightly more formally, they'd benefit a lot more from airtight labor markets than they'd be hurt by 0.3 percent faster inflation.

Second, remember, numerically speaking, we can't reliably identify the unemployment rate consistent with full employment, so all of these numbers that economists, myself included, are throwing around are fanciful at best.

Here's a nice bit of history to underscore that point. Back in the early 1990s, the mythology of the time was "Ye who dares to allow the unemployment rate to get too low risks triggering an inflationary spiral." But as unemployment fell below this alleged "too low" rate in the 1990s—thought to be around 6 percent— price growth didn't accelerate at all. How could this be, came the economists' chorus?

---

[21] See Chapter 3 of Baker and Bernstein for a more detailed discussion of these estimates. http://www.cepr.net/index.php/publications/books/getting-back-to-full-employment-a-better-bargain-for-working-people

The answer came from—of all people—Alan Greenspan, chair of the Federal Reserve back then. Greenspan recognized that because productivity growth was accelerating, full employment-induced faster wage growth didn't obviously have to feed into price growth. Because firms were producing more output per hour, they could maintain healthy profit margins and still raise pay.

As mentioned in passing above, in the last few months of 2000, the unemployment rate fell below 4 percent and inflation was still well-behaved. Economists' estimates of full employment were way off.

Next, speaking of those at the Federal Reserve, they've been hyper-vigilant about maintaining their inflation target of around 2 percent to the point where everyone who pays attention to this sort of thing expects them to pounce—i.e., raise interest rates to slow growth—if inflationary pressures should build. In the lingua Franca, we say inflationary expectations are "well-anchored." Considerable research has revealed how well this anchor holds, such that it is now partially preempting the role of slack as a determinant of inflation.[22]

Finally, those who fret about inflation are not worried solely about that 0.3 percent nudge noted above. They're worried that unless the job market loosens up, we'll get another 0.3 percent, and another, and so on, until inflation is spiraling out of control. But here again, the evidence is thin and getting thinner. As I show in Figure 10 in the next chapter, in early 2015 the unemployment

---

[22] Larry Ball, forthcoming.

rate was around the mid-fives, and as such, was creeping closer to the Fed's estimate of full employment (as of April 2015, this estimate is about 5.1 percent). For the inflation-acceleration story to be credible, we'd have to have seen some pick-up in the rate of price or wage growth as the actual unemployment rate moved closer to the Fed's full employment rate.

The fact that we did not see any acceleration in price or wage growth suggests yet another great disconnect in today's economy. The growth in both prices and nominal wages were completely unresponsive to the alleged tightening in the job market.

There are at least three possibilities explaining the lack of the expected reaction. One, as I've suggested, the full employment unemployment rate is lower than the Fed thinks. Two, we're mis-measuring labor market slack and the unemployment rate doesn't tell the whole story. And three, economists don't quite understand these dynamics.

I believe all three are true. The natural rate is lower than we think (and very difficult to reliably estimate). There is more slack in the US job market than the measured unemployment rate reveals. And our traditional understanding of such dynamics is incomplete, in part because we've paid too little attention to a key wage determinant: workers' bargaining power.

The point is that sure, of course the possibility of economic overheating exists, but given the costs of slack job markets on the vast majority of working households, it would be deeply foolish to let that possibility block our path to full employment. The Fed has inflation expectations tightly controlled and can act if the jobless rate falls low enough to trigger faster price growth. And let's be appropriately humble about our knowledge of these dynamics. We don't know how low is too low on the unemployment rate, nor do we have a reliable sense of how far reduced slack will push inflation. The empirical record strongly suggests that this reaction function has been weak for years.

None of this means we can ignore inflationary pressures, but as the Greenspan example from the late 1990s reminds us, the tendency of US policy makers has been to overweight inflation concerns and underweight the deep problems engendered by slack labor markets.

Um . . . Aren't the Robots Going to Take All the Jobs (part 1)?

There is an advancing line of thinking that maintains it will be increasingly hard to achieve full employment because, in common parlance: the robots are coming. Or, if you prefer the econo-mese, the rate at which labor-saving technology is entering the workforce is accelerating. (In Chapter 5 I revisit this issue in the manufacturing context.)

It's a tempting path to go down. I'm old enough to have been impressed when calculators started making graphs. The fact that I've now got this little computer in my pocket that can both access much of human knowledge and history and allow me to call my wife to remind me which toothpaste we like still blows my mind.

Also, some smart and perhaps even visionary futurists make this argument in ways that are pretty damn compelling.[23]

But consider this anecdote that economist Alan Blinder shared with me:[24]

Say you were Thomas Jefferson's chief economist and you'd just somehow seen a report from the year 2013 showing that 1.5 percent of the workforce was in agriculture, as opposed to the 90 percent in your day. You ran to the President with news of this crisis, telling him we've got to start preparing for mass unemployment.

You would have been wrong, of course. That is, you would have been right that productivity advances in farming led to massive displacement of workers in that sector, but, after considerable disruption that should not be glossed over, other sectors grew in its place, providing ample employment opportunities. The Luddites have always been wrong and, as I'll show in a moment, the "robots-are-coming" advocates don't have much at all beyond anecdote by way of evidence.

On the other hand, throughout this book I've been stressing that over most of the past few decades, job creation has often been inadequate. So again, how do I know the robots aren't here?

---

[23] See *The Second Machine Age*, by Brynjolfsson and McAfee.

[24] Some of the material in this section comes from this piece: http://economix.blogs.nytimes.com/2014/02/17/before-blaming-the-robots-lets-get-the-policy-right/

For that, we need a little bit of simple math, wherein we'll borrow a few numbers from economist Larry Mishel.[25] There's a simple identity in economics—meaning a formula that must hold by definition—that goes like this:

Job growth = GDP growth – Productivity growth

It's actually a pretty common-sense identity. With constant output, or GDP, growth, more efficient production (aka faster productivity growth) means fewer jobs are needed to maintain the constant GDP level.[26] If we can produce the same output in fewer hours, we need less work to hold steady. But of course output has been anything but constant. The intervening variable that has made this identity work out in our favor throughout history is the greater demand for the additional goods and services we can produce by dint of our increasing productivity.

Mishel provides the annualized growth numbers to plug into the little formula above for the last three business cycles: 1979-1989, 1989-2000, and 2000-2007, as well as the period since 2007, though in that case both growth and jobs have been depressed by the Great Recession.

---

[25] See http://www.epi.org/blog/dont-blame-robots-slow-job-growth-2000s/.

[26] Though I've said "job growth" to make this part a bit more intuitive, it's really the growth in annual hours worked.

TABLE 1

Annualized Percentage Growth of Jobs, GDP, and Productivity

	Job growth	GDP growth	Productivity growth
1979 - 1989	1.7	3.1	1.4
1989 - 2000	1.5	3.3	1.8
2000 - 2007	0.3	2.4	2.1
2007 - 2013	-0.4	0.9	1.3

Note: "Job growth" is actually hours of work.
Source: Larry Mishel's analysis of Bureau of Labor Statistics data.

Both the 1980s and 1990s saw decent job growth, but the 2000s look pretty terrible, with job growth at one-fifth the rate of the 1990s. The question for the technology story, however, is quite specific: was this slower job growth due to the faster productivity growth you'd expect to see if the pace at which technology was displacing workers was ramping up?

Productivity sped up a little in the 2000s—by 0.3 percent--but the big negative was slower GDP growth (otherwise known as weak demand), which fell almost a point (to 2.4 percent from 3.3 percent). Had growth remained constant at 3.3 percent, we would have added jobs at a rate of 1.2 percent per year (3.3 percent minus 2.1 percent) instead of a measly 0.3 percent. That fourfold difference would have amounted to seven million more full-time jobs and a much better shot at full employment.

Moreover, since 2007, the robot story gets even weaker. Productivity doesn't accelerate as robots dispassionately hand workers pink slips. It slows further. How could this possibly be consistent with an acceleration of labor-saving technology? Shouldn't that, by definition, be boosting output and cutting hours of work, the very definition of faster productivity growth?

It should, and there's other evidence that the tech story is overhyped: capital investment that businesses make in the interest of boosting their productivity growth has also declined in recent years, and the slowdown is particularly notable in IT industries. Again, wouldn't the robot story suggest the opposite investment story?[27]

Still, even after all that, I'm not saying the robots are assuredly *not* coming for our jobs. I'm saying that for reasons you'll read about in coming chapters, we've made policy choices, by omission and commission, and having nothing to do with technology, that have kept us from getting to full employment. The 2007 crash, which still reverberates through the global economy even as I write today in early 2015, didn't help either.

So what exactly am I claiming here? It's this: there's no solid evidence that technology is blocking the path to full employment. Our economy has made striking technological advances since its inception and yet we've often had periods of tight labor markets. Barring evidence, we must resist the impulse of Jefferson's chief economist and not cite labor-saving technology as an excuse for failing to pursue full employment.

---

[27] See John Fernald's work on this point: http://www.frbsf.org/economic-research/publications/working-papers/2014/wp2014-15.pdf

Can You Get There—to Full Employment—from Here?

Much of what follows explains how to raise the height of that post-1980 bar in Figure 1, the one that shows we've been at full employment less than a third of the time since 1970. As alluded to above, one important way to stay on the path is for the Federal Reserve to keep us on it, as Greenspan did in the 1990s. Another way is to bring down trade deficits that have led to significant employment losses and weak demand for decades.

But a punchline of this book, motivated by both the importance and scarcity of full employment labor markets, is that if the market doesn't create the necessary quantity of jobs, the government will need to correct this market failure.

Before you wince—"but our government can't even launch a website!"—allow me to point out that government—at the federal, state, and local level—is already very deeply embedded in our economy. It's accounted for about a fifth of the total economy for decades now, including over $3 trillion in the most recent quarter.

Add to that another trillion in spending through the tax code through so-called tax expenditures like breaks for specific businesses (R&D tax credits), investments (mortgage interest deduction), or wage subsidies for low-wage workers in private sector jobs (the Earned Income Tax Credit). That comes to one-quarter of our GDP with government fingerprints on it.

So the question is not: "should government be in the economy?" That may be a fun debate for libertarians with too much time on their hands. But that train left the station a long time ago and it's heading down the tracks (built with large government subsidies, I should note).

The correct question is: "are we getting the biggest bang for the government bucks that are in the economy?," where "bang" refers to opportunities for those who most need them. There, I suspect you'll agree, we could do a whole lot better.

Chapter 4

Fiscal and Monetary Policies that Work for Working People

We economists make all kinds of assumptions, many of which are unwarranted, but I'm going to climb out on a limb here and assume you're with me all the way out to the end of the branch on the importance of full employment to the reconnection agenda. I mean, unless you're someone who's either just downright mean-spirited or who benefits from a bunch of surplus labor, or both, you'd probably like to see everyone who wants a job get a job, and a decent one at that. Which again, means we need to have tight enough labor markets to give workers the bargaining power they need to claim a fairer share of the growth they're helping to generate.

In modern, advanced economies, the two biggest tools to achieve full employment are fiscal and monetary policy. And since what we're up to here is putting the right tools in the reconnection agenda toolbox, then these two are the biggest and most essential, the veritable hammer and drill, the tools without which we will be unable to reconnect growth and more broadly shared prosperity.

Fiscal policy is taxing and spending, something with which we're all pretty familiar. It occurs at all three levels of government; in 2013, government receipts were around $3.1 trillion at the federal level and $1.5 and $1.2 trillion at the state and local level, respectively (that's 19, 9, and 5 percent of GDP). So yeah, there's some real money in play here that we use for social insurance programs like Medicare and Social Security, defense, our public infrastructure, public education, and the one we're going to be diving into pretty deeply here: temporarily stabilizing the economy when markets fail.

Monetary policy may seem a bit more mysterious, though that will no longer be the case after a few painless and entertaining minutes of your time (OK, "entertaining" may be a bit of a stretch, but I'll try). But it's really nothing more than the actions of the nation's central bank—that's our Federal Reserve, or the Fed—to try to control two opposing forces: unemployment and inflation. Though the negative correlation between these two variables has lessened in recent years (meaning they've become somewhat less likely to move in opposite directions), it is still generally the case that slack in an economy—weak demand, lots of people out of work—leads to lower price pressures, or less inflation.

Of course, other factors can and do come into play. As I write this, the price of a barrel of oil is down by more than half over the past six months, largely due to increased supply. In a country like the US that's still a net oil importer, lower energy costs will tend to boost growth, leading to a situation of lower prices (due to the positive oil shock) and lower unemployment. But interestingly, as I'll show later on, when Fed economists measure inflation, they leave out oil prices, not because such prices are immaterial to the Fed's mandate of balancing inflation and employment, but because they're both volatile and more of a function of global forces. Our central bank is more interested in the underlying trend in inflation and its connection to the movements of other domestic variables, like wages.

The Fed's main tool in its efforts to manage its dual mandate—maintaining both full employment and stable prices—is the interest rate it controls, called the federal funds rate, which I'll just call the Fed rate. Based on its extensive analysis of the economy—the Fed employs over 300 economists! . . . What could go wrong?—it adjusts that rate up to slow growth and inflation and down to try to speed it up.[28]

OK, enough with the niceties. I've obviously got an angle here and it's this. You'll note I mentioned "market failure" up there

---

[28] The Fed moves the interest rate up and down mostly through its "open market operations," printing money to finance its purchase of government bonds from commercial banks or conversely, selling securities back to banks to reduce the money supply. Instead of printing or burning cash, the Fed just credits or debits bank X's account, showing that they've either increased or decreased their holdings (or "reserves" in Fed-speak) at the Fed. In expansion mode, the increase in loanable funds, as well as the Fed-induced increase demand for government bonds, lowers the interest rate (because bond rates move inversely to their prices). And vice versa when the Fed wants to "tighten."

regarding the role of fiscal policy. It's the same with monetary policy—the business cycle (booms and busts) used to be much more volatile before central banks came on line. It is my not-at-all-humble-opinion that Figure 1 in the previous chapter, the one showing how we've been at full employment only 30 percent of the time in recent years, is representative of a persistent and deeply damaging market failure, one that looms behind the negative trends documented in Chapter 2 that have been tremendously costly to working families. And I'm here to argue that better—much better—monetary and fiscal policy can help a lot here.

So let's dive in. I'll start with an overview of how the two policies can and should work together, provide evidence of their effectiveness, and suggest a variety ways they can be more complementary to the reconnection agenda.

Fiscal, Monetary, or Both?

As a "listy" kind of guy,[29] I'm tempted in this sort of exposition to give each of these two policy areas their own section. But in this case, even while they're pretty different, there's an important substantive reason to at least begin the discussion in unison: there are times, and the last few years in the US and Europe serve as exhibits A and B, when growth-oriented fiscal and monetary

---

[29] It may be sort of obnoxious, but I've found when you say to someone, e.g., "there are three reasons why X is true," they just pay closer attention to your argument. Of course, you have to remember your three reasons, as I, a la Rick Perry, decidedly did not do the other night on national TV (well, cable . . . but still). In that case, your argument will be somewhat less effective.

policy must work together. At such times, they are not substitutes but essential complements, each boosting the other's effectiveness.

See the box in Table 2. Before we get to its relevance re the one-two punch of fiscal and monetary policies working together, let me explain the hydraulics in terms of growth and contraction. Again, fiscal is simple because it's so direct: government spending, by definition, adds to economic growth.

To those skeptical of that claim, stay calm! That is far from saying "all government spending is well spent" or asserting that we can get whatever growth rate we want through fiscal policy (and, in fact, I pursue in some detail in Chapter 8 this question of what "well spent" means in this context). Spending more than you take in (deficit spending), while essential in recessions and a few other specific times, is misguided at others and, if you do too much of it, unsustainable in the long run. But the fact that at first blush government spending unquestionably adds to growth is what you need to know to understand the box.[30]

Monetary policy, as alluded to above, is less direct but can also be a powerful growth inducer (or dampener). The fact that the Fed can lower or raise borrowing costs is of course a big potential growth factor, whether a household is borrowing to redo the kitchen (you'll see that analogy again in these pages; it's because I'm living that particular dream) or a business is planning to open

---

[30] Since GDP = consumption + investment + net exports + **government spending**, this assertion is definitional.

a new branch. And many other influential interest rates in the economy, from car loans to student loans to home loans (mortgages), key off of the Fed rate.

The takeaway, then, is that both fiscal and monetary policy can be in either growth, contraction, or neutral mode (the latter wherein they're neither nudging nor suppressing the underlying growth rate). Now, turn to Table 2 below. When we're in box 1, both government spending and Fed interest rate policies are trying to raise the growth rate, goose investment and job creation, and lower unemployment. Both fiscal policy and monetary policy are in expansionary mode.

TABLE 2

Fiscal and Monetary Policy Should Work as Complements

| | | Monetary Policy | | |
		Growth	Neutral	Contraction
Fiscal Policy	Growth	1	2	3
	Neutral	4	5	6
	Contraction	7	8	9

The last time that happened was back in 2009-10, in the throes of the Great Recession, when the deficit rose to between 9 and 10 percent of GDP and the Fed rate was headed for about zero.[31] But, unfortunately, we didn't stay there for long.

---

[31] Fed aficionados will recognize that I'm talking about the federal funds rate (the rate set by the Fed that banks charge each other for overnight loans of balances parked at

The Fed kept rates low, enabled in no small measure by their political independence, an absolutely critical advantage afforded to our central bank. But fiscal policy went all "austere," by which I mean it shifted into contraction/deficit-reducing mode, as in the third row of Table 2. Instead of employing government spending in the business of temporarily offsetting the private-side market failures in countries across the globe, governments turned to "consolidating their fiscal accounts," i.e., lowering their budget deficits. Thus, by 2012-13, we were in box 7, with monetary policy in growth mode but fiscal policy pushing the other way. And many of the victims of the Great Recession, still trying to claw their way back, paid a steep price in terms of weaker job and wage growth than would otherwise have prevailed. For example, European policy makers went in for fiscal austerity measures far more than here in the US and unemployment there in early 2015 was north of 11 percent.

In fact, US fiscal policy went neutral in 2014, so with the Fed still in growth mode, the economy moved to box 4. The result was a considerably more robust year for growth.

A Bit of Context Involving Meatless Meatballs

I'll get to the evidence in a moment, but it's hard to really absorb, or even believe, such evidence without a common sense context within which to place it. Moreover, I find such common sense to be particularly elusive in this area of fiscal and monetary policy,

---

the Fed), not the discount rate, the latter being the rate the Fed charges commercial banks for short term loans.

because fiscal in particular is so politicized and monetary is so obscure. The famed chair of the Fed for many years, Alan Greenspan, famously quipped, "If I seem unduly clear to you, you must have misunderstood what I said."

The Fed's gotten much better in this regard since G-span left in 2006, as his successors, Ben Bernanke and Janet Yellen, have made more of an effort to explain their actions in ways that normal humans can comprehend, should they care to do so. Still, readers less ensconced in this material might benefit from some context as to why we'd want to be in one of the other boxes.

Think of the economy as a restaurant. Things have been really slow of late, but the owners of the restaurant have a great idea for a new menu featuring meatless meatballs. Yet they lack the resources to get the new tofu/tempeh combo required to realize their dream (I chose this example because I figured it wouldn't make you hungry). Luckily, there's a bank willing to lend them the money to give it a shot, and because the bank is tasked not with making a profit but with stimulating economic activity when times are tough, they make the loan at a near zero rate of interest.

Our vegetarian chefs blissfully get down to work, and in a matter of days they're ready for the grand opening, featuring every enticing meatless meatball dish you can imagine. The owners invite the lending officer from the bank to opening day, they cut the ribbon, and . . . nothing happens. To their surprise, there's no line waiting around the block, and, frankly, that's what they might have expected if they'd thought about the key phrase above about how "things have been really slow of late." The problem is not solely one of expensive credit. It's also a problem of weak demand (I guess it could also be that nobody likes meatless meatballs, but suspend disbelief on that point for now).

When the Fed is Double-teamed, You Dish to Fiscal

That's where fiscal policy comes in. When the economy is weak—growth is too slow, unemployment too high, real paychecks stagnant—consumers reel in their spending. This is an especially tough problem in the US economy, where consumer spending is 70 percent of GDP, compared to about 55 percent in Europe and 35 percent in China. So you can make the absolute best can't-possibly-tell-the-difference meatless meatballs you want, but if people don't have discretionary money jingling around in their pockets, they will not partake.

Not to put too fine a point on it, in a down economy, the Fed can set the table, but it takes fiscal policy—a temporary boost in stimulative government spending—to get people in the restaurant. That's box 1 in Table 2 and it's the only one that reliably works when consumers are just crawling up off the mat after a knockout recession.

This insight regarding box 1 is both an old and a new one. It is obviously one associated with British economist John Maynard Keynes from back in the 1930s, but it is one that most economists put aside in recent years for two reasons. First, it was believed that the Fed was all you needed. Back in 1997, no less than economist Paul Krugman, someone who understands Keynes' contributions better than most, wrote the following: "if you want a simple model for predicting the unemployment rate in the United States over the next few years, here it is: It will be what [then Fed chair] Greenspan wants it to be, plus or minus a random error reflecting the fact that he is not quite God."[32]

Second—and unlike the "Fed-is-all-you-need" rap, this one has some validity—it was and is believed that fiscal policy takes too long to launch and is hamstrung by formulas that don't always funnel resources to the places where they're most needed.[33] Even when the nation is in recession, there are of course some places feeling the brunt of the downturn more than others. Yet discretionary fiscal spending in recessions doesn't always account for such variance, though that's not a hard problem to fix and I suggest solutions later in the chapter.

On the other hand, the too-long-to-launch problem certainly wasn't the case in America's most recent adventure with fiscal stimulus targeted at a market failure: the Recovery Act. As noted in Chapter 1, I was there at the time as a member of President Obama's economics team, and my boss VP Biden was implementer-in-chief. While no one's saying the Recovery Act

---

[32] http://web.mit.edu/krugman/www/vulgar.html

[33] Let me be specific about "where they're most needed" because I think this provides a bit of insight into the economics of why this sort of fiscal policy is so important to have in the toolbox. I'm not so much worrying here about the problem of a boondoggly member of Congress seeking resources to build a "bridge to nowhere." If that member's district is facing high joblessness then, while I'd much rather see them build something they need, the fiscal stimulus will still be valued. Instead, I'm saying we want to avoid spending resources in places where the economy is doing okay.

worked perfectly, the measure passed less than a month after the President took office, and some of the most important funding streams get out the door in weeks. Others, including some infrastructure spending and energy projects, took a lot longer, but even there the fiscal boost was still timely, given the length and depth of the downturn.

Leave-it-to-the-Fed was also motivated by the belief among too many economists and policy makers (certainly not Krugman) that the best thing fiscal policy can do is make sure deficits stay very low, if not disappear. While this may sound like a detail or political arguing point, it has in fact served as a critical barrier to a reconnection agenda and to achieving full employment. The drive to reduce deficits regardless of the need for continued fiscal support played, and continues to play, a large role in keeping the US and much more so the nations of Europe out of box 1 and in boxes 7 (Europe) and 4 (US). Or to get out of the box(es) and talk about what actually matters, such fiscal austerity consigned millions of households to unnecessary economic pain.

Summarizing the importance of relearning old lessons, economists Larry Ball, Brad DeLong, and Larry Summers recently pointed to three old-but-new-again insights germane to our economic era: "Keynes's view that the liquidity trap, or zero lower bound on short-term nominal interest rates, can sharply limit the efficacy of monetary stabilization policy; President Kennedy's 'Economics 101' view of the desirability of fiscal stimulus during a slump; and the possibility that a prolonged episode of weak demand and high unemployment in an economy may have destructive consequences for aggregate supply."[34]

I'd argue that if we hope to elevate monetary and especially fiscal policy to their proper position in the reconnection agenda, these insights must be well understood by economists and policy makers. They also fit nicely into this theme about how fiscal and monetary policy must work together if we are to get back to full employment.

We've already discussed the second insight, the econ 101 part about stimulus in a slump. But it's essential that we relearn insights one and three. The "liquidity trap," which sounds like some sort of economic water torture, can be a serious problem indeed, and it's one where fiscal policy is not merely complementary; it's a big part of the solution.

Again, for all the obscure-sounding terms about zero lower bounds and nominal rates, the liquidity trap is simple to describe. It's what happens when, in order to further incentivize lending and the ensuing economic activity that engenders, the Fed needs to further lower interest rates but cannot. Since interest rates don't go below zero—if they did, lenders would be paying you for the

---

[34] http://www.pathtofullemployment.org/wp-content/uploads/2014/04/delong_summers_ball.pdf

privilege of lending you money, which doesn't make much sense—the Fed is trapped by zero.[35]

By early 2015, the Fed rate had been about zero for about five years. Though the recovery was finally strengthening, many economists believed that given investor sentiment, even at a zero Fed rate, borrowing was too expensive. The Fed pulled a few other tools out of their bag of tricks over the course of the recovery (quantitative easing—the purchasing of longer-term bonds to lower longer-term interest rates), but there's just no getting around the fact that when the main interest rate the Fed controls is stuck at its lower bound of zero, the central bank's impact on the economy is severely constrained.[36]

Luckily, there's a way out. When Fed policy is neutralized by the zero lower bound, fiscal policy must step up. It's no more complicated than the old basketball move: when your top player is double-teamed by the D, you dish to the open man (of course, if your open man is covered by anti-Keynesian conservatives,

---

[35] We're talking about nominal interest rates, before accounting for inflation. Since the real interest rate is the nominal rate minus the rate of inflation, it is possible--and when trapped by zero, desirable--to have negative real interest rates.

[36] The problem of chronically weak demand even in the face of zero interest rates is often referenced as evidence of "secular stagnation," a concept reintroduced by Larry Summers (see http://www.voxeu.org/sites/default/files/Vox_secular_stagnation.pdf for an extensive discussion of these issues). As stressed throughout, I strongly concur with the idea that demand, particularly for labor, has been weak for decades in the US, but argue that the "zero lower bound" is but one dimension of the problem. Large, persistent trade deficits, high inequality, inadequate financial market oversight, unresponsive fiscal policy, misconceptions about the full employment unemployment rate, and the other topics covered throughout this book are equally important aspects of the deficient demand diagnosis.

you've got a whole other problem, one we'll return to in the last chapter).

In fact, as Ball et al. argue, this stuck-at-zero problem actually magnifies the positive impact of fiscal policy. The impact of fiscal policies that boost consumer or investor demand can be particularly effective (in econo-mese, fiscal spending has a "large multiplier" at the zero lower bound) because the economy is flush with underutilized resources and borrowing is and will remain cheap.

Think back to the restaurant example above. It's not that people don't want to eat out; it's that they can't afford it. Give them some resources from a fiscal stimulus—say, an unemployment construction worker gets a job fixing a highway—and they'll eat all the meatless meatballs you can throw at them. And as long as so much slack persists in the economy, the Fed won't step in and bust up the meal by raising rates.

The point is, once again, that fiscal and monetary policies are essential complements in weak economies, and we've seen an awful lot of weak economies in recent years.

Permanent, or At Least Long Term, Damage

The other old/new insight by Ball et al. in favor of aggressive use of fiscal policy in pursuit of full employment is "the possibility that a prolonged episode of weak demand and high unemployment in an economy may have destructive consequences for aggregate supply." Let's unpack that one.

Again, for all the econ rhetoric, all they're saying is that if policy makers put us in the wrong box, the damage will be lasting. Too many of the unemployed, after being jobless for too long, will leave the labor market for good. Productive investments in equipment, structures, R&D, and so on will get short shrift, with negative consequences for future productivity growth. And the combination of a diminished and less productive workforce means slower growth in living standards, not for the top 1 percent— they've been doing swell in times good and bad—but for the middle class and poor.

If that sounds at all theoretical or fanciful, I assure you it's not. It's an accurate depiction of the reality of what's happened in the US and many other economies in recent years as a result of protracted recessions, themselves a function of getting these policies wrong. Moreover, the importance of recognizing these dynamics reappears later in the chapter when we ponder ways to make fiscal and monetary policies more effective from the perspective of those hurt most by weak labor markets.

Figure 3, for example, shows the number of long-term unemployed (people who have been jobless for at least six months) as a percentage of the total unemployed population. This percentage reached heights in recent years heretofore unseen in the history of the data, including the early 1980s double dip recessions. Just a few years ago, 45 percent of the unemployed had sought work for at least half a year, almost double the percentage during the previous peak. Moreover, as I discuss further in Chapter 6, there's evidence that simply being unemployed for this long leads employers to discriminate against you.[37]

FIGURE 3

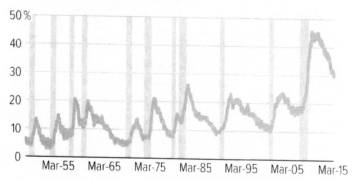

The Long-Term Unemployed

Of total unemployed, percent unemployed 27 weeks and over

Source: Bureau of Labor Statistics.

Too many of these long-termers ultimately left the job market, and the share of the working-age population participating in the labor force fell more sharply in recent years than in any other period on record, as Figure 4 shows. Study the end of the figure carefully and compare the trend in the labor force with past recessions. Not only was there a sharper decline in this downturn, but it also kept going, only stabilizing in 2014, the fifth year of the recovery (hard to see in the figure, but that's what happened). There's an important caveat to this point: a part of the decline,

---

[37] http://www.washingtonpost.com/blogs/wonkblog/wp/2013/04/15/companies-wont-even-look-at-resumes-of-the-long-term-unemployed/

perhaps as much as half, is due to the aging of the labor force—
i.e., people leaving for retirement—as opposed to weak labor
demand and the inadequate availability of jobs. But that still
leaves more than two million weak-demand-led dropouts.

FIGURE 4

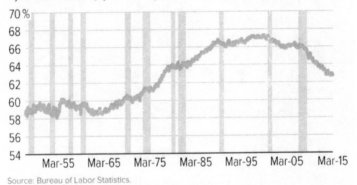

Civilian Labor Force Participation Rate

The share of the working-age population employed or actively looking for
a job fell more sharply in recent years than in any other period on record

Source: Bureau of Labor Statistics.

We've also skimped on capital investment, which grew about half
as fast since 2010 as in the previous decade.[38] Put these supply-
side losses together—fewer workers and less productive
investment—and you end up with precisely what Ball et al. warn
of: a "permanent" scarring of the growth rate (the reason for the
quotes is a very important point to which I'll return below: it's as
necessarily permanent as people think it is).

---

[38] See Fernald's series on capital investment: http://www.frbsf.org/economic-
research/publications/working-papers/2012/wp12-19bk.pdf

The reluctance to use fiscal policy to try to generate more demand for workers and investment is at fault here and it is responsible for literally millions of hours of unemployment by people who could have been contributing to the economy and getting themselves and their families ahead. Central banks, both here and to a lesser extent in Europe, have been doing their best but, as noted, they were stuck at zero. The government officials who refused to apply temporary fiscal stimulus are responsible for economic scarring effects that have reduced the long-term growth rates of economies in countries across the globe. According to follow-up work by Larry Ball, if you sum up the costs of this policy neglect across most of the advanced economies, it comes to over 8 percent of their cumulative GDP, or $4 trillion.[39] That's one measure of the cost of being in box 8 (i.e., the Fed rate is constrained at zero and austere fiscal policy is pushing the wrong way) when we should have been in box 1.

Evidence for the Effectiveness of Fiscal Policy

That last bit of analysis shows you the costs of getting fiscal and monetary policies wrong, but before you're convinced these tools deserve the privileged position in the reconnection agenda that I say they do, you might want to see more evidence of their efficacy. Let's start with the largest infusion of fiscal policy into the economy in recent years, the American Recovery and Reinvestment Act of 2009, an $800 billion Keynesian stimulus

---

[39] http://www.pathtofullemployment.org/wp-content/uploads/2014/03/Laurence-Ball_long-term_damage_May-2014.pdf

unleashed in late February of that year in order to repair some of the damage done by the Great Recession.

ARRA had three basic parts about equally endowed: tax cuts, fiscal relief to states, and investments in various public goods (e.g., infrastructure), energy projects, and people (Chapter 6, for example, features an unheralded employment program for low-income workers that I argue should be scaled up). There are a number of ways to evaluate its effectiveness, and here are a few, from the most simple to the more statistical. None are anywhere near perfect—this is economics, not science—but together they paint what I think objective observers would agree is convincing re ARRA's positive impact.

The easiest way to see if and how ARRA worked is to just take three key variables—GDP growth, job growth, and unemployment—and plot them over this period, drawing a vertical line in late February 2009, when the bill was signed by the new President. As you see in the next three figures, real GDP stopped falling and soon began to grow, employment losses diminished and then turned positive, and unemployment at least stopped rising.

This is, admittedly, not a strong test, as there are no controls for what would have happened absent the Recovery Act. But for those, like myself, who like a clean shave with Occam's razor, it's at least the first thing you want to see. All else *not* equal, ARRA clearly had its intended effect.

FIGURE 5

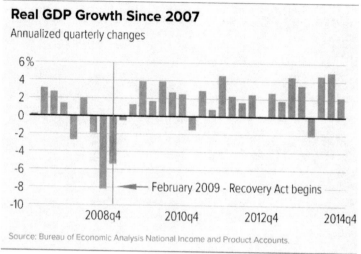

Real GDP Growth Since 2007
Annualized quarterly changes

February 2009 - Recovery Act begins

Source: Bureau of Economic Analysis National Income and Product Accounts.

THE RECONNECTION AGENDA | JARED BERNSTEIN

FIGURE 6

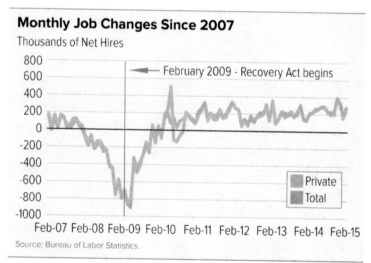

Monthly Job Changes Since 2007
Thousands of Net Hires

February 2009 - Recovery Act begins

Private
Total

Source: Bureau of Labor Statistics.

THE RECONNECTION AGENDA | JARED BERNSTEIN

FIGURE 7

Unemployment Rate Since 2007

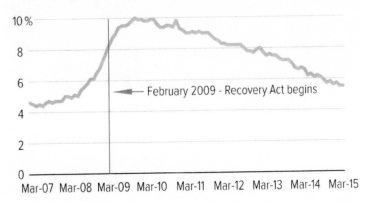

February 2009 - Recovery Act begins

Source: Bureau of Labor Statistics.

The next level of analysis is to try to guesstimate an alternative reality using statistical methods and compare actual reality to your alternative one. This was the practice of a wide variety of analysts, including the White House Council of Economic Advisors, who made Table 3.[40] Based on their estimates of how GDP and jobs would have evolved absent the stimulus, what actually happened was that by early 2010, GDP was more than two percent higher than it would have been otherwise and there were over two million more jobs compared to their estimate for no-ARRA world.

---

[40] http://www.whitehouse.gov/sites/default/files/microsites/CEA-3rd-arra-report.pdf

TABLE 3

Estimates of the Effect of the ARRA Using CEA Multiplier Model

	2009:Q2	2009:Q3	2009:Q4	2010:Q1
GDP Level (%)	+0.7	+1.7	+2.1	+2.5
Employment Level	+380k	+1,095k	+1,742k	+2,230k

Source: Council of Economic Advisors calculations.

You might fairly argue that White House economists had a thumb on the scale, and it's not hard to find opposition research that finds the whole thing to have been a big waste. But non-partisans found results similar to those of the White House economists. The Congressional Budget Office, the well-established non-partisan arbiter of all things economic in DC, undertook the same type of exercise described above and came up with a range of results, which actually makes sense in this context, since it's statistical guesswork.[41] Many of their average estimates look much like that of the White House economists. For example, their GDP impacts in the first quarter of 2010 were between 0.9 percent and 4.3 percent, for an average impact of 2.6 percent, almost exactly the same as the White House economists' estimate. CBO's job estimates were lower than the above table for that quarter—1.6 million on average—but for the next quarter they were up to over two million, so part of the difference there appears to be how the

---

[41] https://www.cbo.gov/sites/default/files/05-25-Impact_of_ARRA.pdf

models handle the timing with which ARRAs various programs made it into the field.

One study from back then struck me as particularly convincing, in a methodological sense. A useful way to get the variation you need to more closely evaluate the impact of the Recovery Act is to compare what happened across states. While all states got hit by the downturn, some got hit harder than others. However, there's a statistical problem here: as you'd expect, the states that got hit the hardest often took the longest to recover, so if you just compare them to the less-hard-hit states, you'd mistakenly conclude that ARRA didn't work that well. That is, you'd find that the states that got the most fiscal relief took the longest to recover when, in fact, the results were biased down by the depth of the downturn in those states.

Economists Chodorow-Reich et al. adjusted for this bias in an interesting way.[42] They recognized that one big ARRA component—FMAP, or Federal Medical Assistance Percentages, which is just a confusing name for extra federal help to states to finance their Medicaid programs during the downturn—were partially a factor of the size of state Medicaid programs *before* the recession. Thus, this ARRA component would be uninfluenced by the impact of the downturn on the state's economy. It's also important to note that a) unlike the federal government, states have to balance their budgets every year, and b) FMAP funds, which amounted to almost $90 billion, were completely fungible.

---

[42] http://scholar.harvard.edu/files/chodorow-reich/files/does_state_fiscal_relief_during_recessions_increase_employment.pdf

States used them to patch holes in Medicaid, but that wasn't all they did with the fiscal aid. The authors report that "ARRA funds were at least partially used to avoid program cuts, since a concentration of the employment effects appears to have occurred in sectors (government, health, and education) which are reliant on state funds."

At any rate, their punchline finding was that for every $100,000 in FMAP fiscal relief, states created just under four jobs per year, at the cost of $26,000 per job per year. In this business, that's a *very* high bang-for-the-buck, which I raise in part to underscore the point made above in all that theorizing about the potency of fiscal policy when the Fed's interest rate mechanism is jammed by the zero lower bound.

Doesn't All this Fiscal Policy Raise the Budget Deficit?

But what about the budget deficit? As noted, the federal budget deficit went to almost 10 percent of GDP in 2009, though of course not all of that was discretionary (i.e., newly legislated) fiscal stimulus; revenues also decline in downturns and there's automatic safety net spending kicking in that isn't counted as part of ARRA. But in the spirit of all of that discussion about why we want to be in box 1, that's a good thing. One of the central points about fiscal policy as part of the reconnection agenda is that you want budget deficits to temporarily expand in recessions due to both higher spending on stabilization programs and lower tax receipts. And the deeper the downturn, the bigger the necessary deficit. This rule holds even more when the Fed is at least partially sidelined by the zero lower bound.

Given the economic amnesia around this simple point, I and others have written extensively about it, and you're welcome to read up on it, but let me cut to the chase.[43] The policy we want in the reconnection toolbox vis-à-vis fiscal deficits is **CDSH**: cyclical **d**ove, structural **h**awk. Again, very simple: when the private sector economy is malfunctioning to a significant degree, meaning large enough to move big quantities like GDP, job growth, and unemployment in the wrong direction, then we want to turn dovish on the deficit—make ourselves perfectly comfortable with its expansion. When the private sector is back and all the gaps that developed are closed, or at least solidly moving towards closure, then we want deficits to come down.

Moreover, as economist Dean Baker and I stress in joint work we've done on full employment, if you actually follow the movements of deficits and surpluses over time, you'll see that they're often driven more by expansions and contractions in the real economy than by the taxing and spending policies that partisans freak out over.[44] Most notably, we show that in the last time we had a budget surplus, the late 1990s, the biggest driver

---

[43] See, for example, chapter 7 here:
http://www.boeckler.de/pdf/p_restoring_shared_prosperity.pdf
[44] See chapter 4: http://www.cepr.net/documents/Getting-Back-to-Full-Employment_20131118.pdf

was clearly economic growth, not legislated changes in fiscal policies.[45]

Those examples all show the benefits of fiscal policy against market failures, but here's one that shows something equally important: the costs of austerity. Figure 8 shows the impact of fiscal contraction on real GDP growth for three recent years.[46] The middle bar for 2013 is particularly notable, both for its magnitude and the factors that drove it. At 1.6 percent of lost GDP, that's over a million jobs lost based on historical relationships and about three-quarters of a point added to unemployment, at a time when the US economy was still trying to recover from the residual pull of the Great Recession. The negative fiscal impact was caused largely by the pre-emptive sunset of a temporary paycheck booster (the "payroll tax holiday") and a bunch of mindless and unnecessary spending cuts—that's not just my opinion; it's the opinion of politicians on both sides of the aisle—called "sequestration."

---

[45] Confusion around this point was what famously got economists Rogoff and Reinhart into trouble a few years ago, when they asserted that when the debt-to-GDP ratio gets too high (above 90 percent), it slows growth (that and a spreadsheet error, though I'm afraid we all make spreadsheet errors—this causal confusion is the much bigger deal). As the text in this section suggests and my work with Dean corroborates, this is backwards. Economist Arin Dube provides statistical evidence for the correct causal flow: http://www.nextnewdeal.net/rortybomb/guest-post-reinhartrogoff-and-growth-time-debt.

[46] Technically, the fiscal factor in play here is "fiscal impulse," which is the change in fiscal policy from one year to the next.

FIGURE 8

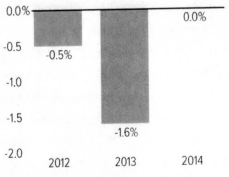

The Cost of Austerity

GDP growth lost due to preemptive fiscal tightening

Source: Goldman Sachs Global Investment Research.

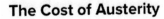

Related work by the IMF is interesting because it shows that, far from an American obsession, destructive fiscal policy was and is much more common in Europe.[47] Economists Blanchard and Leigh show that European economists consistently and systematically underestimated the damage done by austerity measures, even once the results were in. That is, Blanchard and Leigh's research showed the difference between the economists' forecasts—what they thought would happen to GDP growth and unemployment if they reduced their deficits—and what actually happened. The economists were off by a factor of between two and three, meaning that's how much they underestimated the positive impacts of fiscal stimulus on growth and unemployment

---

[47] http://www.imf.org/external/pubs/ft/wp/2013/wp1301.pdf

(they thought the fiscal multiplier—the bang-for-fiscal-buck—was 0.5 when it was actually between 1 and 1.5).

OK, that's Fiscal. I Suppose You're Going to Tell Me that Monetary Policy Also Works.

What about monetary policy? What's the evidence of its effectiveness? That's actually a more complicated question. First, monetary policy has been a constant factor in advanced and emerging economies for many decades (our own Fed was born about a century ago) and thus doesn't often provide the discrete policy interventions you get in fiscal policy, as with ARRA. Second, the Fed's main tool is a "price," an interest rate that affects the price of borrowing throughout the economy, so we broadly assume it must have an impact, much like we correctly assume that the rise and fall in gas prices must have an impact.

There's empirical evidence to back up such assumptions. People my age remember the Volcker recession of the early 1980s when Fed Chair Paul Volcker took the Fed rate up to 20 percent to break an inflation rate that was in double digits. When the big man (some macroeconomists, like my friend Dean Baker, are actually kinda small; Volcker really is a big guy) took his foot off of the brake and lowered rates aggressively, the 1980s recovery took off. Note also how by dint of raising the Fed rate so high, the 1980s Fed had a highly elevated perch from which to lower rates. From interest-rate mountain tops of 20 percent, the "zero lower bound" simply couldn't be seen with the naked eye.

And then there's the full employment period of the 1990s, widely understood to have been facilitated in no small part by Alan Greenspan. As Baker and I observed:

> . . . in the summer of 1995 then-Federal Reserve Board Chairman Alan Greenspan made a remarkable break with the orthodoxy within the profession. He insisted that he saw no evidence of inflation in spite of the fact that the unemployment rate, at 5.7 percent, was below the conventional range of estimates for the structural rate of unemployment. As a result, he pushed through a cut in interest rates that opened the door for a speedup of the economy and further declines in the unemployment rate. By the summer of 1997 the unemployment rate had fallen below 5.0 percent. It fell below 4.5 percent the following summer and finally stabilized near 4.0 percent, the year-round average for 2000.[48]

And that was the last time we were at full employment.

Finally, economists Blinder and Zandi, in an exhaustive review of the full spate of measures that the government and the Fed took throughout the Great Recession, found that in the years during and after the Great Recession, interventions by the Fed (and related actions in financial markets) lowered unemployment by two to three percentage points and raised GDP by as much as 2.7 percent.[49] Historically speaking, those are large effects.

---

[48] http://www.cepr.net/documents/Getting-Back-to-Full-Employment_20131118.pdf
[49] https://www.economy.com/mark-zandi/documents/End-of-Great-Recession.pdf

OK, They Work. But Can We Make Fiscal and Monetary Policies Work Better?

No question, the Fed can be an important part of a reconnection agenda, as can fiscal policy. In fact, to be most effective they must work in tandem, especially in periods of economic weakness. But beyond making the case as I've tried to do above with both theory and evidence, what specifically is the "ask" here? What needs to change to make sure these two behemoths of economic policy are prominent and useful components of the reconnection agenda?

In both cases, there are technical fixes with the potential to lift the effectiveness of both fiscal and monetary interventions. Let's start with fiscal, where it's all about getting the triggers in place, and move to monetary, where the key improvements involve asymmetric risk and getting the natural rate—the lowest unemployment rate consistent with stable prices—right. Or . . . if not "right," then less wrong.

The fiscal ask: "Countercyclical" fiscal policy—deficit-financed, temporary government spending designed to offset demand contractions—should a) turn on and off in a timely manner, and b) use its resources for high bang-for-the-buck projects where they're most needed.

The first part—turning on and off—must be a function of measurable triggers and not of political whims. We already have programs that automatically respond to need. Think of the way Unemployment Insurance automatically responds to increasing joblessness or nutritional support (food stamps) to income losses among the least well-off. Right now, other programs like subsidized jobs or state fiscal help are discretionary (i.e., left up to Congress to legislate), which leads to considerable waste. There's no reason why these other fiscal interventions shouldn't be similarly keyed off of state or even sub-state economic indicators. In fact, to not do so is to risk sending the fire trucks to the wrong house, or almost as bad, to risk having the fire trucks leave before the fire is out.

I happen to disdain the hyper-partisan congressional gridlock that has dominated politics for years now and shows no sign of letting up. But if they insist on feckless squabbling when the economy's doing fine, that's one thing. When they engage in that sort of thing when we're in crisis, it's obviously quite another. The political system in general, then, and the countercyclical system in particular, needs a mechanism to prevent congressional gridlock from keeping the fire trucks in the station when someone's house is burning down. In fact, such a mechanism would be an important tool in the reconnection agenda toolbox.

In addition, you want the trucks to head for the right house—the one with the fire—and, if you'll allow me to stretch the analogy to the breaking point, the fire department has the added problem that everybody wants the trucks to come to their house, even if they've barely got a spark ablaze. That is, members of Congress have obvious and understandable incentives to want fiscal relief to flow to their constituents, regardless of need.

Triggers can help avoid this, and, as budget expert David Kamin has pointed out, can do so in a way that's fair and maybe even politically acceptable. He notes that "if the triggers are enacted before we actually enter recession, policy makers are essentially behind the veil of ignorance. They don't know which states will most benefit from the future relief. Thus, no one will feel cut out and all could potentially benefit—it's an insurance policy for the country as a whole."[50]

As noted, the alternative to triggers in this case is discretionary fiscal policy, which is what we do now (except, of course, for the automatic stabilizers, like UI or food stamps). That is, you wait until it's clear that recession is on the land, squabble with Congress for fiscal policies to help, and end up having to buy off members with goodies for their districts.

So far, I've largely focused on how and where fiscal help should trigger on, but such triggers can also help on the other side of the downturn, when the fire is reliably out. I saw close-up the importance of this function—rather, the damage done by the lack of it—in the slow recovery out of the deep recession that began in late 2007 and was officially declared to be over by mid-2009. Officials in the Obama administration were anxious to turn to deficit reduction, motivated more by politics than economics. So they convinced themselves—ourselves, as I was a member of the econ team at the time—that "green shoots" of recovery were

---

[50] The quote is from personal correspondence with Kamin. See also: http://www.brookings.edu/research/papers/2014/12/15-legislation-responds-fiscal-uncertainty-kamin

breaking out all over (I recall a call-in show I did at the time where a listener said that if we thought the economy was really improving, we must be "smoking green shoots").

To be fair, we on the economics team did try to go back to the fiscal well, but the political doors were to some degree closed (though not as much as you might have thought).[51] The use of fiscal triggers thus has the potential to avoid this problem by providing real time indicators of when fiscal help is needed and when it isn't; in other words, triggers can help distinguish when green shoots are real and when they're imaginary.

Thus far, this exposition has assumed timely and reliable indicators off of which the triggers get pulled. Are such statistical indicators available? If not, could we create them?

The obvious trigger is unemployment, a consummate cyclical variable. It's very timely on a national level: on the first Friday of each month, we learn the jobless rate (and many related labor market indicators, like job growth, labor force participation, and under-employment) for the previous month. Towards the end of the month, we get state level unemployment, and a few weeks later, metro-level estimates. So, for example, in early January 2015, we learned the national unemployment rate for December 2014 (which happened to be 5.6 percent, since you asked), on

---

[51] That "to some degree" is important and underappreciated, as I explain in this post: http://jaredbernsteinblog.com/there-was-more-to-the-stimulus-than-the-stimulus/. In fact, we were able to go to the fiscal well more than people in this debate generally realize or acknowledge. But still, as I note in the post, not enough to avoid "negative fiscal impulse."

January 27 we got state rates for December, and on February 4 we got December's city rates.

That's not bad, and the historical record shows that an unemployment trigger[52] would fairly quickly signal to policy makers that a downturn was underway. In fact, certain extended unemployment benefits are already keyed to increases in the jobless rate. The timing record also shows that recent recoveries have begun as "jobless" (GDP growth arrives well before job growth). Some folks who think about this sort of thing worry that an unemployment rate trigger would not trigger off soon enough. That is, it might risk keeping fiscal relief flowing after an official recovery has begun.

I'd argue that this is a feature, not a bug. If anything, my concern would be that the unemployment rate would fall too quickly, signaling the fire was out when live sparks were still burning. That's because of a measurement problem inherent in the way we measure unemployment, the one I discussed above in some detail. To remind you, if unemployed persons give up the job search because they can't find work, the jobless rate goes down, making it look like the job market is tightening up when in fact the opposite is occurring.

In 2010, for example, the decline in the unemployment rate from 9.8 percent to 9.2 percent occurred because of a fall of the same magnitude in the labor force. Imagine a fiscal trigger that shut off

---

[52] Specifically, an unemployment trigger would be an increase above some recent average so as to distinguish a cyclical rise from a structural one.

a subsidized jobs program for the long-term unemployed based on that trend, when in actuality it was telling the opposite story: unemployed job seekers giving up and leaving the labor market.

So we need other triggers, and a recent study by economists at the Chicago Federal Reserve provides one set of possibilities.[53] These economists recommend the use of composite indexes of state business cycle indicators tracked by the Philadelphia Fed, which include "nonfarm payroll employment, average hours worked in manufacturing, the unemployment rate, and wage and salary disbursements deflated by the consumer price index." They show that these State Coincident Indexes may hold promise in terms of reliably catching cyclical turning points. For example, as shown in Figure 9, the indexes captured some of the differences between states that did relatively well during the recession (like Wyoming and North Dakota) and states that did poorly (like Nevada).

At the same time, the results were counterintuitive for California, a state that saw a comparatively large 5.4 percentage point rise in unemployment over the course of the recession to a rate of 11.3 percent in June 2009, the sixth highest rate in the nation. California also had one of the highest foreclosure rates in the nation[54] and, according to the Economic Security Index developed by Yale professor Jacob Hacker and colleagues, only five states saw a larger share of their citizens lose at least 25 percent of their

---

[53] https://www.chicagofed.org/publications/economic-perspectives/2010/3q-mattoon-haleco-meyer-foster

[54] http://www.realtytrac.com/landing/2009-year-end-foreclosure-report.html

available household income each year between 2008 and 2010.[55] In other words, by just about any metric, the state was whacked hard by the Great Recession. Yet the State Coincident Indexes showed similar results for California and states that were less affected by the recession (like Maryland and New Mexico), meaning this metric alone would likely be an inadequate trigger.

FIGURE 9

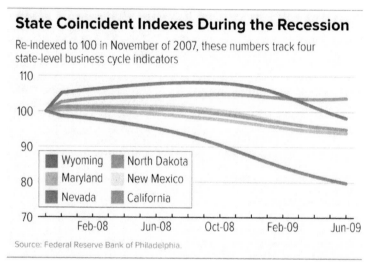

State Coincident Indexes During the Recession

Re-indexed to 100 in November of 2007, these numbers track four state-level business cycle indicators

Source: Federal Reserve Bank of Philadelphia.

SNAP, or food stamps, caseloads offer another data source that conveys information about need quickly, and are thus a good trigger candidate. SNAP has been consistently found to be responsive to nutritional needs during recessions and, unlike the unemployment rate, it doesn't turn off too soon. Also, SNAP data are available with quite short lags (about a month) at the state

---

[55] http://www.economicsecurityindex.org/assets/state_reports/CA_dated.pdf

level, so they can provide some of the geo-variance we need in a targeted trigger.

It would be smart trigger policy to tie together some of the lessons discussed above regarding the importance of fiscal policy when the Fed rate is stuck at zero. An effective fiscal trigger might include this macro-constraint, in tandem with others noted above. If policy makers were on the fence regarding the utility of stimulative fiscal policy based on unemployment, the SNAP rolls, etc., factoring in the problem of the Fed rate stuck at zero might be enough to push them towards doing more and vice versa.

Once we get fiscal relief to the right places and at the right time, we'd like to get the biggest bang for the buck from it. My own experience, corroborated above by the research I cited about multipliers (that stuff about FMAP), suggests that state fiscal relief is a strong candidate. The key observation here is that unlike the federal government, states must balance their annual budgets. Thus, when job and income losses begin to weigh on state budgets, they must raise taxes or cut services, a surefire recipe for making a bad situation worse.

Think of the nation's economy as fifty states and Uncle Sam, all in a boat taking on water. Sam's the only guy with a bucket. By dint of his essential ability to run budget deficits, Sam's states' best hope against sinking.[56] More concretely, I vividly recall a trip

---

[56] By the way, that right there is one of the main reasons you want to very strongly oppose the push that flares up every now and again for a balanced budget amendment for the federal budget. That would ensure that no one, not even Uncle Sam, had a bucket.

with VP Biden to tout our fiscal relief efforts. We attended a ceremony wherein the mayor of the town we were visiting showed the audience a bunch of pink slips for teachers in one hand and a new Recovery Act check in the other. He (the mayor) then dramatically ripped up the pink slips. That's state fiscal relief at work.

Later, in Chapter 6, I feature another Recovery Act program I'd significantly scale up and not just in the next downturn, but in any part of the country where pockets of joblessness exist even in the midst of expansion: a direct job creation program through subsidized work. It's a simple and effective way to apply fiscal policy to job creation, but you'll have to wait a few pages to learn more about it.

The monetary ask: Because of its political independence and limited tools, the monetary ask—policy changes that would make monetary policy more effective in getting to full employment—is simpler than the fiscal one. It's all about getting the weights right.

As discussed, the mandate at the Fed is to balance the dual goals of full employment and stable prices. Sounds pretty straightforward until you consider the following: first, as stressed in the full employment chapter, no one knows with the requisite precision what number corresponds to the "natural rate" of unemployment. Second, though the tradeoff between unemployment and inflation is real, we don't know the magnitude of that correlation. In part, our ignorance is due to the fact that both of these quantities move around with economic conditions,

Fed actions, productivity growth, global supply issues, and who knows what else. End of the day, these constraints make it very tricky indeed to find the right balance for Fed policy in the interest of meeting the dual mandate.

That's all technical stuff of the sort that economists work on and argue about all the time. We actually travel to conference centers and squabble about what's the natural rate and the slope of the Phillips Curve (the relationship between unemployment and inflation). I'm sure you're jealous. But even were we to resolve these gnarly technical questions, there's still another factor in play, one that's actually been huge in breaking the connection between growth and broadly shared prosperity: the power to influence the Fed's actions in ways that favor one side or the other.

I said the Fed was politically independent. I didn't say they exist in a vacuum. In the real world, there's tremendous pressure on the central bankers from heavily moneyed interests to settle that balancing act in favor of low inflation, not full employment. This dynamic stems from the difference between people who depend on paychecks and thus on tight labor markets, and a smaller but more powerful group of people who depend on asset portfolios, which get eroded by inflation. What matters here is who benefits from higher labor costs—again, paycheck earners—and whose profits are squeezed by those costs.

At any rate, when the Fed is engaged in stimulus through low rates and the expansion of its balance sheet, meaning the Fed's governors are injecting money into the economy, there's often great pressure on them to cut it out and get back to the business of fighting inflation, even if inflation's nowhere to be seen.

For the record, both the Yellen and Bernanke-led Feds have resisted much of this pressure, but as I write in early 2015, the pressure to raise rates and the uncertainty around key parameters are coming together. Let me show you what I mean.

Figure 10 plots three recent trends and a constant: unemployment, inflation,[57] wage growth, and the Fed's most recent estimate of the lowest unemployment rate consistent with stable inflation (I call this the full employment unemployment rate, or FEUR). As unemployment rose sharply in the Great Recession, you can kind of see inflation and wage growth slow a bit, but they clearly don't budge at all as unemployment falls, even—and here's the punchline—as it approaches the Fed's own full employment rate.

Now consider this for a moment. If the Fed's 5.1 percent is an accurate benchmark signaling to monetary policy makers that they'd better start raising rates to slow the economy in advance of inflationary pressures, then surely we should see some, any, a hint, of such pressures as we near that benchmark. Instead, we're seeing nothing.

And yet, not only does one typically hear at such times the usual caterwauling from the outside to preempt this phantom menace of forthcoming inflation, we often hear some Fed officials

---

[57] That's the "core" personal consumer deflator, the Fed's benchmark inflation rate. "Core" means it leaves out volatile food and energy prices.

themselves making sounds like they're buying such admonitions. At the time the data story you see above was unfolding, one of the Fed's regional bank presidents, a voting member on interest rate policy, said this:

> We are going to conceivably have to make a judgment that the outlook, even in the absence of realtime inflation readings that are rising, that inflation is nonetheless converging to target.[58]

FIGURE 10

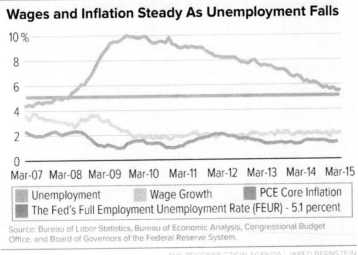

Wages and Inflation Steady As Unemployment Falls

Unemployment | Wage Growth | PCE Core Inflation
The Fed's Full Employment Unemployment Rate (FEUR) - 5.1 percent

Source: Bureau of Labor Statistics, Bureau of Economic Analysis, Congressional Budget Office, and Board of Governors of the Federal Reserve System.

It's convoluted Fedspeak, so let me interpret, at least the way I understand it: "Even if inflation isn't going up, we're going to have to act as if it is." I wish I'd had that one back in grade

---

[58] http://www.nytimes.com/reuters/2015/01/12/business/12reuters-usa-fed-lockhart-inflation.html?src=busln&_r=2

school: "even though my homework assignment is not ready, I'd like you to proceed as if it is." And this guy's not alone. Another member of the Fed board has predicted five of the last zero inflationary outbreaks.[59]

In order to be a more effective tool in the reconnection agenda toolbox, the Fed needs to be able to assess not just the risks of both sides of the mandate, but their relative weights. As I write this passage, even five-and-a-half years into an economic expansion, those risks are highly imbalanced, or asymmetric, as Fed wonks like to say. The risk of not actually getting to and staying at full employment is much greater than the risk of inflationary pressures.

And yet, other than the stalwart determination of our pretty awesome Fed chair, Janet Yellen, who seems to get pretty much everything I'm laying out here, there's nothing other than hot air like my own pushing the institution to assign the correct asymmetric weights. Given the critical importance of their independence, I of course want to tread lightly here. I'm not suggesting that some outside body tell them what to do and not do re macro-management. That route may sound appealing to those of you who share the reconnection agenda I'm building here, but I guarantee you there are others out there with their own agendas for the Fed that look very different than the one described in these pages.

---

[59] http://www.newrepublic.com/article/118870/five-times-richard-fisher-has-wrongly-warned-inflation-2011

So what would help the Fed resist pressure to not nip full employment in the bud? Four things: a more realistic view of the natural rate, wage targeting, "reverse hysteresis" (sounds mysterious, but we've actually already discussed it without naming it), and a people's campaign.

On the first three, I must invoke help from my fellow economists. The Fed must remain immune from political pressure but it must be, and it is, an evolving institution when it comes to absorbing the work of academic economists. A quick look at Figure 10, along with much more careful statistical research, suggests that we don't have a good bead on the natural rate, which is an extremely important limitation to implementing the optimal monetary policy.[60]

If we as economists are invested in having monetary policy achieve its intended effects of maximizing employment in the context of stable prices—and don't get me wrong, that latter goal is also essential—then we need to stop writing down numbers that don't make much sense, like the Fed's natural rate of unemployment (and this isn't meant to pick on them; the Congressional Budget Office's natural rate is even more out of touch). A concerted effort by researchers challenging the conventional wisdom around the natural rate is warranted and my bet would be that eventually such research would rub off on the Fed.

---

[60] See references in this piece: http://economix.blogs.nytimes.com/2013/11/20/the-unemployment-rate-at-full-employment-how-low-can-you-go/

Another very important part of the economic research agenda, one that links quite directly to the reconnection agenda, should be looking into the utility of wage targeting by the Fed. That is, instead of keying an increase in interest rates to price growth, the Fed keys off of wage growth. Especially in a global economy with large and growing inequalities in many advanced economies, it should not be assumed by default that economic expansions lead to pervasive wage pressures, or even price pressures. In fact, that's a poignant message from Figure 10: even with unemployment close to the "natural rate" by early 2015, neither wages nor prices had yet accelerated at all. Thus, targeting not just earnings, but the extent to which wage growth feeds into price growth, would be a reliable way to connect Fed policy to workers' paychecks.

Look at it this way. As Figure 10 reveals, and as economic history of the past few decades confirms,[61] real wage growth, particularly for middle and low-wage workers, has been a key missing ingredient from recent recoveries (see also Table A1). In this recovery, which if history is any guide is at least middle-aged if not older,[62] wages have been uniquely flat. In the 2000s the story was similar, as real compensation for the typical worker grew about half-a-percent per year.[63] Working families simply cannot keep losing decades of wage growth like this, at least not without

---

[61] See this chapter on the history of US wage developments by Mishel et al.: http://www.stateofworkingamerica.org/subjects/wages/?reader

[62] The average postwar expansion lasted about five years. As of the first quarter of 2015, we're on year six. http://www.nber.org/cycles/cyclesmain.html

[63] Data underlying Figure A4.

a strong and persistent policy response. I recommend wage targeting by the Fed in that spirit.

I'm not alone. No less than the researchers at Goldman Sachs, who do high-level analysis of monetary policy (believe me, GS has the bucks to hire some serious economists), recently wrote the following in a piece on Fed policy:

> . . . we find that the benefits of focusing on wage inflation are substantial when slack is difficult to measure and wage growth acts as a reliable cross check for the true amount of spare capacity . . . Although our analysis is subject to a number of caveats, we conclude that increased emphasis on wage developments would likely be beneficial for Fed policy. This would be a strong argument for a continued accommodative stance as current wage growth [in 2014] remains stuck at only 2 percent.[64]

Now, let's relate this back to this sickly sounding condition introduced above: "hysteresis." It's the problem that occurs when persistent slack in the economy in general and the job market in particular leads to "permanent" damage. It's when cyclical problems last long enough that they become structural problems. You encountered the idea above first in the discussion of the three old/new fiscal insights by Ball et al., and then again in the

---

[64] "The case for a wage Taylor rule," Stehn, June 4, 2014.

discussion of how labor force dropouts distort the unemployment rate by making the job market look tighter than it is.

Since the growth of the labor force is a key factor in the economy's potential growth rate, a slower growing labor force maps onto slower real GDP growth. But if running a sagging economy for too long leads to long-term damage, can running a hot economy reverse some of the damage? Is there such a thing as "reverse hysteresis?"

I believe so and there's at least some evidence to support my hunch. For example, in the same analysis from which Figure 10 is drawn, I show that if you assume the existence of reverse hysteresis, you can explain the behavior of recent wage trends much better than if you deny that possibility.[65]

But far more important than my own musing and number crunching, check out this quote from a speech by a VIP in 2014:

> Some 'retirements' are not voluntary, and some of these workers may rejoin the labor force in a stronger economy . . . a significant amount of the decline in participation during the recovery is due to slack.[66]

That's another way to say that reverse hysteresis is a real possibility, and this is the opinion of one Janet Yellen, our own Fed Chair. A Fed that considers this dynamic to be a real

---

[65] http://www.washingtonpost.com/posteverything/wp/2015/01/12/heres-why-wages-arent-growing-the-job-market-is-not-as-tight-as-the-unemployment-rate-says-it-is/
[66] http://www.federalreserve.gov/newsevents/speech/yellen20140331a.htm

possibility should be one that is willing to keep its feet off of the economic brakes long enough for hysteresis to shift into reverse, thus undoing some damage that other, less re-connective agendas would simply write off.

Finally, there's the need for a people's campaign targeted at the Fed. Even though I think we often overestimate the power of the Fed to shape economic outcomes,[67] by dint of its control over a critical variable in our economy (the Fed rate) as well as its role as bank regulator (a topic I return to in Chapter 7) it holds tremendous sway. As such, its actions have considerable impact on the lives of working people, and yet few know much about it, especially compared to bankers and those in finance. And yet, there is absolutely no question—in fact, both Yellen and Bernanke were explicit on this point—that working households are a key Fed constituency.

But while more enlightened central bankers may recognize that obligation, for it to become something they feel more acutely, they need to interact with those at the receiving end of their policies. To be fair, there's some of that going on already, but more recently, a group of activists organized by the racial and economic justice group Center for Popular Democracy took this pursuit to another level. Their mission statement in this space echoes some of the same ideas and concerns I expressed above:

---

[67] http://economix.blogs.nytimes.com/2013/11/15/yellen-impresses-but-feds-powers-are-finite/

The Federal Reserve has tremendous influence over our economy. Although our communities continue to suffer through a weak recovery and economic inequality keeps growing, corporate and financial interests are demanding that the Fed put the brakes on growth so wages don't rise. There is a real danger that in early 2015, the Fed will cut the legs out from the recovery before the economy reaches full acceleration, costing our communities millions of jobs and workers tens of billions in wages.

But for the first time in 20 years, community organizations, unions, and consumer advocates are mobilizing around the Federal Reserve for a national economic policy that prioritizes full employment and rising wages.[68]

The organization is also pushing the Fed to devote some of its economic research staff's considerable firepower to more work on reconnection-style ideas; though again, while the Fed banks don't say a lot about it, more of that already goes on than you might think. The Boston Fed, for example, is working on a project called the Working Cities Challenge, where Fed research and expertise combines with stakeholders in troubled communities to build human and investment capital targeted at low-income households.[69]

---

[68] http://populardemocracy.org/campaign/fed-national-campaign-strong-economy

[69] http://www.bostonfed.org/news/speeches/rosengren/2014/101814/index.htm?wt.source=res_agenda

But the CPD group has an even more ambitious idea:

> Under its quantitative easing program, the Fed supported the economy by purchasing bonds and financial securities . . . Now that that program is over, it should explore the possibility of using its legal authority to purchase state and municipal bonds. Zero interest rate lending to cities and states would help them reduce their debts and invest in public works projects – like renewable energy generation, public transit, climate change adaptation, and affordable housing – that will create good jobs and strengthen our communities.

Wait up . . . can the Fed do that, i.e., buy state and local bonds? I asked a Fed president, one sympathetic to CPD's cause, that very question. He said no—their charter forbids it. But when I relayed that answer to a CPD official, he assured me that this wasn't their lawyers' interpretation of the charter. So, who knows? I see a fight worth having coming soon.

The point is that like any other institution that hopes to survive and flourish, the Fed must evolve. I've offered what I hope are a number of ideas, both in research and advocacy, that can move that evolution in the direction of reconnecting growth and prosperity.

Conclusion

In sum, fiscal and monetary policy are absolutely essential tools in the reconnection toolbox. In fact, they have to work together, especially when monetary policy—specifically the Fed's key interest rate—is jammed up against zero. The evidence reveals solid potential for both types of interventions, and there are a variety of ways to ratchet up their effectiveness when it comes to getting to full employment, boosting wage growth, offsetting cyclical downturns, avoiding permanent damage to the economy and the people in it, and providing states with budget relief in recessions.

Those ideas include fiscal triggers based on not just the unemployment rate but broader indicators of state economic conditions, wage targeting at the Fed, running a tight enough job market to pull sideliners back in, and a people's campaign such that folks from all walks of life can interact with an institution that has real sway over their economic lives.

OK, glad that's over and we now have some kick-butt macroeconomic tools in the reconnection toolbox. Let's turn to another area where policy can help to generate not just more jobs, but more good jobs: revitalizing the manufacturing sector through going after our persistent trade imbalances.

Chapter 5

Reducing the Persistent American Trade Deficit, a Steep Barrier to Full Employment

I started the last chapter with the assumption that, like me, you want to get to full employment. Hopefully at this point you're with me on wielding the tools of fiscal and monetary policy to get there and stay there. In this chapter, we break down yet another barrier standing between us and a robust reconnection agenda: the persistent US trade deficit.

Yes, that implies reducing the amount of stuff we buy, on net, from other countries (that "on net" is not in there to sound wonky; those little words are extremely important as I'll explain in a moment). But let me either warn or reassure you that what follows has nothing to do with protectionism, by which I mean raising barriers to the flow of goods, services, and even people between countries. I am a committed free trader for numerous reasons.

First, I'm all for the USA, but I think the Bangladeshis, the Haitians, and the people of all other developing countries also deserve a chance to pull themselves up, and globalization, by which I mean expanded trade between countries, should give them an opportunity to do so. In fact, a significant part of what you'll read below documents the process by which, under the current trade regime, developing countries that could be investing more in their own people are lending their capital to us, thereby sacrificing longer-term investments for short-term growth. I argue that we'd both be better off if instead of lending so much to us so we can consume more than we produce, these countries invested more in their own well-being at home.

Second, it seems inconceivable to me that this global genie would go back in the bottle, so blocking trade is a pretty fruitless endeavor (shaping trade agreements to protect workers as opposed to just investors, on the other hand, is an important pursuit in this space). And given how much global trade has expanded the supply of goods while holding down their prices, why would we want to restrict trade? Third, as the dad of two kids adopted from China, I wake up every morning in a global household (often earlier than I'd like).

OK, so if I'm not going to suggest protectionist measures, what can be done to improve our trade balance and give our manufacturers a fighting chance to compete in global markets (as you'll see, our trade deficit is fully in manufactured goods and oil—we run a surplus in services)?[70] The answer has to do with

---

[70] Actually, there's good news here on the energy front regarding our trade balance. While we still import more crude oil than we sell abroad, we recently began to run trade surpluses in refined energy products.

the good old US dollar, but let's not get ahead of ourselves. There's a fair bit of ground to be covered before we get there.

One Little Word . . . Three Little Letters

Suppose I told you I went to the see the Wizards (DC's much-improved basketball team) last night. I gleefully reported that it was a great game and our squad scored 97 points! As I start to walk away, you ask the obvious question: "Hold up! What did the other guys score?"

You've just asked the "net" question (having nothing to do with the basketball net, just to be clear), one that is critical in the trade debate. Let me explain its importance by taking you back to my days in the Obama administration.

My tenure occurred during the Great Recession that began in late 2007, when the economics team was understandably obsessed with getting the US economy growing again. Well, not to get into too much arithmetic (though it turns out that adding and subtracting are actually pretty much all you need to get the fundamentals of this trade argument), but exports are a plus to our economy (i.e., they add to GDP) while imports are a negative. Exports are points for your team; imports are points for the other team (the analogy breaks down in that I want poor countries to prosper through trade—"score baskets"—but table that thought for a moment).

So it made sense that we wanted to expand exports to help increase economic activity among businesses that produce goods to sell abroad, along with the upstream firms along the supply chain that provide them with the inputs they need to make their outputs. So in his 2010 State of the Union speech, President Obama announced the national export initiative, the goal of which was to double our exports by 2015.[71]

"We mean *net* exports," I said when I first heard about the idea, "Right?" Actually, no. The National Export Initiative, as it was called, was just about our score, not the other team's.

The problem with this formulation is that what matters to growth and jobs is not exports. It's *net* exports, or exports minus imports. If your squad scores 97 and their squad scores 100, you lose. If we import more than we export, then trade is, by definition, a drag on growth. That doesn't necessarily mean that at the end of the day, we'll grow more slowly. There are, of course, other offsets, as I describe in a moment, and we've had periods of fast growth amidst large trade deficits. I've often noted, for example, that the last time we were at full employment in this country was the year 2000. Well, in that year we had 4 percent unemployment along with a historically large trade deficit of -4 percent of GDP (we also had a dot-com bubble, but again, I'm getting ahead of this story). Still, just based on the simple GDP identity, trade deficits by themselves subtract from growth and jobs, and good jobs at that.

In fact, let's look at the simplest definition of Gross Domestic Product, the most commonly referenced measure of the total

---

[71] http://www.whitehouse.gov/the-press-office/remarks-president-state-union-address

dollar value of the economy (and yes, it leaves important things out, but that doesn't affect the analysis that follows). It's:

$$GDP = C + I + G + (EX - IM)$$

C is consumer spending, I is investment in businesses and homes, G is government spending, and EX and IM are the focus of this chapter, exports and imports. As you see, if IM > EX, then net exports are a drag on growth.

OK, that's the theory, but what's the reality? Surely, a kick-butt producer like the US typically exports more than it imports, or to put in econo-mese: our trade accounts are usually in surplus, right?

Wrong, as shown in Figure 11. From the 1950s through the late 1970s, the trade balance as a share of GDP was about zero. But since then, it has averaged -2.5 percent.

What do such numbers mean? Well, here's where basic arithmetic comes in handy. For one thing, just glancing at that GDP equation above, it means that all else equal, there's less growth. And while it's alarming how elusive this point is to many who should know better, the point itself is not arguable. It's definitional.

As noted above, all else isn't equal; there are other moving parts and we've had lots of growth periods over the years since the trade balance went south. Referencing once again the equation above, that must mean C, I, or G—the "offsets" mentioned above—worked overtime to offset the fact of IM > EX.

FIGURE 11

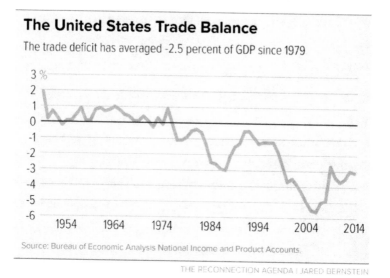

The United States Trade Balance

The trade deficit has averaged -2.5 percent of GDP since 1979

Source: Bureau of Economic Analysis National Income and Product Accounts

Again, that's just definitional. One of those other letters had to expand to make up for the persistent trade deficits you see in Figure 11. If that were the end of the story, we'd stop here. Reducing our trade deficit would not appear to be a particularly promising way to get to full employment. But, in fact, our trade imbalances have been problematic for at least three reasons.

First, by spending our money on so many things made abroad, we're not just exporting jobs, we're exporting good jobs. As noted, our trade deficit is in manufactured goods, meaning it's costing us factory jobs. It's true that the compensation premium in that sector isn't as large as it used to be, but it's still significant and positive, especially when you include benefits. For example, in 2013, average compensation in manufacturing was about 10 percent higher than the economy's average.[72] That's not huge, but remember, that average includes the highest paid bankers. For low-wage factory workers, the wage premium is about 15 percent.[73]

Second, the manufacturing sector is responsible for important spillovers to the rest of the economy, punching well above its weight, for example, in terms of productivity and research and development (R&D). In recent years, manufacturing has accounted for about 10 percent of our output but 70 percent of our R&D. Output per hour, or productivity, also tends to run higher in the factory sector, though the difference is smaller than the official statistics suggest, a point I'll return to below.[74]

Also, and this is highly germane to the goal of full employment, manufacturing has a large employment multiplier relative to other sectors, creating almost twice as many jobs in other parts of the economy as office jobs.[75] A key reason for this is supply chains. The big factory at the end of the line—the one that churns out cars, for example—by no means makes all the inputs it uses. Increasingly over time, it gets them from other shops, such that

---

[72] http://jaredbernsteinblog.com/talking-manufacturing-and-its-wage-premium/

[73] Using the same data described in http://jaredbernsteinblog.com/talking-manufacturing-and-its-wage-premium/, this estimate comes from a quantile regression at the 20th percentile of the wage distribution.

[74] See http://www.brookings.edu/~/media/research/files/papers/2012/2/22%20manufacturing%20helper%20krueger%20wial/0222_manufacturing_helper_krueger_wial.pdf re these points.

[75] http://www.epi.org/publication/wp268/

there are many more jobs in the manufacturing supply chain than in the final factory.

In auto production in 2013, for example, there were over 500,000 workers in the supply chain providing batteries, glass, rubber, transmissions, and so on, to the 300,000 that were building frames and assembling cars and trucks. Then there were 1.8 million car and parts dealers in the retail sector, and another 800,000 in repair.[76] And that's just the folks directly employed in making, selling, and fixing cars. When they spend their income in the broader economy, they of course create employment in other industries (that's the multiplier effect noted earlier).

Trade Deficits, the Shampoo Cycle, and the Savings Glut

The third reason why persistent trade imbalances are so problematic deserves its own section. It's a problem I've labeled *the economic shampoo cycle*. I'll get into it in some depth in Chapter 7 as it's an important part of our story, but the shampoo cycle is simple. It's just bubble, bust, repeat. The reason it matters to our story is that it's extremely hard to get to and stay at full employment long enough for the benefits of growth to be broadly shared if every few years, big financial bubbles inflate and explode.

When an economic expansion begins, GDP starts growing, unemployment starts coming down, and so on (though it's taking longer these days for growth to lead to jobs, leading to the need

---

[76] http://www.bls.gov/iag/tgs/iagauto.htm

for the new oxymoronic term: *the jobless recovery*). But then some bubble forms in some sector, like the housing market or the stock market. The bubble is big fun at first, as it spins off tons of demand, boosting jobs (think construction workers and the housing bubble), income, and wealth, but since bubbles are a toxic mixture of excessive speculation and underpriced risk, they must pop, leaving a big mess, usually in the form of a recession, in their wake. You work through the recession (boy, there's a world of pain squeezed into five words) and you start the cycle again. So there's your "bubble, bust, repeat."

But what does that have to do with trade?

As I pointed out above in our discussion of the GDP identity, growth-slowing trade deficits can and are offset by the other parts of the system. In the 2000s, we overinvested in housing; before that, in the 1990s, it was information technology (the dot-com bubble). Moreover, this doesn't just leave you with empty housing in the Nevada desert or an excess of fiber optic cable. It creates and feeds into a vicious cycle.

In 2005, Ben Bernanke, who was on the board of the Federal Reserve and soon to become its chairman, wrote a paper called "*The Global Saving Glut and the U.S. Current Account Deficit.*"[77] Sounds obscure and technical, but in fact, it was so simple that few, myself included, caught its significance (the "current account deficit" is just a broader measure of the trade deficit). But I came to view Bernanke's analysis as fundamentally important in the

---

[77] http://www.federalreserve.gov/boarddocs/speeches/2005/200503102/

quest for lasting full employment. In fact, I'm not sure we can break the shampoo cycle and reliably get to and stay at full employment without understanding his analysis and acting upon its implications.

Here's my interpretation of what Bernanke was arguing and, most importantly, how it links up to the core idea of this chapter. His message has two parts: First, it will be very tough to get to and stay at full employment unless we deal with the drag on growth created by our persistent trade deficits. Second, to a significant extent, these trade imbalances are being thrust upon us by the actions of our trade competitors.

It's pretty conventional wisdom in economics to blame the trade deficit on the people in the country with the deficit. Such profligates are choosing to consume more than they produce, which is the definition of a trade deficit. Instead of saving more of our income, we've consumed it all and then some. Why can't we be more like those thrifty [insert those from trade surplus country here—Chinese, Germans, South Koreans, etc.]?

But the truth, as Bernanke began to get at and others, most notably economist Michael Pettis and economics journalist Martin Wolf, have since developed and amplified, is more complicated. (Which reminds me: I've often been bugged by how regularly economic theory blames something on someone that's simply not that person's fault. Perhaps the most common example is the assumption that if your earnings are flat, it must be because you've got low productivity, as opposed to just low ability to bargain for a fair wage.) It turns out that when it comes to trade balances in global economies, we are not always the masters of our fate.

Suppose, in a global economy like ours, a country wants to boost its net exports in order to quickly create more growth and jobs (this approach to growth is often termed "mercantilism"). How would they go about it? The best way to do it is to make their exports cheaper and others' exports to them more expensive. That is, the country would want to subsidize their exports and tax imports. This sounds like it involves messing around with exchange rates—the value of one country's currency relative to that of another country. But there are so many different currencies out there in the world, so how could any one country pull this off?[78]

It's easier than you'd think because, while there are lots of countries with their own currencies, there are only a few so-called "reserve currencies" with the good old US dollar being the foremost example (a "reserve currency" is a currency that most countries and international businesses prefer to use when doing business with one another because they trust its value and recognize its worth). So by making your currency cheap relative to the dollar, you should be able to boost your exports and block others' imports.

---

[78] Some of what follows was originally in a *New York Times* oped I wrote called "Dethrone King Dollar." http://www.nytimes.com/2014/08/28/opinion/dethrone-king-dollar.html?hp&action=click&pgtype=Homepage&module=c-column-top-span-region&region=c-column-top-span-region&WT.nav=c-column-top-span-region

Also, it doesn't hurt that the same country that prints dollars is a country with literally hundreds of millions of highly acquisitive consumers, which is a nice way of saying we shop 'til we drop a lot more than our counterparts abroad. Consumer spending as a share of GDP is about 70 percent in the US, 55 percent in Europe and 35 percent in China. That makes us steady customers for export-led economies.

When a country wants to boost its net exports, its central bank accumulates currency from countries that issue reserves. To be very concrete, say a Chinese factory makes and assembles computers under contract with a US firm. The owner of that Chinese factory now has dollars, which the People's Bank of China borrows from him. The PBoC then uses the dollars to buy US debt, like Treasury bills, which, due to the increased demand for a dollar-denominated asset, keeps the value of the dollar up in international markets. Remember, the goal here is to make stuff that's priced in dollars more expensive than stuff that's priced in yuan.

Note that in order to support this process, the countries that accumulate dollar reserves suppress their consumption and boost their national savings. The PBoC could invest the computer factory's profits in schools or roads. Or the Chinese factory owner could have given her workers a raise and they could have consumed the profits.

But, and here's the key part that suggests this isn't all our own doing, since global accounts must balance, when one country saves more and consumes less than they produce, other countries must save less and consume more than they produce. That is, they must run trade deficits.

Squeezing the Balloon: Some Basic Trade Relationships

This always confuses people, myself included, and since it's so central to what follows, let's stick with these basic relationships for a moment.

To lock down the mechanics of the problem, let's start with a very simple economy with no trade at all. In order to grow (to build factories, roads, airports, homes, etc.) our simple, closed economy needs investment dollars. And sure enough, it gets them from savers. Savings don't just sit in vaults; they're lent out to investors. The key point is that in closed economies with no trade, savings equals investment and thus investment is constrained by the level of savings.

But add another country into the mix and things get interesting. Now neither investment nor consumer spending in our formerly closed economy is bound by domestic savings. As long as our newly added country doesn't use up all of its savings through its own consumption or investment, it can lend its extra savings to us. In fact, and this is key to the whole argument, the income generated by a country's production of goods and services must all be consumed, invested, or saved. And since that holds for every country, it holds for the aggregate of all global income.

OK, now we're really getting somewhere (are you as excited as I am?!). So we have this big lump of income that has to all be saved or spent (either consumed or invested). But what happens if a country saves more than it invests? By definition, it has a trade surplus, and that surplus doesn't just sit there: it must be spent or invested somewhere else. It's like squeezing a balloon—if one country runs a surplus, someone else must run a deficit. If one country saves more than it consumes or invests, another country must do the opposite: consume or invest more than it produces.

These are simple, rock-solid relationships, well-established for years and taught in every textbook on international accounts. The technical terminology used by Bernanke says it this way: the current account must by precisely offset by the capital account, which is just giving labels to what I just told you. When one country saves more than it uses, another country uses more than it saves and borrows to make up the difference. The saver has a trade surplus. The borrower, a trade deficit.

And yet, despite their long use, a fundamental and I hope now obvious point is widely overlooked by economists, policy-makers, pundits, and especially scolds: we do not, by ourselves, determine whether we run deficits. We do not, by ourselves, determine our savings rates. We're part of a global system where these determinations are made both by us and for us. Just like you can't squeeze a balloon and have it not get bigger somewhere else, you can't have surplus and excess savings in one country and avoid deficits and lower savings in other countries.

Given that we're not yet trading with other planets and global income must be spent, saved, or invested, then individual countries must adjust to one another. What Bernanke pointed to—what he called a "savings glut"—was that some trade-surplus countries, mostly developing economies in Asia, but also Germany and Japan, were generating and exporting their excess savings to trade-deficit countries.[79]

And not just here and there, but systematically, a fact that constitutes a very important wrinkle. You'll note that I often label our trade imbalances as "persistent." That's because there's absolutely nothing wrong with the occasional savings surplus or trade deficit. But when the same countries generate economically large surpluses and deficits year in and year out, it's a signal of a seriously unhealthy global imbalance.

The punchlines from this dynamic articulated by Bernanke are as follows: First, Americans alone do not determine their rates of savings and consumption. When other countries under-consume and under-invest in order to generate excess savings with which they can buy dollar reserves, our savings rates must fall. Second, when other countries export their savings to us, our trade deficit must grow. From the perspective of full employment, this point is

---

[79] Note that as the dollar is a primary reserve currency, America's trade deficit can worsen even when we're not directly in on the trade. Suppose South Korea runs a surplus with Brazil. By storing its surplus export revenues in Treasury bonds, South Korea nudges up the relative value of the dollar against our competitors' currencies and our trade deficit increases, even though the original transaction had nothing to do with the US.

key: it means we're exporting jobs, and not just any old jobs, but factory jobs.

Third, getting back to the shampoo cycle point raised above, the reason we've had decent growth amidst large trade deficits is because we've offset them with other parts of that GDP formula above, including investment, consumer spending, and government spending. But that's just a nice way of saying what's really happened: we offset them with bubbles.

Bernanke, who was on the board of the Federal Reserve and would soon chair it, becoming for all intents and purposes the globe's chief economist, worried about this back in 2005 in language that almost seems quaint today:

> . . . much of the recent capital inflow [the excess savings discussed above] into the developed world has shown up in higher rates of home construction and in higher home prices. Higher home prices in turn have encouraged households to increase their consumption. Of course, increased rates of homeownership and household consumption are both good things [*sure . . . up to a point! JB*]. However, in the long run, productivity gains are more likely to be driven by nonresidential investment, such as business purchases of new machines. The greater the extent to which capital inflows act to augment residential construction and especially current consumption spending, the greater the future economic burden of repaying the foreign debt is likely to be.

That's cautious central banker for "all this money pouring in from abroad is not as helpful as it seems. It's potentially leading to over-investment in unproductive stuff, otherwise known as a bubble, and if/when that should burst, it's gonna be a mess."

Those of you who recall any econ 101 might be bothered by something else about these international dynamics. Why is it that developing countries are lending to developed countries? Shouldn't those flows go the other way, from capital-rich countries to capital-poor ones? Add in the insight (also from Bernanke's paper) that we've got aging populations relative to many of those surplus countries, and thus we should be the ones with rising savings rates, and you get a feel for what I mean when I referred to these imbalances as "unhealthy."

Not to lose the thread, my point is simple and direct: Those persistent trade imbalances that you see in Figure 11 are keeping us from getting to full employment, or at least from doing so without bubbles that then pop, leaving us with recessions, high unemployment, and again—the absence of full employment. Moreover, these deficits are in manufactured goods, so we're importing excess savings and production from abroad while we're exporting good, middle class jobs.

What should we do about it?

Dollar Policy: A Linchpin of a Full Employment Strategy and Thus of the Reconnection Agenda

So far, we've established that our persistent trade deficits are a drag on growth and good jobs and a source of financial bubbles, and that they're caused not solely by consumer-crazed Americans but by the strategy of some of our trade partners to essentially subsidize their exports and tax their imports. That's the diagnosis. Here's the prescription.

The key to fixing these imbalances is attacking their cause: the exchange rate. Other countries manage their currencies—or "manipulate" them if you want to get nasty about it—to get a trade advantage, and while we occasionally get annoyed with them for doing so, we don't do much to stop them (I don't really think "manipulate" is nasty; I just think it implies a shadowy secrecy to the currency strategy when, in fact, it's out there for all to see).

We need to fight back, to implement one or a number of the simple ideas articulated below that will level the currency playing field. The knee-jerk reaction is that "if we do that, we'll start a trade war." I must say, I don't even know what that means. China will stop trading with us? Yeah, right. They're just going to stop selling us $300 billion per year more than we sell them (that's the magnitude of our annual trade deficit with China in recent years;

it's about 2 percent of our GDP and over 3 percent of their GDP).[80]

There's already, if not a trade war, a perfectly obvious and easy-to-see set of competitive trade battles going on out there in the real world. We're only losing because we refuse to see them for what they are: strategic efforts to manage the price of your goods in international markets in order to boost your growth and jobs at the expense of those same variables in your trading partner's country.

We could impose a tax on the imports from offending countries.[81] In fact, congressional majorities, even in our recent highly partisan Congresses, have voted in support of just such a plan,[82] one that would allow us to place tariffs on goods that benefit from export subsidies. In fact, US administrations already have restricted leeway to "countervail" export subsidies—meaning offset the subsidy through a tariff or some other penalty, like blocking currency managers from procuring US federal contracts or low-cost financing from US government sources. But the Commerce Department has typically refused to use their authority to do so, in part because the definition of allowable action is

---

[80] This statistic may sound off to those who've heard that China's GDP is now larger than ours. But that's not the case when you use market exchange rates, which is the correct metric for this comparison.

[81] Some of this material was developed in this NYT op-ed:
http://www.nytimes.com/2015/01/10/opinion/jared-bernstein-how-to-stop-currency-manipulation.html

[82] http://www.bloomberg.com/news/2011-10-03/china-currency-measure-sending-a-message-advances-in-senate.html

extremely narrow.[83] While the plan from Congress makes it easier for the administration to bring such cases forward, it's still actually quite mild and does not take sweeping actions against currency-managing countries. Instead, it works item-by-item, as in "we find that rubber tires, grade four, are being unfairly subsidized by managed currency." That's simply not the stuff of trade wars.[84]

Since we have trade deals with some of the countries who are known to manage their currencies, like South Korea, we could also temporarily cancel their trade privileges until they allowed their currencies to re-appreciate. This option is particularly germane in that as of this writing, the US and 11 other countries are in what may be the late phases of negotiating a multilateral trade agreement called the Trans-Pacific Partnership, or TPP. It should definitely contain a currency chapter specifying that signatories who are found to manage their currencies will temporarily lose privileges granted under the treaty.[85]

A final idea to block currency management, lower our trade deficits, and get back to full employment is one of my favorite because it's simple and could be very effective without being too

---

[83] If the exporter can show that the subsidy doesn't just benefit exporters but also benefits non-exporters, like an upstream firm in the supply chain that sells exclusively to the exporter, Commerce maintains that it cannot bring the case. This legislation would get rid of that archaic and confusing rule.

[84] Note that such actions mean we need to be able to clearly identify currency management by our trading partners. The op-ed in footnote 80 discusses solutions to this challenge.

[85] http://www.nytimes.com/2015/01/10/opinion/jared-bernstein-how-to-stop-currency-manipulation.html

heavy a lift: reciprocal currency intervention.[86] Currency management rests on the ability of countries to go into international currency markets and buy the currency, often dollars, against which they want their own currency to depreciate. But—and this is not widely known—various countries engaged in this strategy employ "capital controls," meaning they don't put their own currencies up for sale in those same markets.

Reciprocity just says, "if you can buy ours, then we must be able to buy yours." That's it. But that simple move would block China, for example, from buying hundreds of billions of our Treasuries in order to boost the value of the dollar to lower the cost of their exports to us. As economist Daniel Gros puts it, our own Treasury "will limit sales of their public debt henceforth to only include official institutions from countries in which they themselves are allowed to buy and hold public debt." China and other developing economies with outflow restrictions on their currencies would either have to stop their purchases of US debt, or they'd have to let our central bank buy similar amounts of their own debt.

What's potentially efficient about this idea is that it gets around a lot of technical challenges invoked by the other ideas I've noted. You don't have to figure out who's managing their currency to get a trade advantage or distinguish between who's stockpiling dollars for legitimate reasons (e.g., to cover debts valued in dollars) versus who's trying to manipulate their exchange rate.

---

[86] See Daniel Gros: http://www.voxeu.org/article/how-avoid-trade-war-reciprocity-requirement

You just level the playing field, or if you want to get technical about it, the global market for foreign exchange.

I'm not suggesting that any of these interventions are without risk, of course. But the current system doesn't just embody potential risks. It is fraught with actual, living risks that have been playing out in the forms of global savings imbalances (as Bernanke recognized a decade ago), persistent US trade deficits, the loss of manufacturing jobs, and the economic shampoo cycle.

When I was a White House economist in the first few years of the Obama administration, I learned that all of my colleagues shared these concerns about currency management and its negative impact on our trade deficits and manufacturing sector. But like every other administration, they believed the only way to do something about it was through quiet diplomacy—our Treasury secretary sits down with theirs and they agree to make nice in currency markets.

But diplomacy hasn't solved the problem and it's long past time to try one or more of the direct approaches I've just listed.

Finally, there's one other argument against taking the type of actions recommended in the text: if we put any such currency rules in trade agreements, like the TPP mentioned above, it will allow our trading partners to take action against our Federal Reserve. As discussed in the previous chapter, in order to lower the cost of borrowing and stimulate demand in weak economies, the Fed lowers the interest rate it controls or engages in "quantitative easing" to lower longer term rates. One side effect of such actions is to lower the value of the dollar. But that doesn't imply currency management by a long shot. In fact, it is not at all hard to distinguish between domestic demand management and currency management: one, is the central bank loading up on foreign currencies, and two, is the country running a persistent and large current account surplus? We do neither, and given the fact that the dollar is the globe's most prominent reserve currency, it is hard to imagine we ever would—we don't buy dollars, we print them! In other words, this is not a serious argument against the pushback-against-currency-measures I advocate.[87]

The Robots Redux: OK, I Heard You in the Earlier Chapter. But Surely They're Taking Manufacturing Jobs?

What's the point of going through all this exchange rate mishegos (Yiddish for gnarly economics) in order to boost US manufactures when technology, like robotics, is just going to wipe out all the jobs in the industry anyway?! In 2014 there were 12 million workers in the sector, about 9 percent of the workforce, down from about 14 million in 2007. Isn't that evidence of increased automation?

As discussed already in Chapter 3, not so fast. In fact, there's no evidence to support the claim that the pace at which labor saving technology is replacing workers is accelerating. If anything, and

---

[87] For an expanded version of this argument, see here: http://jaredbernsteinblog.com/tpp-and-the-fed/. I point out that while our central bank could not plausibly be caught in the crosshairs of a rule to distinguish demand management from currency management, the central banks of other countries certain could be. I view that as a feature, not a bug, of this strategy.

I'm none too pleased to say this, the trend in the growth of output per hour, or productivity, is actually going the wrong way (it's slowing down, not speeding up), and that makes the robots story very hard to sustain beyond the level of anecdote. True, the plural of anecdote is data, so maybe the formula here is anecdote + time = displacement of significant swaths of manufacturing workers. That is, I want to firmly note that I'm not dismissing the possibility of what Keynes called "technological unemployment" but there is nothing in the data that leads me to believe technology is a large and binding constraint on expanding our manufacturing footprint in the world.

What we somehow seem to forget in this space is that technological progress has always been part of the landscape of economies across the globe, especially our own. But here's what else has always been a central part of the economy: demand for the goods and services we produce. Especially cool new stuff that makes this process of going through life better, of which I can see numerous great examples from where I'm sitting, including my smart phone (OK, maybe that's a bit of a mixed bag, but you know what I mean), an amazing-sounding little Bluetooth speaker, wifi, laptop, wireless printer (which cost 99 freakin' dollars and does all kinds of tricks), mp3 player, and stapler (whoops—old school, but fact is I use it a lot).

Yes, we import a lot of that stuff from abroad, I know, but that's kinda the point of the whole damn chapter, right? We here in America have robust demand for manufactured goods and, as I'll point out in a moment, it still takes people to make those goods (and even if it didn't, somebody would have to make the robots!). But because of many of the dynamics discussed above, we're meeting too much of our demand for manufactured goods from abroad, and exporting good jobs in the process.

The correct lesson to take from economic history in this area is not that productivity is the enemy. It's that we need enough robust consumer and investor demand to absorb our productivity gains through broadly shared prosperity and improving living standards across the income scale.

To be clear, I'm not suggesting we make a serious play for, say, assembling consumer electronics. China's cornered that market and we're beneficiaries in the form of cheap electronics. Nor am I implying that we can radically alter a characteristic employment trend in advanced economies from manufacturing toward services. But the citizens of the world will continue to demand manufactured goods, and there's no reason why our manufacturers shouldn't have a fair opportunity to compete with others to meet that demand. And unless we fight back against currency management, that "fair opportunity" will continue to elude us.

Now, let's look at some evidence behind these arguments for the increased prevalence of technological unemployment. If machines were replacing workers at a faster clip than in the past, we'd see an increase in the growth rate of labor productivity (aka output per hour). That is, we'd be increasingly producing more output with fewer workers (or fewer hours of work), and that would, by definition, show up as faster productivity growth. And yet, productivity growth has slowed considerably in recent years.

Figure 12 shows the actual yearly changes in productivity growth, which are pretty erratic. In order to get a better look at the underlying trend, I've plotted a smooth trend through the jigs and jags of the underlying data. This smooth line should be interpreted as the underlying trend in productivity growth and, as you can see, it has gone from around 3 percent in the late 1990s and early 2000s to around 1 percent in recent years.

FIGURE 12

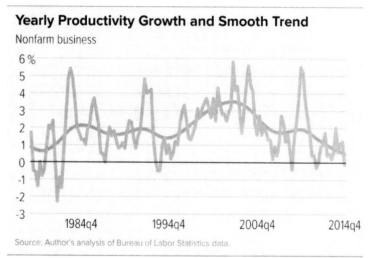

Yearly Productivity Growth and Smooth Trend
Nonfarm business

Source: Author's analysis of Bureau of Labor Statistics data.

Now, you'd probably like to know what explains that deceleration in this critically important variable. I'll tell you: I don't know. And neither does anyone else—such changes in productivity growth are notoriously hard to puzzle out. I do find it intriguingly suggestive that the one period where productivity growth accelerated—the late 1990s—corresponds to the period we moved towards full employment. There's a coherent story behind that: since employers face higher labor costs in tight labor markets, they strive for efficiencies in order to maintain profitability, something you might think of as a full employment productivity multiplier. But for now, my simple point is this: the fact that there's no faster automation story in the productivity accounts casts doubt on the idea that labor-replacing technology is wiping out significant numbers of jobs.

What about a more narrow manufacturing productivity story? It's possible that when you mix different sectors together as in Figure 12, you're losing an acceleration in factory productivity. Manufacturing productivity growth is even noisier than overall growth and the data only go back a few decades, so it's hard to pull a smooth trend, but there's no obvious recent acceleration in the trend.

The economist Susan Houseman has looked carefully at this question of whether automation is responsible for the loss of manufacturing jobs. She reports that while:

> . . . automation undoubtedly has displaced some workers in manufacturing, a growing body of research suggests that trade and the decline of the United States as a location for production have accounted for much of the sector's job loss. In addition, the employment effects of manufacturing production extend well beyond that sector.

The breakup of vertically integrated firms and the growth of complex supply chains mean that a large share of the workers needed to produce manufactured goods— currently about half—is employed outside the manufacturing sector. A strong domestic manufacturing presence also is critical to innovation and the growth of high-skilled jobs . . . Not only can a resurgence in U.S. manufacturing be an important component of a jobs recovery, but a vibrant domestic manufacturing sector is essential for the global competitiveness of American workers.[88]

FIGURE 13

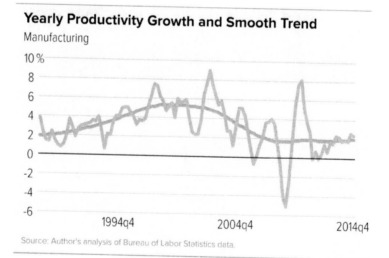

Yearly Productivity Growth and Smooth Trend
Manufacturing

Source: Author's analysis of Bureau of Labor Statistics data.

---

[88] http://www.pathtofullemployment.org/wp-content/uploads/2014/04/houseman.pdf

The economist Dean Baker estimates that there are 4-6 million lost jobs embedded in trade deficits of the magnitude we've been running.[89] It's not that we don't want or need the goods those displaced workers could be making. It's that we're getting them from abroad, exporting those jobs year in and year out, as we allow trade deficits to block the path to full employment.

So, in the interest of getting to and staying at full employment, a robust reconnection agenda depends on a concerted effort to correct these persistent trade imbalances and give the American factory worker a chance to compete on a level playing field. The key action implied by this analysis, and I've suggested numerous ways to go about it, involves actively pushing back against currency management whereby our competitors subsidize their exports to us and tax our exports to them. Starting with the 2005 Bernanke paper, and thinking through the simple growth identities and interdependencies in global markets, the weight of the analysis seems awfully convincing: adding such tools to the policy toolbox is one important way to reconnect growth, good jobs, and middle class prosperity.

---

[89] http://www.pathtofullemployment.org/wp-content/uploads/2014/04/BAKER.pdf

Chapter 6

A Full Employment Agenda that Reaches Everyone

Suppose we did everything I've suggested so far. We established full employment as a national goal. We used smart fiscal and monetary policies to move the economy towards full employment when market failures were upon the land. We fought back against currency manipulation to level the playing field for our exporters. And as long as we're into such luscious fantasy, let's say it all worked as I think it would and the unemployment rate fell to . . . oh, I don't know . . . let's say 4 percent, like in the year 2000 (the last time we were at truly full employment), and real wages were growing across the board, not just at the high end of the scale.

We'd be done, right? Mission accomplished.

Nope. Sorry, but we'd still have pockets of underemployment, particularly among the folks facing the tallest barriers to entry into the job market. I'm talking about the long-term unemployed, folks with low skill levels and little workplace experience, older displaced factory workers who haven't been able to find their way back in, the millions with criminal records, and those who face labor market discrimination.

I fear we cannot reliably get to full employment without a strategy for these groups as well, and this chapter presents such a strategy: a set of policies designed to reach any and every able-bodied adult who wants to work. They include subsidized employment, or direct job creation; apprenticeships, or "earn-while-you-learn" programs; so-called "sectoral employment training"; youth employment programs; and fair chance hiring practices targeted at those with criminal records.

All of these ideas are important in not just getting to full employment but also in allowing a lot of disadvantaged folks to realize their potential; they're essential supports for families and communities. But my personal favorite is direct job creation, a commonsensical and obvious solution to the problem of inadequate employment opportunities. That's not to say it's costless or simple. As with any public policy, the potential for unintended consequences abounds. But while we should respect and evaluate such concerns, let us not be aspirationally hamstrung by them.

One final introductory point, especially as regards direct job creation: anti-poverty policy in this country is increasingly conditioned on work. Simply put, and glossing over a lot of nuance, decades ago a poor person did not necessarily have to be employed in the paid labor market to get various government benefits. Now, with some notable exceptions (i.e., nutritional support[90]), the largest non-health benefits are tied to employment.

It's important for poor families to have ample opportunities in the job market that would allow them to work their way out of poverty. I remember my days long ago as a social worker in New York City when I worked with poor families with kids, and I assure you, they all wanted a decent job. I don't mean some. I mean all. They of course recognized that their public benefits would never provide them with anything beyond subsistence incomes. Illegal opportunities to earn real money often presented themselves, but these were parents, often single parents, and this was the 1980s in NYC, where getting busted meant being sent away for a long time.

So trust me when I tell you that low-income parents and the most conservative Tea Partiers you can imagine agree that it's great when people are able to work their way out of poverty.

Yet when one hears conservatives talk about the importance of work as a path out of poverty, they implicitly assume that the only thing you have to do to get a job is want one. But labor supply doesn't create labor demand. If it did, we would not have one of

---

[90] Even SNAP, or the Supplemental Nutrition Assistance Program (food stamps), limits benefits to able-bodied childless adults unless they are working or in a job training program, though this is sometimes waived in areas of high unemployment. States may also require additional SNAP recipients to participate in employment and training programs.

the problems that motivates this book: the American labor market's inadequacy in terms of job quantity and job quality.

These insights have led me to the following policy conclusion: *If you believe that work should be a ladder out of poverty for able-bodied adults, then you must be willing to provide the working poor with enough jobs of requisite quality to back up that goal.* And that is the agenda I describe next.

The Need for Employment Programs Even When Unemployment is Low

Before getting into the details of how these policies that reach those who are at best marginally attached to the job market might work, how do we know that they are needed? A good place to start is in the year 2000, the last time we were at full employment, with very low unemployment and broadly shared real wage growth. The overall unemployment rate was a historically low 4 percent that year, but let's look at both that rate and other indicators for some of the groups of folks targeted by ideas in this chapter.

Table 4 compares just a few economic indicators across different groups, mostly whites and African Americans, though I put one line in there on those who haven't finished high school (this indicator is for people 25 years and up). Though full employment prevailed in the overall job market in 2000, you still see some considerable variation around the overall jobless rate; the 2014 column shows the most recent full year data and has some poignant examples of cases of quite high rates of unemployment or underemployment five years into the economic expansion that began in the middle of 2009.

TABLE 4

Selected Job Market Indicators

	2000	2014
Unemployment (%)		
All	4.0	6.2
Whites	3.5	5.3
African Americans	7.6	11.3
High-school dropouts	6.3	9.0
Underemployment (%)		
All	7.0	12.0
Whites	5.6	9.7
African Americans	12.4	19.5
Long-term unemployment as share of unemployed (%)		
All	11.4	33.4
Whites	9.6	32.1
African Americans	15.0	39.7

Sources: Bureau of Labor Statistics and Economic Policy Institute

Black unemployment in 2000 was 3.6 percentage points above the economy-wide average, black underemployment rates were in double digits (underemployment adds in part-time workers who want full-time jobs), and 15 percent of unemployed blacks had been jobless for at least half a year (that's the definition of long-term unemployment).

In 2014, unemployment was more than 50 percent higher (6.2 percent vs. 4.0 percent), adults without high school degrees faced 9 percent unemployment, and black underemployment was almost 20 percent. On underemployment, even whites were just below 10 percent, and blacks were at twice that rate. One third of the unemployed were long-termers, though for African Americans that statistic rises to two-fifths.

As I've noted in various places, ad infinitum if not ad nauseam, I don't think unemployment rates in the 5 to 6 percent range really equate with full employment. But, as stressed in Chapter 4, lots of highly influential people do believe this. Looking at the 2014 data, the table shows that even in a job market where unemployment is less than a percent above even lower bound estimates of full employment, about 40 percent of the black unemployed had been so for at least half-a-year, almost 20 percent of blacks were jobless or couldn't find the hours of work they wanted, and 9 percent of high school dropouts were unemployed.

So I'm not backing down for a second from my claim that tight job markets are an essential part of the reconnection agenda. I'm just saying we can't stop there.

Direct Job Creation

It is widely recognized that when credit markets fail, advanced economies require that the central bank (in our case, the Federal Reserve) temporarily stand in for the private system of credit, making sure loanable funds are available to investors at prices (interest rates) low enough to stimulate demand. What I'm proposing here is a simple corollary: when labor markets fail, the government has the same responsibility to temporarily fill a critical economic gap by directly providing jobs.

Sometimes that market failure will be acute, as in a recession. But at other times it will persist as a slow drip even amidst a normal economic recovery, affecting specific groups of workers by making it more difficult for them to find and sustain employment. Simply put, for a disadvantaged worker with few marketable skills and a criminal record, the job market is always in a deep recession.

There are two ways to go about direct job creation. One, the government (federal, state, or local) carries out a discrete project, like building a dam or setting up a new ball field, and they directly hire workers to do so. Sounds very 1930s New Deal-ish, I know, though the Census Bureau actually does this every 10 years as they temporarily staff up to carry out the decennial census.

In 2010, for example, the Bureau hired about 560,000 census takers.[91] In fact, I was a White House economist back then, and given that this hiring spell took place during the Great Recession, we were, as you can imagine, very happy to see those jobs. It so happened that the completion of their work on the census coincided with the terrible BP oil spill, and I recall a number of people wondering if we could just keep them on the government payroll and detail them to cleaning up beaches on the Gulf Coast.

---

[91] http://www.bls.gov/opub/mlr/2011/03/art3full.pdf

The problem with this very direct approach is that the federal government has been committed to outsourcing such work for so long that it is not clear there exists adequate administrative/oversight infrastructure to pull it off (though over the longer term, it would be worthwhile to invest in building such infrastructure). Thus, the second approach to direct job creation, though admittedly somewhat less direct, is to use government funding to temporarily subsidize employment in any sector: private, non-profit, or government.

What's that? Again with the 1930s?! Wake up and smell the 2010s!

I assure you, I am awake. Though it was totally unheralded, a few years ago the federal government ran just such a program as part of the Recovery Act, one that in its heyday placed "more than 260,000 low-income adults and youth in temporary jobs in the private and public sectors," according to poverty scholar Donna Pavetti.[92] Yes, that's one month of US job growth in a decent labor market, but stick with me here. I'm going to advocate for significantly scaling this idea up.

Since this is your federal government at work, there of course must be an opaque acronym nearby; in this case it's the TANF EF, or Temporary Assistance for Needy Families Emergency Fund. And it really was a fund (a stream of funding that flowed to intermediaries who worked with employers to find subsidized job

---

[92] http://www.offthechartsblog.org/new-evidence-that-subsidized-jobs-programs-work/

slots), meaning it paid most, often all, of the wages for targeted populations of unemployed people, for a set number of months.

Here's an overview of what the program accomplished across the land, from Pavetti:

> In all, 39 states, the District of Columbia, Puerto Rico, the Virgin Islands, and eight Tribal TANF programs received approval to use $1.3 billion from the fund to create new subsidized employment programs or expand existing ones. States used the TANF EF funds to operate programs for both adults and youth. A total of 33 states operated programs targeted to adults, and 24 states and the District of Columbia operated programs targeted to youth. The 260,000 subsidized job placements were split almost equally between year-round programs that served mostly adults and summer and year-round programs that served youth (up to age 24). California, Illinois, Pennsylvania, and Texas operated the largest programs, each placing more than 20,000 individuals in subsidized jobs. Illinois operated the largest year-round program, placing almost 30,000 adults in subsidized jobs in less than six months. California and Texas operated the largest summer youth programs, placing about 27,000 and 22,000 youth in jobs, respectively. Pennsylvania's placements were almost equally split between adults (14,000) and youth (13,000).[93]

---

[93] http://www.pathtofullemployment.org/wp-content/uploads/2014/04/pavetti.pdf

Florida had one of these programs, called Florida Back to Work, run on the ground by local government workforce boards that contracted with employers; it targeted workers from families with incomes below twice the poverty level, about $40,000 for a parent with two kids. As Pavetti reports, the program placed individuals with "for-profit, non-profit, and government agencies at the prevailing wage for the occupation, up to a maximum of $19.51 per hour, and reimbursed employers for 80 to 95 percent of the cost of wages and related payroll costs. An individual could stay in the placement for up to 12 months."

Unfortunately, and despite the fact that my colleagues on the White House economics team and I, along with Vice-President Biden, tried to get Congress to extend the program, TANF EF ended when the funding expired in the fall of 2010, so many participants in Florida and numerous other states never got to stay on for the full number of months for which they were eligible.

Thankfully, however, researchers were able to evaluate some of the programs. In at least one setting, in Florida, they were able to evaluate the outcomes for people in subsidized employment against a group of people who wanted to get into the program but never got a subsidized job. That creates a kind of natural experiment, which is always the best way to see whether an intervention worked as intended.

The results, which I'll review in a moment, were quite positive. Importantly, there were positive effects not just in the short run, but also for regular employment after the subsidized job ran out.

This last point should not be overlooked, especially as the long-term benefits were realized by workers, like the long-term unemployed[94] or those with criminal records, that employers tend to discriminate against. In these cases, the subsidy lowers their cost enough—often to zero!—such that prejudicial employers will give them a shot. And that's often all it takes for a worker to prove herself as someone worth keeping on when the subsidy ends.

Pavetti reports that TANF EF subsidized employment programs raised participants' employment and earnings during the programs and in the Florida pseudo-experiment noted above, "participants earned an average of $4,000 more in the year after the program than in the year before it, compared to a $1,500 increase for people in the comparison group."[95]

Remember all those long-term unemployed shown in Table 1 and my point above about how employers clearly took long-term joblessness as a negative signal? Well, the subsidized employment programs "were especially effective for the long-term unemployed. In Mississippi and Florida, average annual earnings of the long-term unemployed rose by about $7,000 after participating; in Los Angeles and Wisconsin, they rose by about $4,000. In all four sites, earnings rose much more among the

---

[94] http://www.washingtonpost.com/blogs/wonkblog/wp/2013/04/15/companies-wont-even-look-at-resumes-of-the-long-term-unemployed/

[95] http://www.offthechartsblog.org/new-evidence-that-subsidized-jobs-programs-work/

long-term unemployed than among people who had been unemployed for shorter periods."[96]

All sounds pretty spiffy, no? Well, here's something to worry about in these sorts of programs, especially in the context of trying to nudge us closer to full employment: displacement. It comes in two flavors, really bad and less bad. "Really bad" displacement is when an employer replaces a perfectly fine unsubsidized worker with a subsidized one. Clearly, we've neither added a new worker nor reduced unemployment. We just wasted the subsidy by paying an employer to substitute one unemployed person for a different, newly-unemployed person. The less bad version is when the employer creates a net new job for a subsidized worker, but they would have created the job anyway, even without the extra incentive.

So it's important to have rules that prohibit these inefficiencies, such as only subsidizing net new hires, to avoid the "really bad" version of displacement (some TANF EF programs had employers sign pledges that they would not displace existing workers). And it is of course essential to enforce those rules. Follow-up interviews with employers from various TANF EF jobsites did find that the program led to more hiring than would otherwise have occurred—two-thirds of the employers said they created new positions—and that the subsidized workers they hired had considerably less experience than their incumbent

[96] http://www.offthechartsblog.org/new-evidence-that-subsidized-jobs-programs-work/

workforce.[97] Of course, since TANF EF was in place during the heart of the Great Recession, one is less worried that the subsidized marginal hire is one that would have occurred anyway.

Still, while this "less bad" form of displacement is hard to avoid, especially in stronger economies, there's another good reason not to worry too much about it: even if the worker would have been hired anyway, it probably wouldn't have been the worker we're talking about here. That is, the key attribute of the subsidized employment program is that it targets someone facing a steep barrier to entry into the job market. Yes, employer X was going to hire someone anyway, but it took the subsidy to get them to hire someone with a criminal record or a big gap in their resume due to a long spell of joblessness.

There's no reason why we couldn't scale up TANF EF to be a robust national program ready to trigger on when unemployment or underemployment goes above a certain level. A smaller version could be permanently in place to help people facing steep barriers in good times, including those from the groups I turn to next. Yes, that would involve new resources, but here's a smart thought from a scholar (Elizabeth Lower-Basch of the Center for Law and Social Policy) who's looked closely at the effectiveness and bang-for-the-buck of TANF EF and come to the same conclusions that I have. We could pay for the program I'm envisioning by eliminating the Work Opportunity Tax Credit (WOTC), a far less effective existing credit that in recent years has channeled around

---

[97] http://economicmobilitycorp.org/uploads/stimulating-opportunity-full-report.pdf

a billion dollars in tax breaks to try to get businesses to hire disadvantaged workers.[98] My back-of-the-envelope math, based on what we spent on TANF EF in 2009-10 through the Recovery Act, suggests that this is in the ballpark of what it would take to scale up the program in the way I suggest above.[99]

So there you have it: a national direct job creation fund based on pretty extensive evaluations of a multistate pilot, paid for by shifting existing resources out of a much less effective program designed to accomplish similar goals. As my grandma might have said, "What's not to like?"

Fair Hiring Practices for Those with Criminal Records

Back when I actually did stuff instead of, you know, writing about stuff, I volunteered in a prison in Queens, New York to help long-term inmates get ready for release. There was clearly a selection bias in play—I only saw inmates who wanted to work with me. But two things were very clear. They wanted a good job on the outside and they viewed their chances of getting one as very low.

I volunteered there decades ago, but these inmates were right then and their contemporary cohort, which has of course hugely swelled in numbers, is right today. According to one recent

---

[98] See http://www.clasp.org/resources-and-publications/publication-1/Big-Ideas-for-Job-Creation-Rethinking-Work-Opportunity.pdf. Lower-Basch: "WOTC is not designed to promote net job creation, and there is no evidence that it does so."

[99] Actually, I think it would take between $1-2 billion to scale up a national subsidized employment program. But there's also about half-a-billion dollars in the current TANF Contingency Fund that could be usefully and legitimately applied to this scale-up.

analysis, over 70 million people have some sort of a criminal record that could be picked up by a background check for employment, and 700,000 return to their communities from jail each year.[100]

Clearly, there's a lot to be said about the implications of these alarmingly large numbers. According to policy analysts Mitchell and Leachman (M&L), corrections spending "is now the third-largest category of spending in most states, behind education and health care. If states were still spending on corrections what they spent in the mid-1980s, adjusted for inflation, they would have about $28 billion more each year that they could choose to spend on more productive investments . . . 11 states spent more of their general funds on corrections than on higher education in 2013. And some of the states with the biggest education cuts in recent years also have among the nation's highest incarceration rates."[101]

M&L also point out that "men with a previous criminal conviction worked roughly nine fewer weeks, and earned 40 percent less, each year than otherwise similar non-offenders . . . by age 48, [earnings] are less than half among men who have been incarcerated than among comparable men who have not been incarcerated."

---

[100] http://www.nelp.org/page/-/SCLP/2014/Guides/NELP_Research_Factsheet.pdf?nocdn=1
[101] http://www.cbpp.org/cms/index.cfm?fa=view&id=4220

OK, that's a serious problem. But there's more people and more crime, right? So surely, even accepting the negative labor market impacts, some of this higher spending on locking people up is justified? But the largest factors driving up incarceration rates are neither the crime rate nor the ratio of arrests per crimes. It's the share of offenders that do jail time and the length of their sentences. Moreover, as M&L show, there's no clear correlation between crime and incarceration rates over time, so the whole deterrent argument has less to back it up than you might imagine.

Like I said, we could go on about the wrong-headedness of our existing practices in this space and I'm usually all for getting to the roots. But in this case, in the interest of getting to full employment given the huge numbers were talking about here, I'd like to focus solely on two issues. One, what changes can we make within the criminal justice system itself to minimize skill atrophy and recidivism and maximize educational opportunity? And two, what hiring practices can be implemented on the outside to help those with records get in and stay in the workforce?

Within the justice system, if we can keep people out of jail who don't belong there, that avoids unnecessary addition to the number with criminal records. So decriminalizing and reclassifying minor offenses, like possession of small amounts of marijuana, could help. Similarly, shorter sentencing for lesser offenses could help reduce both prison terms and probation periods.

In addition, there needs to be more of the type of initiatives I participated in long ago in Queens to provide some work-based education and training for people in prison. There's good evidence that these programs can be effective: a comprehensive meta-analysis (evaluating a bunch of studies while giving heavier weight to the most rigorous ones) found that "inmates who participated in correctional education programs had *43 percent lower odds of recidivating* than inmates who did not."[102] Yet, you won't be surprised to learn that we're doing less of that sort of thing over time. That's despite the fact that the same research just noted finds that such interventions "far exceed the break-even point" in terms of cost-effectiveness.

As regards the second question—what can be done on the outside so that those with records get a fair look in the job market?—I need to introduce you to the work of the National Employment Law Project (disclosure: I'm a board member). NELP's been engaged in important work to reduce legal barriers to employment stemming from the stigma associated with criminal records.

For example, here's something you may not know. There are a bunch of people out there with criminal records who either shouldn't have records at all or for whom their records inaccurately represent the magnitudes of their crimes. The problem is that a significant minority—about one-third—of felony arrests do not lead to conviction (a similar share are

---

102

http://www.rand.org/content/dam/rand/pubs/research_reports/RR200/RR266/RAND_RR266.pdf

charged but convicted of lesser crimes than the original charge) but, as NELP discovered, while "law enforcement agencies are diligent about fingerprinting and charging individuals who are arrested or even merely detained, [they] are far less vigilant about submitting the follow-up information on the disposition or final outcome of the arrest." The group estimates "that more than half a million workers a year may be severely prejudiced in their employment search by the flaws in the FBI's criminal records system."[103]

There are straightforward administrative fixes to this problem. The correct information exists and either laws or common practices by the FBI when they engage in background checks could be updated to reflect the correct information about an individual's record. At the same time, everyone subject to a background check should of course get a look at their rap sheet, which is not the case for employment checks conducted by the FBI today.

But here's the thing: when it comes to applying for a job, the *existence* of a criminal record is just about as damaging as anything on it. NELP points out that "the likelihood of a callback for an interview for an entry-level position drops off by 50 percent for those applicants with an arrest or conviction history."[104]

---

[103] http://nelp.org/content/uploads/2015/03/Report-Wanted-Accurate-FBI-Background-Checks-Employment.pdf

[104] http://www.nelp.org/content/uploads/2015/03/Seizing-Ban-the-Box-Momentum-Advance-New-Generation-Fair-Chance-Hiring-Reforms.pdf

That's where "fair chance hiring" and policies like "ban the box" come into play. The "box" is a checkbox on job applications that asks about an applicant's criminal record. Fair chance hiring practices do not—I repeat, do not—demand that this information is kept from employers. The argument is that this question should be excluded from the initial application. Employers should be of course be free to conduct background checks, but "ban the box" laws move that activity to a later stage of the interview process, after employers have developed impressions of candidates from meeting them and learning about their qualifications and skills.

NELP recommends, as do I, that the background come late in the game, ideally after a conditional offer of employment (which, to be clear, is the way it's often been in my own experience—the background check is a formality after the job offer).[105]

I mean, this ain't rocket science. Say an employer looks at two initial applications and sees that box checked in one of them. Which one of us wouldn't toss that one and proceed with the other? The goal of banning the box is thus to "ensure that employers take into account other important factors when considering an applicant's conviction history, including the age of the offense, the relationship of the individual's record to the job duties and responsibilities, and evidence of rehabilitation."[106]

---

[105] Even at the White House, that's how they do it. And in that case, the FBI drops in on your friends and has a little talk with them about you. Seriously.
[106] http://www.nelp.org/page/-/SCLP/2014/Seizing-Ban-the-Box-Momentum-Advance-New-Generation-Fair-Chance-Hiring-Reforms.pdf?nocdn=1

This fair chance hiring work is relatively new, but the available data suggests the policies are helping. In Minneapolis, postponing the background check until after a conditional offer of employment "resulted in more than half of applicants with a conviction being hired." In Durham, the employment rate for the affected population quadrupled, and in Atlanta, affected individuals made up "10 percent of city hires between March and October of 2013." In 2010, Massachusetts extended its policy to private employers, and Minnesota, Rhode Island, Illinois, and New Jersey have since joined them.

I don't know if that qualifies the idea as a juggernaut, but it makes sense—remember, banning the box just delays the background check, it doesn't block it—and it appears to be catching on. From my perspective in building the reconnection agenda, it definitely deserves a slot in the toolbox.

Sectoral Training, Apprenticeships, and Earn-While-You-Learn

Youth unemployment has grown particularly high in recent years. Narrowing the lens down to 23- to 24-year-olds not in school, Harry Holzer and Bob Lerman, two economists who think a lot about this problem, find that "28 percent were not employed in 2013, up from about 20 percent in 2000-01 . . . As of 2013, about one in three black 23- to 24-year-old men were neither working nor in school."[107]

---

[107] http://www.pathtofullemployment.org/wp-content/uploads/2014/04/holzerlerman.pdf

So here again, we need a strategy to help connect young, often minority, and often male workers to the job market. Of course, a subsidized jobs program will help some and fair chance hiring will help others, but it's a big toolbox (if needed, we could change the analogy to a "toolshed") and the more useful measures we put in there to get hard-to-employ people into work, the better.

This section briefly presents a few ideas in this spirit, one in particular—apprenticeships—that has shown real promise in other countries and in a few scattered examples here in America. Apprenticeships can provide young people who might not be successful in traditional college with a chance to master an occupation where there's demand for skilled work and to make some money while they're learning the trade.

That point just made—"where there's demand"—may seem like an incredibly obvious component of any effort to help people get into the job market. But for decades, many of our training programs failed in this regard. Sometimes they took their cues from students. Instead of telling them "here's where the jobs are" they asked them "what would you like to learn?" Sometimes they just focused on soft, generalized skills that, again, didn't link up to actual opportunities in the labor market.

Of course, in a book partially premised on the insufficient quantity of jobs, readers have a right to wonder why I'm straying into assumptions asserting that "demand" and "actual opportunities" exist in the labor market. Very fair point, and as I showed in Chapter 2, slack labor markets have been the norm for the past few decades. But that doesn't mean we can ignore the supply side of the labor market. In fact, the training and apprenticeship programs quite consciously press on both "edges of the scissors" (as we used to call supply and demand curves back in the day).

That is, we've finally discovered that effective training programs are "sectoral" in that they work with employers to identify the sectors where future labor demands will need to be met by future labor supply. And then they provide workers—often less advantaged youths—with the soon-to-be-demanded skill sets. According to recent government research on what works in this space—part of an effort to consolidate the myriad training programs that exist across different government agencies—more than half of the states "are implementing sectoral training strategies," working with regional employers to identify future pockets of demand, and, in tandem with community colleges, fill skill deficits in local workforces.[108] Evaluations of the approach typically report employment and earnings gains relative to controls. Unsurprisingly, since they helped set the agenda, employers report high levels of satisfaction with the workers who come out of these programs, and there's evidence of higher retention and less turnover. Worker satisfaction has also been found to respond positively to increased wages associated with successful sectoral training and placements.

---

[108] http://www.dol.gov/asp/evaluation/jdt/jdt.pdf

Sectors like health care, information technology, and human services (e.g., child care, teaching) are likely to expand, especially if we get the macro right (Chapter 3), and even skilled manufacturing work could potentially be in greater demand if we get the dollar policy right (Chapter 5). Believe it or not, even throughout the Great Recession when we were hemorrhaging jobs across the labor market, health care added jobs every month. That's in part because demand for those services can be "inelastic," meaning that you can't put them off the way you can replacing an old car or fridge. But it's also because the public sector pays half the freight for health care in this country, a share that will rise due both to demographics and the Affordable Care Act (and, as I discuss in later chapters, the ACA is helping to both increase coverage and slow cost growth, so this rising share is good news on various fronts).

So I'm pretty confident that the demand will be there in some of these sectors. But can these training and apprenticeship ideas (I'll get to the latter in a moment) really make a difference? Well, imagine a home health aide working with elderly outpatients. As a terminal high-school grad, she'll be able to provide minimal services, e.g., checking vital signs and, if not administering meds, at least organizing them (as a child of a 92-year-old mother, I speak from experience). But if she has two years of gerontology training from a community college or an apprenticeship program, she can do much more for her clients, including changing dressings, administering meds, helping to sustain cognitive functioning, and eventually supervising others. What we're really talking about here are interventions that can turn an okay job into a good job.

Apprenticeships, or work-based learning, provide another vital tool in this space. Holzer and Lerman (H&L) define apprenticeships as "contractual arrangements between private employers and workers that prepare workers to master an occupation."[109] An advanced manufacturer, for example, might contract with a worker to spend a number of years (most such programs take two to four years) to learn laser welding, programmable machine tools, 3D printing, etc. The apprentice will experience both classroom and production floor training, and, critically, as employees they are expected to contribute to the production process and are compensated as such.

As H&L point out, "persistence rates in such programs tend to be higher, as are completion rates. Students see a direct link between what they learn in the classroom and problems in applied settings; put succinctly, they engage in *contextualized learning*, a successful learning environment for young people, especially those not entirely successful in traditional academic settings." And yet, America is a big laggard when it comes to apprenticeships; they make up only 0.2 percent of our workforce compared to 2 percent in Canada, 3 percent in Britain, and about 4 percent in Australia and Germany. Not huge numbers, I grant you, but remember, in our labor market 4 percent is over six million workers. Remember also that unlike some of the other tools in the

---

[109] http://www.pathtofullemployment.org/wp-content/uploads/2014/04/holzerlerman.pdf

reconnection toolbox, like the fiscal and monetary policies discussed in Chapter 3, these ideas are designed to reach the harder-to-reach corners of the job market.

Apprenticeships are largely funded by private employers (small amounts of public funds sometimes supplement pay or coordinate education services), so the usual reason proffered for why we don't do more of the sorts of things we should be doing—we're broke!—doesn't hold here (neither are we broke, by the way, but that's a different argument; see Chapter 8). You ask me, I think there are two reasons we under-provide apprenticeship slots relative to other countries:

First, unions have much less of a presence here than abroad. Collective bargaining covers about 60 percent of the German workforce compared to about 12 percent here in the US. That matters in this space because from the days of the ancient guilds, unions have embraced apprenticeship programs, both to boost membership and to pass along skills. Second, compared to these other advanced economies, the US suffers broadly from a disease you might call short-termism. Investing in a worker for a number of years just comes less naturally to US employers. That's partly a rational reaction to the fact of greater turnover in our labor markets. Why invest in an apprentice when she might go work for a competitor once her training is complete? But what we're starting to see in these programs is that firms get a big, lasting payback from such investments. A well-trained and well-compensated worker with a skill set unique to the firm is pretty obviously likely to stick around.

Reaching the Hard-to-reach: Putting It All Together

In closing out this part of the reconnection agenda, let's think for a moment about the interaction between the ideas put forth in earlier chapters—using fiscal and monetary policy to achieve full employment, reducing trade deficits—and the focus here on reaching specific groups of hard-to-reach persons. To my thinking, a 2012 evaluation of a job placement program in various cities across France helps pull these ideas together. The results were on the discouraging side, with only transitory impacts and considerable displacement. Except for one thing: the program worked a lot better in places where labor demand was strong.[110]

The ideas I've presented above have a lot going for them. I've featured them based on their inherent logic—there should be no question that the obstacles faced by literally tens of millions of people with criminal records are a significant barrier to full employment, a barrier that we'd better try to surmount if we want a robust reconnection agenda. But I've also looked for ideas that have a track record based on evaluations, like the TANF EF program in Florida that mimicked a randomized trial.

On the other hand, we must never lose sight of the demand side of the equation: there's always a danger in these training, placement, and even apprenticeship programs that participants risk being all dressed up with nowhere to go. They've got the training but there are not enough jobs. Even a subsidized worker stops looking good

---

[110] http://economics.mit.edu/files/8514

when there's nobody on the shop-room floor to buy whatever it is you're selling.

Though the real-world debate too often breaks down into the demand camp or the supply camp, it will of course take both to achieve full employment. We could have a Fed committed to hitting a low "natural rate," fiscal policy that offsets downturns in bad times and makes the requisite investments in public goods in good times, dollar policy to lower the trade deficit . . . and still have large groups of underemployed people, many with obvious barriers to entry into the job market.

A reconnection agenda worthy of support thus must be one that reaches all corners of the economy. Adding the policy tools articulated above to those of earlier chapters designed to increase the quantity and quality of jobs is thus an essential part of the solution.

Chapter 7

Maintaining the Reconnection with Policies to Sustain the Booms and Bust the Busts

The previous chapter argued that even at full employment, there are still pockets of under-employment that must be considered if we want everyone to get a chance to contribute to their own and their family's well-being, not to mention the nation's output. So let's say we fill those pockets, such that the job market is at full employment, our manufacturers are competing on a level playing field, working stiffs (supported by pro-growth fiscal and monetary policy) have some real bargaining clout, and real wages are rising with productivity growth for many if not most in the workforce.

Sounds great, right? But our goal is not just *getting* to truly full employment. It's *staying* there. Just as keeping a light bulb shining requires not just establishing but also maintaining an electrical connection, an economic reconnection requires not just getting to full employment but also avoiding the bubbles and busts that have characterized the US macroeconomy in recent years. That is, not just getting to but staying at full employment has become particularly germane in our era of "the economic shampoo cycle," wherein regular implosions of the financial sector spill over into the rest of the economy and undermine the best efforts of the reconnectors. This chapter will define and explore that issue and related gnarly problems and prescribe solutions designed to promote steady growth that doesn't fall prey to bubbles, inflated by risky finance, that burst every few years at great cost to the rest of us.

The Economic Shampoo Cycle: Bubble, Bust, Repeat

The last two recessions (including the so-called Great Recession, the uniquely long and deep downturn that began in late 2007) were born of financial bubbles. In the 1990s it was the dot-com bubble, followed in the 2000s by the housing bubble. The early 1990s recession is also a candidate for being bubble-driven, as per the 1987 stock market crash, a mini housing bust, and the savings-and-loan banking collapse. The fact that these earlier recessions were relatively mild compared to the "great" one is a side point I'll revisit briefly below—for interesting reasons, recent recessions borne of equity bubbles haven't been as bad as the one borne of bad debt. But the key point for now is that bubbles and busts are ending expansions with what appears to be some degree of regularity.

The term "bust" is clear; it's a synonym for recession, a large market failure leading to loss of GDP, jobs, and incomes, along with rising unemployment. But defining a bubble in a particular economic variable—stocks, homes, the Internet—is trickier. In this context, it means a persistent and large deviation from a fundamental price. (Now, we're enough pages into this book that you'll be excused if that definition raises an eyebrow or two, and I applaud you if you've adopted a somewhat skeptical position about free and unfettered markets delivering perfect information about fundamental prices. But even if prices are distorted, it's still the case that a bubble is a persistent, significant departure from trend.)

Home prices are a great example. Considerable research has shown that US home prices are inflated by tax policies that subsidize housing, most notably the ability to deduct mortgage interest payments from your income tax. But that didn't stop a precious few economists—Dean Baker, most prominently, spotted and wrote about the housing bubble well before others[111]—from noting the large and persistent departure from both trend home prices and from rental prices, signaling a housing bubble. Unfortunately, Baker and literally one or two others were ignored by the masters of the universe, like then Federal Reserve Chair Alan Greenspan, who just saw the housing market doing its thing in some benign way, assuming self-correction would occur before anything got ugly.

In the 1990s there were actually numerous financial analysts who recognized that internet stocks were overvalued, but they played along, basically trying to time the bubble. Remember, if all you're trying to do is make money buying and selling securities, you

---

[111] http://www.cepr.net/index.php/reports/the-run-up-in-home-prices-is-it-real-or-is-it-another-bubble/

couldn't care less about whether *underlying* valuations are actually lying. You just need to find the next sucker down the line to unload the inflated asset onto before the casino implodes. Meanwhile, there's very strong evidence that these bubbles spin off massive "wealth effects"—that's the phenomenon showing that when the value of your assets go up, even if it's just on paper (i.e., "unrealized capital gains" in the lingo), you feel richer and spend more. Such effects added hundreds of billions of dollars to consumer spending during the inflation of the housing bubble.[112]

These dynamics all might amount to a big "so what?" if it were just a bunch of traders selling junk back and forth, or homeowners' incomes getting a boost from cash out refis every time the bubble got a little bubblier.[113] But, of course, what actually happens in these cases is far less benign. The 2000-01 recession, partially a function of the bursting of the dot-com bubble, ended the full employment economy of the 1990s, and while the recession itself was not that deep or long at all, the recovery that followed was terribly weak on many key metrics that loom large in the reconnection agenda, including jobs, wages, incomes, and the growth in inequality.[114]

---

[112] On wealth effects, see, for example:
http://cowles.econ.yale.edu/P/cd/d18b/d1884.pdf
[113] Cash out refinancing is a way to pocket increased equity in your home. When the value of your home increases, you replace your old mortgage with a new, larger loan (typically at a lower interest rate), and pocket the difference between what you owe on the home and the new, larger loan.
[114] In comparing the 2000s recovery to past cycles, Bivens (2008) finds that "[m]easures of total output, investment, consumption, employment, wage and income growth, all rank at or near the bottom when compared with past business cycles."

The 2000s expansion was also, as noted, fueled by a housing bubble which was, in turn, inflated by reckless finance. That story has been told many times over and my point is not to revisit it in detail here, though I will highlight aspects relevant to my key point, which is this: expansion-killing bubbles are . . . um . . . killing expansions before working people have a chance to make up their losses and maybe even get ahead. Even if we can pull off the reconnection we need, the bubbles break that (re)connection.

One of the main motivators for building a reconnection agenda is to try to steer more of the growth to households for whom growth has been so elusive. Well, for growth to reach the middle class, we need lasting, robust expansions that don't depend on volatile bubbles that will, by definition and by experience, deflate, often at great costs. And, ironically, the way things are set up today, those costs are too often borne not by the engineers of the bubble—the financial "innovators"—but by working households who are left holding the bag.

Therefore, part of the reconnection agenda must be to figure out what's behind the shampoo cycle and prescribe ways to break that cycle.

---

http://www.epi.org/publication/bp214/. Employment, for example, grew 23 million in the 1990s cycle and 6 million in the 2000s cycle. On an annualized basis (so that we don't penalize the 2000s cycle for being shorter), job growth was three times as fast in the 1990s than in the 2000s. And for the record, this chapter argues that you should penalize recoveries for not lasting longer. As was the case in the 2000s, a shortened cycle is not some natural, organic outcome; it's the result of a policy failure (in that case, ignoring a housing bubble goosed by reckless finance).

A Deeper Dive into the Shampoo Cycle

The obvious solution, and it's one to which most people now appropriately subscribe, is to provide adequate oversight to financial markets so that they don't keep going off the rails. Though there are of course holdouts who still maintain the old Greenspan view (one he himself has jettisoned) that these markets will "self-correct," they are either economists with obscure theories about "perfect information" or lobbyists paid— handsomely, I should add—to take this position. Both are scary, and both, especially the latter, are much more influential than they should be.

For that reason—the strong influence of the well-financed deregulatory advocates—our historical approach to financial market oversight has been demonstrably inadequate. Let me explain by use of a diagram that both gets into the guts of the shampoo cycle and highlights a critical dimension familiar to all who seek a reconnection agenda—that of high levels of income and wealth inequality.

The Economic Shampoo Cycle

The schematic of the shampoo cycle on the next page starts out with the trends laid out in Chapter 2, specifically rising income inequality and middle-income stagnation. This in turn leads to income and wealth accumulation by those at the top of the income scale. As less growth reaches them, middle class households turn to credit markets to maintain their living standards, and as their borrowing increases relative to their incomes, their debt-to-income ratios begin to rise.

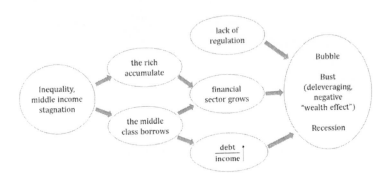

As researchers Michael Kumhof and Romain Ranciére wrote about this part of the process: "the bottom group's greater reliance on debt – and the top group's increase in wealth – generated a higher demand for financial intermediation."[115] Thus we expect, and particularly in the decade of the 2000s we got, an expansion in the financial sector. At this point, the other important dynamic enters the mix, itself a function of high wealth concentration and money in politics: the absence of sufficient financial market oversight.

This combination of forces is a potent recipe for a dangerous bubble. A large supply of cheap loanable funds is made available to a large group of borrowers not supported by much in the way of income growth while financial market regulators snooze on the

---

[115] https://www.imf.org/external/pubs/ft/fandd/2010/12/pdf/kumhof.pdf

sidelines. And as if that mixture wasn't volatile enough, the system's near-term incentives actually encourage this cycle. Shoddy underwriting by mortgage brokers who could securitize (bundle together) risky loans and sell them down the line (sell the bundle to investors who knew little about the actual quality of the loans) was a highly profitable line of work in the 2000s.

As the final "bubble" in the schematic shows, the bubble eventually bursts. Borrowers aggressively deleverage and wealth effects quickly shift into reverse, leading to a contraction in overall demand and recession.

It's a nice, logical story, but is there any evidence for it? In fact, one study by economists Barry Cynamon and Steve Fazzari conducts a careful empirical investigation of this sequence of events wherein the authors conclude that "the rise of inequality is easily large enough that it could *potentially account for the entire increase in bottom 95 percent debt leverage*, an increase that spawned the Great Recession."[116]

On the other hand, history shows that we've had financial bubbles in periods of lesser inequality than we face today. I'm not suggesting this sequence is either inevitable or the only way bubbles work, and one should always be wary of complex, chained arguments. But the growing evidence gels with my own experience as a DC-based economist: these dynamics are afoot. And importantly, our politics reveals that we're not learning our lessons from them. Note, for example, that when Republicans

---

[116] http://papers.ssrn.com/sol3/papers.cfm?abstract_id=2205524

won both houses of Congress in 2014, one of their first votes was to roll back regulations in the Dodd-Frank financial market reform bill.[117]

Underpricing Risk, and Not All Bubbles are Created Equal

Before I turn to the policies implied by all of this, a few more diagnostic observations are required.

As an occasional TV pundit, a creature that many readers may shrink from (after all, you are reading, not watching!), I often get asked big, fat, substantive questions and told I have 30 seconds to answer them (and if you go on for longer than that, as I'm wont to do, they yell "wrap!" in your earpiece). So I try to come loaded with quick responses to some predictable questions. For example, back in the days of the Great Recession, I was often asked for a one-sentence explanation of what caused the downturn. My answer was: "the collapse of a housing bubble inflated by reckless finance in which risk was severely underpriced."

The last bit of that one-liner warrants further discussion, as it's integral to the diagnosis and prescription in this space. Systematically underpriced risk is the helium that fills financial bubbles, and as such, it is the sworn enemy of the reconnection agenda. Such thinking goes all the back to Adam (i.e., Smith) and Keynes, but it is the brilliant work of the late economist Hyman Minsky that has become especially relevant in recent years, as his

---

[117] http://www.nytimes.com/2015/01/15/business/house-passes-measure-to-ease-some-dodd-frank-rules.html?_r=0

understanding of the fragility of financial markets and the cycle of underpriced risk was both deep and prescient.

Apparently, back in 2008, no less than Queen Elizabeth asked academics at the London School of Economics why "no one saw it coming," referring to the financial crisis that birthed the Great Recession.[118] An important part of the answer dates back to Minsky. When he was writing (and even today), many economists and forecasters viewed financial markets as playing not much more than an intermediary function, passively allocating excess savings to their most productive uses. Based on this assumption, their models either omitted or underweighted the impact of the financial sector on the broader economy.

But Minsky identified a financial cycle (or to use my cute update, the shampoo cycle) that evolved pretty predictably within the more widely-accepted business cycle. Lenders who got burned the last time out begin the financial cycle with caution, carefully underwriting loans; venture capitalist investors won't take your meeting if your internet startup sounds hokey. But as the cycle progresses, "animal spirits" take over, bad memories fade, "financial innovation" offering either opaque complexity or new distance between borrowers and lenders ("securitization") becomes rampant, and caution yields to euphoria, hyper-cautious risk-aversion to incautious risk-seeking, and bubble, bust, repeat is underway.

---

[118] http://www.telegraph.co.uk/news/uknews/theroyalfamily/3386353/The-Queen-asks-why-no-one-saw-the-credit-crunch-coming.html

(Photo by Kirsty Wigglesworth; with my comic bubble, btw!)

One final problem to keep in mind before turning to how to dampen if not squelch this financial/shampoo cycle: debt bubbles are particularly pernicious. To understand why, we need to wrap our heads around two phrases you might hear if you listen to CNBC long enough: "mark to market" and "extend and pretend." When a stock bubble bursts, the value of shares in firms inflated by the bubble lose air quickly. Pet rock shares worth $100 at

Friday's close sink like the stones they really are and open on Monday at pennies on the dollar . . . if you're lucky. The market can and does quickly mark down inflated shares. That, of course, happens all the time, and it's not evidence of a bubble; remember, the definition of a bubble is not speculation writ small. It's speculation writ large, across large and critical sectors, like housing or the NASDAQ (the tech-heavy stock exchange).

In fact, comparing the equity-driven dot-com bubble to the debt-driven housing bubble is instructive in this regard. The NASDAQ peaked in March 2000, then fell 20 percent off that peak in April, 27 percent off the peak in May, and 59 percent by March 2001. While it's trickier to measure the "correction" with the debt- (as in mortgage debt) driven housing bubble, note that after the housing bust in 2006-07, it took about three years for household debt as a share of income to fall back to pre-housing-bubble levels and about the same amount of time for mortgage debt to unwind.[119]

One reason why debt bubbles can take longer to mop up relative to other types of bubbles (equity, commodity) is that the losses they engender are not realized as quickly, in part because banks holding the "non-performing" loans have an incentive to kid themselves that the toxic loans will someday be healthy again. Whether or not they will be can be a matter of life and death for a bank because a loan is an asset, and if enough of your assets turn from a source of income to a source of loss, you're looking at

---

[119] See exhibits 1 and 2 here:
http://www.federalreserve.gov/pubs/feds/2012/201214/201214pap.pdf

least at diminished profitability and at most, depending on how leveraged up you are, insolvency.

In some cases, as when a default occurs, banks have to mark their non-performing assets to market in the same way as equities. But particularly when the loans are in real estate, the market simply doesn't mete out the quick discipline it should—Lehman's stock fell 93 percent on the day it declared bankruptcy.[120] But the banks can "extend and pretend"—extend the life of a loan portfolio they know to be no less deceased than the famous Monty Python parrot[121] while pretending it's just resting.[122] For example, after the crash in the last recession, banks were widely observed extending the maturities of loans or lowering interest rates to avoid—more accurately, postpone—defaults. Such restructuring protected their balance sheets and their earnings, as they could maintain, at least on paper, the balance between their assets and liabilities without having to set aside extra reserves to cover the "non-performing" assets.

This might not sound so bad—it's not obviously a bad thing to stagger such losses—were it not for extend-and-pretend's impact, which was to restrain the recovery by constraining access to credit, of which the current economic expansion (the one that allegedly began in late 2009 and six years later is only now beginning to reach broad swaths of Americans) is exhibit A. Credit flows are essential to recoveries and banks with bad loans

---

[120] http://www.investopedia.com/articles/economics/09/lehman-brothers-collapse.asp
[121] https://www.youtube.com/watch?v=4vuW6tQ0218
[122] http://www.wsj.com/articles/SB10001424052748704764404575286882690834088

on their books will be hesitant to lend to anyone without pristine credit. This, then, is the other side of the "Minsky-moment": the flip from underpricing risk to overpricing it. Such risk aversion is not to be trifled with. The failure to resolve bad assets helped keep Japan in an economic funk for at least a decade. And here in the US it has led to years of delay as too-highly-risk-averse credit markets prevented the recovery hitting escape velocity from the gravitational pull of the Great Recession.

What to do about it, however, is also not obvious. For banks to simply accept defeat and default would mean a large write-down of their capital and threats of insolvency, which could lead to the same excessive risk-aversion outcome in terms of credit restrictions. So how do we keep our economic hair clean while killing the shampoo cycle? Which raises the equally pressing question: how long will I torture this metaphor?

How to Keep the Reconnection Agenda . . . Connected!

The way to break the shampoo cycle is to provide adequate oversight to financial markets, but what's adequate? And didn't we recently legislate precisely that solution with the Dodd-Frank financial reform legislation? And isn't this financial regulatory stuff just downright boring?

OK, that last one is a toughie, but one way to keep it at least mildly interesting is to keep it simple.

Yes, Dodd-Frank is the law of the land, but as I mentioned above, the financial lobby didn't all fall on their swords the day it passed.

To the contrary, they recognized that the law had literally hundreds of provisions (about 400, to be precise) that had to be ironed out and specified, and they've been extremely busy in ironing them out in ways that keep the wrinkles they like in place. *USA Today* looked into votes to roll back some rules that financial lobbyists disliked and found that "committee members who voted for one of the amendments received 7.8 times as much in campaign contributions from the nation's four largest commercial banks than members who voted against."[123] The paper also reported that prior to issuing a draft version of the Volcker Rule from Dodd-Frank (which I'll explain in a moment), regulatory agencies spent 93 percent of their meetings with members of "banks, financial institutions and affiliates . . . public interest groups, research, watchdog and labor groups were involved in 7%" of the meetings."

So yeah, we legislated reform, and no, we're not done with it. And for the record, those with a vested interest in keeping the shampoo cycle going would very much like you to perceive it as a crushing bore and move on to something else. Nothing to see here folks . . . move along.

Based on the diagnosis above, here's what's needed to break the cycle:

---

[123] http://www.usatoday.com/story/money/business/2013/06/03/dodd-frank-financial-reform-progress/2377603/

- large capital buffers;

- a strong Volcker Rule;

- a strong, activist Consumer Financial Protection Bureau (CFPB);

- a Federal Reserve that's vigilant around systemic risk underpricing and bubbles.

If that seems like a pretty simple menu, that's because it is. That's not some swipe at Dodd-Frank's almost 900 pages. The details matter and careful articulation of how derivatives should be traded to avoid explosion is also part of the mix. But what I'm trying to do here is to suggest the four walls of a courtyard within which financial markets can safely grow. Various pathways in the courtyard will also need to be drawn up, but my contention is that if we get these four right, we have a decent chance of dampening the destructive cycle.

When a bank gets kicked in its assets, it needs an adequate capital buffer: First, here's an old saw among financial market reformers: "you can get a lot wrong if you get the capital buffers right" (IKR! What a bunch of cutups!). Capital buffers, or capital requirements, are rules about how much equity or capital a bank must hold against potential losses. Just like many other businesses, banks raise money through borrowing, or leverage, through earnings, including profits on services as well as their own trading activities (the latter can also be a problem; we'll address that re the *Volcker Rule* in a minute), and through investments by shareholders. The latter two of these income sources belong to the bank; the former, however, are merely on loan, and creditors have strict, highly enforceable, and often publicly-insured claims on any money they've loaned to or deposited in the bank.

So if a bank gets whacked by significant losses, it needs an ample buffer of equity capital (its own money) to cover the losses and still have enough assets left to cover its liabilities (what it owes depositors and anyone else who's lent it money). After all, once a bank's burned through its capital holdings (its earnings or equity shares), its balance sheet no longer balances out. At that point, its liabilities surpass its assets, which is a nice way of saying it is insolvent. The key idea is that banks should be allowed to lose their own money but shouldn't be able to lose your money. If they do lose your money and can't replenish it with more of their own money, they're toast. Or, more precisely, if they're insured by the FDIC, we're toast, since we as taxpayers backstop the deposits in insured institutions. And if they're highly interconnected to the broad system of global credit as in the last great crash, then we're all extremely burnt toast.

But surely the banks want to avoid such cataclysms too, right? Um . . . not so much. Borrowing is called "leverage" for a reason; it's one way to amp up, or lever, your profits, and while higher capital requirements protect banks and, more importantly, the broader public against shocks, such requirements also make them less profitable, not to mention less sexy and more boring. Proof of this assertion can be seen in the common strategy employed by banks when their assets take a hit and regulators start sniffing around to see if their capital buffers enable them to sustain the hit without tapping the government backstop (FDIC insurance). In such cases, it's common for the institution to reduce the size of its balance sheet, shedding both assets and liabilities and paying down its debt. And that usually leads to considerably diminished profitability.

And yet, and I'm speaking for all of us who lived through the last financial meltdown and/or all the ones before it, the goal of having boring, unsexy banks is one very much worth pursuing.

Now, to state the obvious, we can't count on markets to monitor this sort of thing. Do you have any idea of your bank's leverage ratio? No, I didn't think so. Just as we need food safety rules to feel moderately comfortable walking into unfamiliar restaurants, we need regulators ensuring adequate capital buffers, which are usually expressed as a percent of assets.

Under current rules, large banks must hold around a 7 percent capital share of their assets as a buffer. That's too low for a robust reconnection agenda, and I'm not the only one who thinks so. Dodd-Frank required the Federal Reserve to do a rethink on this critical issue and the Fed's proposed rule adds as much as another 5 percent on top the current standard (for banks whose assets regulators judge to be risky, that percent could go even higher).

There's no magic number here but that's a fine start. However, it looks like the Fed's proposal will only increase capital requirements at eight behemoths.[124] I understand the logic—the Fed's going after "too big to fail." If you're a big-ass bank like JP Morgan or Goldman Sachs, you pose a unique danger to the global financial system, so you of all institutions need a fat buffer zone. But it's not so much size as interconnectedness that matters when banks get whacked in the assets. So I'd extend these higher buffers far beyond the eight largest banks, to medium-sized institutions as well.

Stop making bets with my money! The need for a strong Volcker rule: That would be Paul Volcker, former chair of the Fed and someone who during the last financial meltdown convinced a bunch of policy makers that federally-insured banks should not gamble with taxpayers money. You might think that idea is a no-brainer, but as someone who worked on this piece of the Dodd-Frank bill, I assure you many don't see it that way.

Part of the problem is the truly prodigious power of the financial lobby, of course, but that's not the whole story. Both in this case and the buffer zone stuff just discussed, there's a real reluctance among policy makers to do anything that might dampen the ability of financial institutions to come up with "innovative" ways—and yes, those are scare quotes—to make trades and bets, derivatives whose value is based on those trades and bets, insurance products against losses in those trades and bets, and

---

[124] http://dealbook.nytimes.com/2014/12/09/with-new-capital-rule-fed-nudges-big-banks-to-shrink/

derivatives whose value is based on those insurance products. To the policy makers with whom I argued about this back in the day—and they weren't all Republicans by a long shot—putting the brakes on any of this stuff would dampen liquidity, reduce investment, choke off credit, raise the price of borrowing, and slow the economy. I think that sequence is mostly bunk, and it's certainly nowhere to be seen in the implied statistics, including investment and productivity.

To the contrary, work by finance scholar Thomas Philippon finds no improvement in the efficiency of the financial sector; if anything, economy-wide productivity slowed as these "innovations" became more . . . innovative.[125] Paul Volcker himself—and I promise we'll get to his eponymous rule forthwith—said that the only useful innovation the banking sector has come up with in 20 years was the automatic cash machine.[126]

Moreover, as is the point of this chapter, that framing of the problem is precisely upside-down. The point of blocking those practices is to *preserve* economic growth and jobs. And here's where the Volcker rule comes in: blocking these practices doesn't always mean stopping them. It means hiving them off so they don't hurt innocent bystanders.

---

[125] https://www.london.edu/news-and-events/news/no-evidence-of-financial-service-productivity-gains-in-a-century#.VNwZm_nF_sY; http://www.frbsf.org/economic-research/publications/economic-letter/2015/february/economic-growth-information-technology-factor-productivity/

[126] http://en.wikipedia.org/wiki/Paul_Volcker

In the old days, commercial banks took deposits and investment banks traded securities (e.g., stocks, bonds, derivatives, and bets on Lucky Jim to place 7th at Belmont). The latter invoked profits and losses and the former (deposits in commercial banks) were insured by the government against losses that would occur were the bank to go under. Eventually, these lines became blurred, legislation that created the firewall was repealed, and deposit banks were allowed to do the sorts of things that investment banks did. Thus was born the "proprietary trading desk" in commercial banks, where they engaged in trades and hedge-fund-like activities with their own money, not that of their clients, for their own profit. And own-book trading meant great profits on the upside, but on the downside it meant that if the bank lost big (say, if Lucky Jim failed to place), the FDIC might have to bail out the banks' depositors.

You are once again forgiven if you're scratching your head—you probably have a callous there by now—wondering "who the h-e-double-hockey-sticks signed off on that bright idea?!" Ahh, you're forgetting the magic of self-regulation (perhaps because it doesn't exist) and the power of the banking lobby to convince policy makers that allowing insured banks to expand their scope will boost liquidity, lower borrowing rates, yada, yada. And it's even easier for the lobbyists to convince said policy makers when the politicians are on the lobbyists' payrolls.

By the way, there's another good reason why, if your goal is to kill the shampoo cycle, you want to block this type of proprietary, or "prop," trading with a government backstop. It's even got a name: *moral hazard,* which is an economics problem that emerges when people don't face the true cost of their actions. In this case it is particularly germane because the moral hazard problem feeds into the underpriced risk problem. If I know you've got my back no matter what, I'm likely to make all kinds of risky bets. After all, I'm not putting my depositors at risk, so hey, why not structure a derivative that pays off big if the weatherman on tonight's 6 o'clock news wears a red tie? When we were working on the Volcker rule in the White House and Treasury in 2009-10, it was pretty widely understood that government subsidies of risky trades wasn't exactly smart policy.

OK, following the brief diversion into game theory, we're back live in our little history of "what could go wrong with letting insured deposit banks run wild?" In the go-go 2000s, publicly-insured banks were allowed to run hedge funds, trade derivatives, and all the rest, putting their own book—their capital—in the game. When the music stopped around 2007, they needed bailouts not just to reflate the shocked credit system but to shield depositors from losses against which they were insured through the FDIC. One estimate placed losses from this type of trading by Wall Street banks at $230 billion as the meltdown was unfolding.[127]

The Volcker rule would simply prohibit these sorts of trades. Banks backstopped by the Federal government would no longer be able to trade their own books. Note that none of this would

---

[127] http://www.thenation.com/article/166500/explainer-why-do-we-need-volcker-rule#

stop *actual* investment banks, hedge hogs, currency chop shops, and/or high freak-quency traders from getting their risk on 24/7, 365. It just separates such activities from those of the insured banks.

This rule did not go down easy with the banking lobby and their reps in Congress, who fought hard to carve out all kinds of exemptions. There are lots of trades, they argued, that might look like "prop" trades but are really about hedging risk for a client. Really, they promise!

Thanks to their influence in drafting the rule, which still isn't fully in place as I write this in early 2015 (!), they took what Volcker himself said should be a four-page rule ("I'd love to see a four-page bill that bans proprietary trading and makes the board and chief executive responsible for compliance") and made it 300 pages. Then, in a move Minsky would have loved, they complained it was too hard to wrap their heads around. As the Times reported: "Wall Street firms have spent countless millions of dollars trying to water down the original Volcker proposal and have succeeded in inserting numerous exemptions. Now they're claiming it's too complex to understand and too costly to adopt."[128]

This book isn't the place to go into the fine points about what is and isn't a prop trade. Banks claim, with some merit, that they sometimes need to trade securities to meet the demands of

---

[128] http://www.nytimes.com/2011/10/22/business/volcker-rule-grows-from-simple-to-complex.html?pagewanted=all&_r=0

customers, and there's no good reason they should have to give up that lucrative business. They also argue they need to be able to engage in vanilla hedges to protect themselves against swings in interest rates, an exemption they claimed was essential to manage "asset-liability risk." Predictably, however, while the argument between banks and Dodd-Frank implementers about precisely where to draw these lines was ongoing, JP Morgan Chase lost over $6 billion in a trade that looked exactly like the sort of thing you'd want the Volcker Rule to stop.[129] Following that episode, such exemptions were narrowed somewhat such that the rule, once in place, is slated to allow banks to hedge against risks that are "specific and identifiable."

I can't confidently say I know what that means and I doubt anyone else can either, at least not with the needed specificity. The banks themselves have said they need a few more years to figure it out, leading Volcker to point out the following:

> It is striking, that the world's leading investment bankers, noted for their cleverness and agility in advising clients on how to restructure companies and even industries however complicated, apparently can't manage the orderly reorganization of their own activities in more than five years. Or, do I understand that lobbying is

[129] http://dealbook.nytimes.com/2012/04/06/what-volcker-rule-could-mean-for-jpmorgans-big-trades/

eternal, and by 2017 or beyond, the expectation can be fostered that the law itself can be changed?[130]

Volcker's snark is, of course, on point. The banking lobby is just stalling for time, hoping to hire ever more friendly politicians to further gut the rule. So, we in the reconnection agenda army must be vigilant. But at the same time, complexity is a fact of life in financial markets, and my strongly held view on all of the pieces of Dodd-Frank, including the Volcker Rule and capital requirements, is that we won't know how effective they are until we put them in place and—this part is key—the regulators enforce them.

For our purposes—breaking the shampoo cycle to maintain the reconnection agenda—the key conceptual point is straightforward: if you're a commercial bank and you're exposed to significant risk through trading your own book, you're out of compliance with the rule. Our best move right now is thus to stop futzing around, implement the rule, stay awake at the switches, and see what happens.

Consumer Financial Protection Bureau—protect me!: At the behest of a Harvard law professor who was a scholar on consumer issues and is now a US Senator by the name of Elizabeth Warren, the Dodd-Frank bill created something called the Consumer Financial Protection Bureau. The mission of the CFPB, according to its website, is "to make markets for consumer financial

---

[130] http://jaredbernsteinblog.com/quote-of-the-day-paul-volcker-on-the-new-two-year-delay-in-implementing-his-eponymous-rule/

products and services work for Americans — whether they are applying for a mortgage, choosing among credit cards, or using any number of other consumer financial products."[131]

That's fine, if not anodyne, but its mission according to me in the context of breaking the shampoo cycle is a very particular one: we need a CFPB that will enforce the adequate underwriting of loans. If underpriced risk is the evil genius of financial bubbles, than bad underwriting is the work of her minions.

Risk underpricing and the bubbles it inflates may be a function of ideologically misguided economics of the type that led Fed Chair Alan Greenspan to believe financial markets would self-correct before they would implode. One level down, risk underpricing is a function of financial practices like securitization, where loans are bundled and sold off such that the original lenders can create a wide berth between themselves and not-very-creditworthy borrowers. It is a function of complex derivatives that mask the true riskiness they engender. But at the granular, ground level, underpriced risk means people making money—lots of money— providing loans to people who shouldn't get those loans.

Who am I to say who should and shouldn't get a loan? Fair question. But the ready answer is that you shouldn't get a loan if you can't realistically service that loan without seriously screwing up your financial life. Certainly, a CFPB worth its name would

---

[131] http://www.consumerfinance.gov/the-bureau/

support such a reasonable definition, one quite consistent with its mission statement above.

The housing/real estate bubble, both here and abroad, was a good example of this problem. Developments in the system of housing finance allowed mortgage brokers in the 1990s and more so in the 2000s to convince people that they could afford to take out loans to buy far more house than they could afford, based on the argument that the value of the home itself would continuously appreciate, thus enabling the owner to continuously extract equity and pay the mortgage. You may not think you're rich enough to buy this house, but by buying this house, you're rich enough to buy this house! Who could argue with that logic?

A forensic detective seeking evidence of this pretzel logic at work would begin her investigation with the deterioration of underwriting. Luckily for us, two housing finance scholars, Adam Levitin and Susan Wachter, undertake precisely this investigation in excruciating and painful-but-essential-to-learn-about detail.[132] In language both antiseptic and barely intelligible, Levitin and Wachter indict "mispriced mortgage finance" (what I called above, "giving loans to people who shouldn't get them;" admit it . . . aren't you glad *I'm* explaining this stuff?) as a central culprit, with unregulated "private label securitizers" (investment

---

132

http://georgetownlawjournal.org/files/2012/04/LevitinWachter.pdf&sa=U&ei=KSVj
U-
aILYyVyASc9IDlDw&ved=0CDEQFjAE&usg=AFQjCNFJd_4uh2Ac3P5KtW6k7
YHuq8KGgw

banks bundling loans that did not conform to traditional standards) as a key accomplice. They go on:

> ... the mortgage-finance supply glut [resulted] from the failure of markets to price risk correctly due to the complexity, opacity, and heterogeneity of the unregulated private-label mortgage-backed securities (PLS) that began to dominate the market in 2004. The rise of PLS exacerbated informational asymmetries between the financial institutions that intermediate mortgage finance and PLS investors. These intermediation agents exploited informational asymmetries to encourage overinvestment in PLS that boosted the financial intermediaries' volume-based profits and enabled borrowers to bid up housing prices.

Cutting through their opacity, they're telling a story about how people (or "intermediation agents," including mortgage brokers, banks, and non-bank lenders) exploited a self-perpetuating—at least for a while—system wherein the ability of homeowners to afford the loans they were getting was no longer a function of their ability to pay based on their income or savings, but on the appreciation of their home values. Once gravity began to reassert itself, as it always ultimately does in bubbles, home prices fell, and ... well, you know the rest.

The evidence from Levitin and Wachter is compelling. I've relegated their graphs to Appendix B—parental discretion is advised—but here's what they show:

- PLS securitization went from about 0 percent of the securitization market in the mid-1980s to about 25 percent in 2000. But by the peak of the housing bubble in 2006, it accounted for over half of the market (Figure B1).

- The issuance of Sub-prime and Alt-A ("low documentation"—in our language: crappily underwritten) bundled mortgage securities went from 0 percent in the 1990s to 40 percent at the peak of the bubble (Figure B2).

- Probably the most badly underwritten mortgages (100 percent financing, meaning no downpayment and "no doc" loans) went from about 0 percent of mortgage originations in 2001 to about 15 percent in 2006 (Figure B3).

- In a murderers' row display of toxic loans, "interest only," "payment option ARMs," and "40-year balloons" peaked at about $850 billion in terms of origination volume at the peak of the bubble. Three years later, in 2009, such originations were back to where they belong: at zero (Figure B4).

And here's the kicker: as all this "innovative" borrowing and lending was being transacted by "intermediation agents" and borrowers (or if you prefer, charlatans and suckers), "risk premiums for housing finance fell," meaning the market was pricing these loans as increasingly safe, not increasingly risky.[133] That's what we mean when we say risk was underpriced.

Now, these dynamics unfolded in housing, but the same kind of thing could easily happen in any other area where households borrow, from student loans to SUVs. What's needed is a public overseer whose job it is to watch out for the growth of the type of variables and products that Levitin and Wachter so carefully track, and to intervene to block their growth when they pose a systemic risk to the economy.

When is there systemic risk? When the potential for defaults threatens the financial well-being of significant numbers of consumers and thus the balance sheets of systemically connected banks. Which, from what I can tell, doesn't take much, so a good rule of thumb would be when such risky products account for more than a few percent of the market.

Of course, banning such products outright might be warranted ("Warren"-ted?), but I can see a role for, say, adjustable rate mortgages. I have a harder time seeing one for "interest-only loans," where you defer payments on the principal for a while, meaning your payments will jump bigtime at some discrete point, and I see no role for "no-docs!"

But it doesn't matter what I see. I'm not the CFPB. I/we need them to figure out the safe ratios and products given the frequency of the shampoo cycle. And we need them to do it without the

---

[133] Technically, Levitin and Wachter show that the interest rate spreads between PLS securities and risk-free Treasuries were shrinking over this period.

finance industry breathing down their necks. The reconnection agenda depends on it!

The Fed and the shampoo cycle: Finally, the Fed needs to be a muscular and vigilant overseer of the financial markets, and not just because it's the Fed's job to oversee the health and safety of the banking sector, but also for a specific reason having to do with the material in Chapter 4. The Fed must ratchet up its financial oversight role so that it can preserve monetary policy that promotes full employment. In Fed-speak, it mustn't conflate macro-management with macro-prudential management.

A common argument these days is that by trying to do what I strongly recommended in Chapter 4 (keeping interest rates low to stimulate investment), the Fed is itself blowing bubbles. Since rates on bonds are so low as per the Fed's intervention, investors must pile into other assets to get any sort of decent return, and thus, the argument goes, the Fed's efforts to promote full employment create the very bubble that will destroy full employment.

On the one hand, I'm arguing that keeping the federal funds rate low in weak economies is essential for meeting the full employment side of the Fed's mandate. On the other, I've argued that the shampoo cycle is regularly killing full employment. The counter-argument here is that the medicine suggested in Chapter 4 is causing the disease described in this chapter. [134] If true, this

---

[134] http://www.bloomberg.com/bw/articles/2013-08-12/bubbles-the-fed-cant-ignore

allegation would be pretty damn ironic for the recovery agenda as I've outlined it.

There's some logic to this counterargument, though even as I write in April 2015, with the Fed rate at about zero since 2009, there's been no systematic asset bubble. Still, the problem isn't with the logic; it's with the proposed solution. Those who worry about Fed-induced asset bubbles want the Fed to fight them with monetary policy, i.e., by raising interest rates, even if the economy, the job market, wage growth, and so on are still weak. But from a reconnection agenda standpoint, that prescription is obviously counterproductive. It argues for choking off the recovery before it reaches working families in order to ensure that investors have rich and varied pickings in financial markets. We've seen that movie and we don't like the ending.

The better solution is for the Fed to use different tools for different problems. Monetary policy (moving interest rates up and down) is the correct tool to meet the dual mandate of full employment amidst stable prices. Regulatory oversight is the right tool to break the shampoo cycle.

The good news is that, though it hasn't always been the case, there's considerable evidence today that top Fed officials understand the importance of making this distinction.

Many Fed watchers found Fed Chair Janet Yellen's 2013 Senate confirmation hearing to be a bore, in that she very ably did her job of not slipping up and making any news in ways that could have derailed the process. I, however, vividly remember one exchange between Chair Yellen and New Jersey Senator Bob Menendez that I found downright scintillating:

Menendez: "Some commentators have suggested that in addition to managing inflation and promoting full employment, the Fed should also monitor and attempt to fight asset bubbles. Do you think that is something the Fed should be doing?"

Yellen: "I think it's important for the Fed, hard as it is, to attempt to detect asset bubbles when they're forming."[135]

Now, back in 2002, Ben Bernanke, a member of the Fed board who was soon to be its governor, said: "The Fed cannot readily identify bubbles in asset prices."[136] That same year, the practically deified Fed governor Alan Greenspan agreed:

> . . . we recognized that, despite our suspicions, it was very difficult to definitively identify a bubble until after the fact--that is, when its bursting confirmed its existence. Moreover, it was far from obvious that bubbles, even if identified early, could be preempted short of the central bank inducing a substantial contraction in economic activity . . .[137]

Greenspan's take is particularly revealing because he's implicitly punting on the Fed's regulatory oversight responsibilities, no doubt because he viewed them as counterproductive given self-

---

[135] https://www.saoscapital.com/1004057.pdf
[136] http://www.federalreserve.gov/Boarddocs/Speeches/2002/20021015/default.htm
[137] http://www.federalreserve.gov/BoardDocs/speeches/2002/20020830/default.htm

correcting financial markets. In his world, even if the Fed could identify bubbles, they're left with one and only one tool: "inducing a substantial contraction in economic activity," i.e., jamming up rates to slow the economy in order to burst the bubble. It's a classic example of misguided ideology taking the much preferred option off of the table, leaving our economy with a Hobson's choice of either accepting the shampoo cycle or Fed-induced slow growth.

As I write today, the 2015 Federal Reserve, led by Yellen and her vice-chair Stan Fischer, makes many good noises about precisely these points. Yellen in particular frequently and clearly recognizes that the Fed doesn't have the luxury to ignore bubbles, nor can it punish those who depend on paychecks in order to protect those who depend on portfolios. In her own words (with my bold):

> . . . monetary policy faces significant limitations as a tool to promote financial stability: Its effects on financial vulnerabilities, such as excessive leverage and maturity transformation, are not well understood and are less direct than a regulatory or supervisory approach; in addition, **efforts to promote financial stability through adjustments in interest rates would increase the volatility of inflation and employment. As a result, I believe a macroprudential approach to supervision and regulation needs to play the primary role.**

> . . . it is critical for regulators to complete their efforts at implementing a macroprudential approach to enhance

resilience within the financial system, which will minimize the likelihood that monetary policy will need to focus on financial stability issues rather than on price stability and full employment.[138]

Fed-speak, for sure. But a pretty strong statement of what I would argue are precisely the correct priorities for a Fed that should focus its growth tools on growth and its regulatory tools on breaking the bubble/bust cycle.

We of the reconnection agenda should feel good about that.

And yet . . .

Conclusion: Can the Connection be Maintained in Our Political Economy?

I remain deeply concerned about this part of the puzzle.

While prior chapters played offense, offering proactive ideas to reconnect growth and prosperity, this one played defense, providing a look at the anatomy of the terrifically damaging bubble, bust, repeat sequence, explaining its connection to underpriced risk, and suggesting a framework for financial market regulation to break this economic shampoo cycle.

But just as the offense won't score if we don't shoot—I've coached little kids' basketball, so trust me on this—defense won't work if it's not aggressively applied. And while it's my nature to be upbeat and never give up hope, this area of financial market

---

[138] http://www.federalreserve.gov/newsevents/speech/yellen20140702a.htm

oversight has me worried. As Volcker points out, the banking lobby has earned their keep protecting their clients' profitability against his rule. Similarly, it has taken far too long to get capital buffer rules in place and, as they too cut into profitability, they're not at all safe from dilution.

Our regulatory infrastructure in this space remains fragmented with too many different agencies overseeing their pieces of the puzzle, while some important puzzle pieces—hedge funds, private equity—still face little oversight. The need for capital buffers—as I noted, you can get a lot wrong if you get this right—is widely understood but not yet applied. Regulators apply "stress tests" to determine whether banks are weak links in the systemic chain, but such tests are opaque, and while I don't know that anyone is gaming them, this sector is highly skilled at precisely that sort of game playing.

Basically, the combination of forces in play here is ripe for getting things wrong. You've got a hugely profitable sector that supports policy makers who do its bidding. It's also a complex sector; asking regulators to identify proprietary trades to hedge against risks that are "specific and identifiable" (recall that this is an exemption to Volcker rule) is trickier than, say, setting a minimum wage. Complexity, profitability, and deep pocketed lobbyists will make it awfully hard—they already are doing so—to break the shampoo cycle.

I recently read a story in the paper about a hostile takeover bid by a hedge fund. The deal fell apart, but the hedge fund still walked away with over $2 billion in profit (in making its own bid, the fund bought 10 percent of the target company's stock, which rose sharply when a higher, rival, and ultimately victorious bid was made).[139] I'm not saying that example means the end is near, or even that it provides much in the way of evidence of underpriced risk, bad underwriting, and snoozy regulators, though it is surely a pointed example of why wealth inequality is so historically elevated.

But I suspect up there in economists' heaven, Hy Minsky saw this example—he probably called Keynes over to have a look—and raised an eyebrow. And when Minsky raises an eyebrow, we should all get a little nervous and a lot more vigilant.

There's much we could do to reconnect growth and prosperity—the reconnection agenda is robust, replete with policy interventions designed to return some bargaining power back to working people who've watched the hedge funds rake it in (even when they lose, they win) while they themselves worked their butts off just to keep from falling behind. But it won't mean much if we implement the agenda and start to see economic gains finally flow more broadly, only to lose it all because some banks blew up the economy . . . again.

Breaking the shampoo cycle must thus be right up there with getting to full employment as a primary goal of the reconnection agenda. And that will take more than economic analysis of the

[139] http://dealbook.nytimes.com/2014/11/17/the-luck-of-a-loser-to-the-tune-of-2-2-billion/?ref=international

type you've just slogged though. It will take political power, standing up to the financial sector's lobby, and a vigilance born of both understanding the shampoo cycle and remembering how damaging it has been and will be again if we ignore it.

Chapter 8

The Federal Government and the Reconnection Agenda

The role of the federal government has shown up in many, many places already, and in the final chapter it gets a full-out political treatment. In this chapter, however, I drill down on the part of the agenda that I've not said much about yet: government programs that help to reconnect growth and prosperity.

Though I haven't labeled it as such, throughout the book I've distinguished between what economists call the primary and secondary distributions of income, with the "primary" being market outcomes and the "secondary" being the distribution of income post-tax and transfer payments (like Social Security or the Earned Income Tax Credit). Much of what I've advocated thus far is intended to rebalance the primary distribution on behalf of those who've been left behind for decades. Full employment, I've argued, boosts their bargaining power such that they can claim a fairer share of the growth they're helping to produce. Blocking currency management gives our manufacturers a chance to fight it out on a more level international playing field, before taxes and transfer payments kick in.

My emphasis on so-called market outcomes is intentional and driven by both my diagnosis and political economy. Diagnostically, as pointed out in Chapter 2, since much of the increase in inequality is a pre-tax phenomenon, it cannot be fundamentally corrected through redistributive tax policies. Politically, to leave everything to the secondary distribution means going back to Congress every year or two to beg for another corrective slug of this or that program to replace the lost income to the poor or middle class. And that . . . um . . . ain't much of a plan.

However, there are many important—truly vital—ways in which hard-won government policies directly reconnect less advantaged households to growth. Moreover, and here's why it says "so-called" above, *there are no pure market outcomes*. There's no firewall between the two distributions—they hugely influence each other. The EITC, for example, not only lifts millions of low-income, working households out of poverty, but it's pro-work: it's been shown to quite sharply increase labor supply in private sector jobs. A highly germane point in this space is that when top marginal tax rates were much higher than they are today, executive compensation—*before tax*—was set much lower (and growth was not negatively affected, for the record).[140]

---

[140] http://eml.berkeley.edu/~saez/piketty-saez-stantchevaAEJ14.pdf

In other words, a well-functioning and amply-funded federal sector must be part of an effective reconnection agenda. As such, it can serve as a vital complement to goals like full employment, as I've already stressed in the discussion about fiscal, monetary, and dollar policy. It sets rules of the road that can either help or block the connection between growth and prosperity, as noted in the discussions about labor standards and enforcing union rights to collectively bargain that follow. And it can and does provide direct support to those who lack the means to meet their own and their families' basic needs.

This last function—the safety net—looms large in what follows, but not for the "usual reasons." It's not just that anti-poverty programs help provide necessities like food and housing to low-income families, though that's a critical function of the safety net. Nor is it just that the safety net is necessary for countercyclical reasons, as I discussed in the context of fiscal policy in Chapter 3. In addition to both of those functions, there's a fascinating strain of relatively new research showing that in many cases, the goods and services we provide for low-income households support not just their near-term consumption but play an investment role as well, boosting their outcomes later in life. It's a good example of the role of government in a reconnection agenda and thus one I highlight below, along with a set of others chosen not to capture the full set of government supports, but to highlight some of the ones that are actively helping reconnect growth and prosperity. They thus must be protected and, in some cases, expanded.

The Safety Net: Near-term Consumption, Long-term Investment

Rep. Paul Ryan, a conservative from Wisconsin, is a tireless crusader against safety net programs for the poor. He parrots an old President Reagan line; disparaging the "War on Poverty" begun under President Johnson in the 1960s[141] (Reagan: "poverty won the war"[142]), Ryan compares the safety net to a hammock,[143] suggesting that the "left" is "offering [poor] people a full stomach and an empty soul."[144]

The first talking point, about losing the war on poverty, is just so patently wrong on the facts that anyone who says it should have to live in poverty for a while as a penalty for such obvious malfeasance. The easiest proof is to look at the impact that Social Security benefits have on the poverty rates of the elderly. Without the program, 44 percent of the elderly in this country would be poor. But counting Social Security benefits, 9 percent are poor. If you think that's still a lot of poverty for those past their working years in a rich economy, you've got a point, but you can't call a poverty rate cut of that magnitude a failure without entering a fact-free zone.

---

[141] http://www.politico.com/story/2014/01/paul-ryan-war-on-poverty-failed-102001.html

[142] http://www.presidency.ucsb.edu/ws/?pid=36875

[143] http://money.cnn.com/2012/03/20/news/economy/house-budget-medicaid/index.htm

[144] http://www.washingtonpost.com/blogs/fact-checker/wp/2014/03/06/a-story-too-good-to-check-paul-ryan-and-the-story-of-the-brown-paper-bag/

More broadly, poverty analysts Sharon Parrot, Arloc Sherman, and Danilo Trisi show that once we factor in the full spate of anti-poverty measures, poverty since the 1960s has fallen from about 26 percent to 16 percent.[145] Not a victory, and one of the key points of Chapter 2 is that forces have developed over these years that are pushing hard in the other direction (toward higher poverty rates). But you'd have to be impervious to facts to dismiss the progress we've made.

However, I'm not interested so much in just setting the record straight re foolish things politicians say. We're here trying to build a reconnection agenda, and thus what interests me is the reconnective tissue we're beginning to learn about in many safety net programs that have been historically underappreciated. Let me explain.[146]

In economics, we distinguish between spending for consumption and investment. Buy a meal, go to a comedy show like I did the other night, that's consumption. Buy a house or a car, build a factory, buy a drill press or a computer, that's investment, i.e., spending from which the benefits unfold over extended periods of time. In this sense, the business above about a hammock and feeding the stomach as opposed to the soul is conservatives' way of saying that the safety net focuses on poor people's consumption but neglects to invest in their future. Consumption

---

[145] http://www.cbpp.org/cms/index.cfm?fa=view&id=4070

[146] I first discussed these ideas here: http://economix.blogs.nytimes.com/2014/03/10/how-aid-to-the-poor-is-also-an-investment/

gets you through today; investment sets you up for tomorrow. Consumption's for the stomach; investment is for the soul.

Putting aside the fact that many in Congress, notably Rep. Ryan himself, are themselves reluctant to invest in poor people or anyone else, once again, recent research shows this critique to be wrong on the merits: using longitudinal data that follows people over their lifecycle, a lot of what passes for consumption today works like investment tomorrow.

Start with food stamps, which really does fill the stomachs of the poor. Yet, according to a recent study by economists Hillary Hoynes et al., it does more than that. Back in the 1960s, food stamps was largely a state program. When it began to go national in the 1960s, it did so gradually, and Hoynes et al. tapped a natural experiment of sorts, comparing the outcomes of disadvantaged kids born into families with food stamp access to kids from similarly disadvantaged families who did not receive the benefits (I highlight state policies in the next chapter, with the thought that there might be some good ideas out there today, like nutritional support was way back then, that are nationally scalable). When poor pregnant mothers and their children had access to food stamp benefits, the kids were 6 percent less likely to experience stunted growth, 5 percent less likely to experience heart disease, 16 percent less likely to experience obesity, and 18 percent *more* likely to graduate high school, find work, and avoid poverty themselves once they reached adulthood (see Figure 14).[147]

FIGURE 14

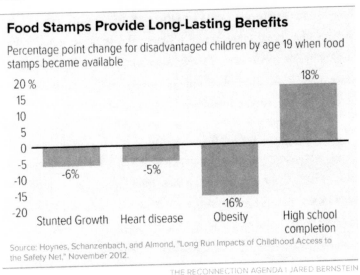

Food Stamps Provide Long-Lasting Benefits

Percentage point change for disadvantaged children by age 19 when food stamps became available

Source: Hoynes, Schanzenbach, and Almond, "Long Run Impacts of Childhood Access to the Safety Net," November 2012.

THE RECONNECTION AGENDA | JARED BERNSTEIN

The Earned Income Tax Credit, as I've already noted, provides a substantial addition to the income of low-income working families with children, and the Child Tax Credit (CTC) has also become increasingly important over time for the same reason. Together, they can add over $5,000 to the income of a single parent with two kids who earns $20,000 a year before taxes. Moreover, research similar to the analysis just noted of nutritional support finds that these programs have lasting, positive outcomes,

---

[147] http://www.nber.org/papers/w18535

suggesting that they too jump the line from consumption to investment.

For example, some research has found that mothers who receive greater benefits from the EITC are more likely to receive prenatal care and less likely to drink or smoke during pregnancy than mothers who received a smaller EITC benefit. As Marr et al. note, infants born to the moms with higher EITC benefits "had the greatest improvements in a number of birth indicators, such as fewer incidences of low weight births and premature births," factors likely to enhance future mobility prospects. The EITC has been linked to higher test scores for children in the year of a family's receipt, and the added income from both the EITC and the CTC has been tied to lasting test score increases for students. Receiving a larger EITC during childhood has also been associated with an increased likelihood of attending and graduating from college. "For children in low-income families, a $3,000 increase in family income (in 2005 dollars) between a child's prenatal year and fifth birthday is associated with an average 17 percent increase in annual earnings and an additional 135 hours of work when the children become adults, compared to similar children whose families do not receive the added income."[148]

Medicaid provides health coverage for low-income households, with an emphasis on kids (half of those with coverage in 2012, about 32 million, were under 18[149]). Research shows that it too

---

[148] http://www.cbpp.org/cms/?fa=view&id=3793
[149] http://www.cbpp.org/cms/index.cfm?fa=view&id=2223

returns investment-like paybacks. Increased years of Medicaid eligibility are associated with lower mortality, higher wages (among women), increased likelihood of college attendance, and higher contributions to public revenues.

By what avenues do each of these consumption channels become investments in the longer-term well-being of their beneficiaries? Income and nutritional support both provide vital resources at critical growth periods in the lives of poor children, and of course, such spending is fully fungible, freeing up other resources. Health analyst Matt Broadus also writes that "enrolling in Medicaid improves access to health care and reduces medically related financial hardships" and "that people more likely to be eligible for prenatal and infant care through Medicaid were healthier in young adulthood."[150]

In addition, and this is another revealing stream of new research, having more financial, nutritional, and health resources reduces what poverty analysts call "toxic stress": lasting stress that arises in response to some of the severe and persistent aspects of poverty. Such stress becomes toxic "when a child experiences strong, frequent, and/or prolonged adversity—such as physical or emotional abuse, chronic neglect, caregiver substance abuse or mental illness, exposure to violence, and/or the accumulated burdens of family economic hardship."[151] Evidence shows that this type of stress negatively affects brain development and other long-term health outcomes of children in utero, during the earliest

---

[150] http://www.ofthechartsblog.org/medicaid-eligible-children-grow-up-to-earn-more-and-pay-more-in-taxes/

[151] http://developingchild.harvard.edu/key_concepts/toxic_stress_response/

years of childhood, and into their teenage years. One study found that children born during times of high maternal stress ended up with "a year less schooling, a verbal IQ score that [was] five points lower and a 48 percent increase in the number of chronic [health] conditions" when compared to siblings who were born during less stressful times.[152] In response to these findings linking toxic stress to childhood and later-life outcomes, the American Academy of Pediatrics raised the importance of anti-poverty policies in this regard in a 2012 statement, and did so citing Frederick Douglass, who resonantly wrote: "it is easier to build strong children than to repair broken men."[153]

In other words, these parts of the safety net function more like a "trampoline" than a hammock. And food for the stomach, when provided in a timely manner to disadvantaged families, can become food for the soul as well. These programs should thus be considered card-carrying members of the reconnection agenda, elevated as such, and protected against those lobbying for their reduction or demise.

Education Policies

For many, more education is the sole response to the fundamental disconnect that motivates these scribblings. While this section is about the importance of education policy, I view the kneejerk invocation of education as a sole solution to be far too reductionist, far too "supply-side only," and thus a woefully

---

[152] https://ideas.repec.org/p/nbr/nberwo/18422.html
[153] http://pediatrics.aappublications.org/content/129/1/e224.full.pdf

incomplete diagnosis. One is reminded of a scene in the movie "Game Change" about Sarah Palin's candidacy, where she was being prepped for the vice-presidential debate. I'm paraphrasing, but her debate coach basically said, "just end every answer with: and that's why educating our children is so important!"

Economist and Nobel Laureate Paul Krugman, writing in early 2015, put it this way:

> . . . there's a new form of issue dodging packaged as seriousness on the rise. This time, the evasion involves trying to divert our national discourse about inequality into a discussion of alleged problems with education. And the reason this is an evasion is that whatever serious people may want to believe, soaring inequality isn't about education; it's about power.[154]

That's true and it's why power is at the heart of the reconnection agenda, like the bargaining power granted to average workers when the job market is at full employment. As Krugman suggests, there's political economy at work here too. It's very comfortable and non-threatening for those few on the in-the-money side of the inequality divide (and the politicians they support) to argue that it all redounds to education and skills. Pay no attention to that declining minimum wage, attack on the safety net, tilted tax policy (that's next), the persistent trade deficit, and high unemployment. Just get some skills, people!

---

[154] http://www.nytimes.com/2015/02/23/opinion/paul-krugman-knowledge-isnt-power.html?_r=0

And yet, real educational barriers persist that must be taken down if people, and I'm thinking largely of children in less advantaged families, are going to have a shot at reconnection. In fact, the high level of inequality that Krugman references and that I document in Chapter 2 interacts negatively with educational opportunity, and thus the reconnection agenda must include actions to offset its impact.

For example, note Figure 15 (also Figure A13). It shows the resources expended by low- and high-income parents on "enrichment activities," the kinds of things that dominate the lives of better-off kids today, including tutoring, sports, books, music and art lessons, and so on. Between 2005 and 2006, the wealthiest 20 percent of families spent about $8,900 per child on such investments, while the poorest 20 percent of families spent only $1,300 per student during the same year. This 7-to-1 ratio was a substantial increase over the early 1970s, when high-income parents spent about four times as much as low-income parents on such "enrichment goods." Note that as this indicator of a particularly important type of inequality has increased, public schools have shed many of these activities, shifting their locus onto families and turning vital public goods into private ones.[155]

---

[155] http://www.russellsage.org/sites/all/files/Duncan_Murnane_Chap1.pdf

FIGURE 15

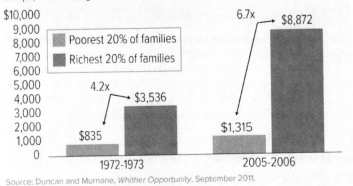

Spending on Enrichment Opportunities for Children

Average spending on books, computers, high-quality child care, summer camps, and other goods and experiences

Source: Duncan and Murnane, *Whither Opportunity*, September 2011.

THE RECONNECTION AGENDA | JARED BERNSTEIN

Relatedly, preschool is another area where inequality of incomes is bleeding into inequality of opportunity. The President's Council of Economic Advisors (CEA) recently reported:

> 60 percent of three- and four-year-olds whose mothers
> have a college degree are enrolled in preschool,
> compared to about 40 percent of children whose mothers
> did not complete high school. Although preschool
> attendance has increased for all education groups since
> the 1970s, children of less-educated mothers are still less
> likely to attend preschool, likely due to the significant
> cost burden of high-quality early childhood care. These

gaps in preschool access exacerbate differences in childhood development outlined earlier.[156]

And such expenditures of course take up a much larger share of poor families' income relative to that of the non-poor.

At the other end of the education life-cycle, college attendance and completion are both significantly more accessible to students from higher-income backgrounds: 80 percent of students born into the top 25 percent of the income scale between 1979 and 1982 went on to enroll in college, and 54 percent of these students completed college. For students in the bottom income quartile, only 29 percent enrolled in college, and only 9 percent earned their degrees within six years.[157]

Part of the problem is costs, and along with and related to the increase in income inequality, student debt burdens have gone up more among those with low and middle incomes than among wealthier households. Federal Reserve data show that in 2013, the mean debt-to-income ratio for the bottom half of households was 58 percent, a 32 percentage point increase since 1995; the same ratio for the wealthiest five percent of households was under 10 percent in 1995 and remained under 10 percent in 2013 (see Figure A12).[158]

[156] http://www.whitehouse.gov/sites/default/files/docs/the_economics_of_early_childhood_investments.pdf

[157] http://www.bostonfed.org/inequality2014/papers/smeeding.pdf

[158] http://www.federalreserve.gov/newsevents/speech/yellen20141017a.pdf

Collecting all these facts suggests that the problem is not "our children's education" in the broad, Palin-esque sense. It's access to educational opportunity for many of the same families facing all of the other economic challenges I've been talking about for many chapters now. Educational quality and access, and the privileges and upward mobility it can provide, are best seen now as another dimension of economic inequality. To be clear, that doesn't mean every middle school in every affluent community is doing a great job. That's not the case, as I know from personal experience. But as the figure on enrichment goods showed above, where schools are failing to provide, upper-income parents are picking up the slack, while parents of limited means often cannot do so.

Thus, in the interest of making things somewhat more equal at the starting gate, the reconnection agenda must include some form of universal preschool. In 2013, the progressive think tank Center for American Progress suggested free preschool for children in families up to 200 percent of the poverty line (about $40,000 in 2015 for a single parent with two kids), and a sliding scale for higher income families.[159] The proposal costs about $10 billion a year to fund, and I'll speak to the price tag of these and related ideas in the next section on tax policy, as that's real money. But there is solid evidence that over the life of the child these investments cover some of their own costs by generating both more tax revenues and lower public costs. CEA describes how "[r]esearchers estimate that the skills gains demonstrated in [high-

---

[159] http://thinkprogress.org/economy/2013/02/07/1555401/universal-pre-k-plan/

quality preschool programs] will lead to income gains of 1.3 to 3.5 percent each year when children are adults . . . In the long run, these earnings gains translate into an increase in GDP of 0.16 to 0.44 percent."[160]

I've said little so far about K-12, in part because I'm writing about federal policy here and even with federal initiatives like "No Child Left Behind" and "Common Core" learning standards, public K-12 is still largely under the purview of state and local governments. Still, and especially given the role of property taxes in funding local schools, income disparities of course play out here as well (getting away from funding schools through local property taxes can also improve funding equity *between* schools and has been shown to improve student outcomes[161]). Ben Spielberg and I recently reviewed channels by which more equitable funding might boost student achievement, including but not limited to reduced class sizes,[162] extended learning time, better

---

160

http://www.whitehouse.gov/sites/default/files/docs/the_economics_of_early_childhoo
d_investments.pdf

[161] Baker notes, however, that whether or not states use additional money to allocate funding more equitably varies state by state:
http://epaa.asu.edu/ojs/article/view/1721/1357. And even states that have made attempts to begin to target funds based on need, like California, will remain far from funding equity until they more completely overhaul their school finance systems (for a discussion of funding inequity in California, see:
http://34justice.com/2014/06/11/informed-student-advocates-pursue-reforms-that-unlike-vergara-v-california-actually-address-inequity/).

[162] While researchers still disagree about whether they are the most cost-effective strategy for promoting student achievement (see
http://www.brookings.edu/research/papers/2011/05/11-class-size-whitehurst-chingos),

facilities (public infrastructure!), more competitive teacher pay that facilitates recruitment and retention, greater investments in extracurricular activities, and expanded instructional coaching opportunities.[163]

A deep dive into the question of public education reform—charter schools, teacher evaluations based on standardized tests, going after tenure—is beyond my scope here. As any parent will tell you, the idea that you must send your kid to a school you believe to be seriously underperforming (especially when you don't have the resources for a private education) is reasonably and extremely unwelcomed. But Spielberg and I examined these debates and found, for example, that, on average, charters have minimal advantage over traditional public schools, though there's important variance around that average.[164] It's also quite difficult to interpret these findings, as even the best charter school studies typically don't distinguish school effects from the effects of student demographics, which include the likely benefit to students of attending small schools with a concentrated group of higher performing peers. Many educators have also raised concerns about potential negative developments at some charter schools, like an overemphasis on tested subjects to the exclusion of other

---

most believe that smaller class sizes have positive effects (see
http://nepc.colorado.edu/publication/does-class-size-matter, for example).

[163] "Outcomes and Opportunity: How inequality and income stagnation are limiting opportunity in America," forthcoming, Peterson Foundation.

[164] http://www.brookings.edu/research/papers/2013/07/03-charter-schools-loveless

types of learning experiences to which higher-income children have access (like physical education and art classes).

There are, however, two important points from this research for education policy in a reconnection agenda. First, better performance in selected charters may be driven in part by better funding. Second, to the extent that student test score results at high performing charters reflect best practices such as extended learning time or enhanced instructional training and support (enabled by higher levels of per pupil spending), the appropriate lesson, as per research by economist Roland Fryer, is to apply these practices in traditional public schools while providing increased financial support.[165] Viewed in this light, charter schools may be seen as the research and development arm of the traditional public school system.

There's another reform which I mention here because it combines various threads of the reconnection agenda. As noted back in Chapter 6, state policy analysts Mike Mitchell and Mike Leachman point out that if "states were still spending on corrections what they spent in the mid-1980s, adjusted for inflation, they would have about $28 billion more each year that they could choose to spend on more productive investments or a mix of investments and tax reductions."[166] I'm not saying all of that could be usefully channeled into education spending. As

---

[165]

http://scholar.harvard.edu/files/fryer/files/2014_injecting_charter_school_best_practices_into_traditional_public_schools.pdf

[166] http://www.cbpp.org/cms/index.cfm?fa=view&id=4220

alluded to above, what I think of as "education reform" goes far beyond schools, into neighborhoods, environments, paychecks, and more. But since getting to full employment requires thinking more creatively about how to help the tens of millions with criminal records get back into the job market and local schools serving low-income kids need more resources, you'd have to be not paying attention not to see an interesting opportunity here.

Turning to higher ed, we've finally discovered that it's not enough to help less advantaged kids get into college—we must focus on completion as well. This is particularly important given the challenges faced by kids who make it to a four-year or a community college without the requisite training to do college-level work. In fact, well under half of community college students complete either two- or four-year programs within six years (and recall the low college completion rate for low-income students cited earlier). Under the Obama administration Pell Grants have gone up considerably, but they still cover a historically low share of college costs.[167] President Obama has proposed to make community college free, which will help some kids, but the fact is that it's not tuition that's the problem at community colleges, which are already close to free for lower-income students when you factor in available aid.

The heart of the problem comes back to the disconnect between growth, jobs, and pay. For those with the drive and capacity, community colleges absolutely should be a gateway to four-year

---

[167] http://www.ticas.org/files/pub/TICAS_RADD_White_Paper.pdf

degrees, and with proper tuition-based support and either solid pre-college course work or quality remedial help, there's no reason why more kids of lesser means shouldn't be able to follow that path. Those remarkably low completion rates just noted are the offspring of a wide variety of problems, many of which exist outside of school. But we're basically sending young people (and I'm talking about the ones with the kinds of aspirations we want to encourage) a set of conflicting messages. On the one hand, it's all "Go to college! That's the way to realize your intellectual and economic potential!" On the other, many of these kids are growing up in families and neighborhoods that persistently suffer from the economic disconnect and the toxic stressors that engenders.

A robust reconnection agenda which promotes not just access to higher ed but also completion is required if we want to put some actual opportunity behind those messages.

Tax Policies

People write books about tax policies, so it's particularly important to corral this one within the reconnection agenda. Plus, I've already talked about a couple of pro-work tax credits—the EITC and CTC—so some of this ground has been covered.[168] I've

---

[168] There is, however, an interesting and important caveat re these credits. While they're very effective in raising incomes and lowering the poverty of working families, they do induce greater labor supply and thus put some downward pressure on wages. Economist Jesse Rothstein finds that about a quarter of the EITC "leaks out" that way as a subsidy to low-wage employers who would have to pay a higher market wage absent the credits. http://www.nber.org/papers/w14966.pdf

also raised many ideas that require revenues, in some cases new revenues, including safety net and education measures (this chapter) and fiscal policies like infrastructure investment (Chapter 3). Even countercyclical deficit spending needs to be paid for at some point down the road once the economy is back firing on all cylinders. All of which suggests that what we need from a discussion of tax policy and the reconnection agenda is a clear and compelling rationale for raising the revenues to support the agenda.

But don't we need to talk about all the loopholes and distortions in the tax code? Mustn't we fight for "comprehensive tax reform," three words that have come to be viewed as some sort of Holy Grail in DC policy circles?

To which I say: meh.

There are definitely big, wasteful loopholes and the taxation of certain types of income (particularly foreign earnings held abroad by multinational corporations and various forms of non-labor income) creates distorted behavioral incentives to shield income from taxation. Fixing these problems is of course smart public policy and a non-trivial part of my day job.[169] But the bigger issue is simply the amount of revenue we raise, which will almost surely prove to be inadequate to meet our needs in the public sector in years to come. Moreover, politicians from both sides of the aisle do not want to go near this reality. These days, a

---

[169] More accurately, it's promulgating the work of CBPP's tax team, Chuck Marr and Chye-Ching Huang.

progressive tax reform is one that's revenue neutral. Proposing something that would expand the pie is verboten and has been for years.

Often you'll hear unenlightened policy makers argue that we can freeze spending at some dollar level. Given the growth in the economy, inflation, and population, surely no one in their right mind would accept a dollar freeze. Except that's exactly what we've done in recent years, at least on the discretionary side of the budget (the 30 percent of the budget for which new spending levels must be legislated each year, in contrast to the entitlement programs that automatically expand with need), under the very unattractive heading of "sequestration." There's no way the government sector can play its needed role in an advanced economy with even just about a third of the budget under such a freeze, something politicians of all stripes are beginning to realize as I write this in early 2015.

A slightly more enlightened, though also highly problematic, view argues that all we need to do is hold revenues at their historical average as a share of GDP (see Figure 16), about 17.5 percent (and then, to balance the budget, hold spending at that level as well). But why should the historical average be taken as a reliable benchmark? To the contrary, I've written about this problem under the heading of "The Tyranny of the Average."[170]

Sounds dramatic, I know, but I mean it. The figure shows federal revenues and outlays as a share of GDP going back a few

---

[170] http://jaredbernsteinblog.com/the-tyranny-of-the-average/

decades, with the averages in there for both sides of the ledger. A few points jump out. One, spending is almost always above revenues as a share of the economy, meaning we usually run budget deficits. This may sound jarring, given that there's more disinformation on this point than on any other in fiscal policy, but that's not a problem as long as a) the money's well spent, and b) deficits don't get too large. Defining "well spent," I admit, is both a tough one and key to my assertion here that the average is not instructive—I'll get back to it in a moment. But "too large" actually has a good definition, and importantly, it's a dynamic one.

FIGURE 16

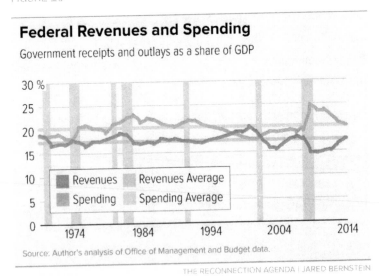

Federal Revenues and Spending

Government receipts and outlays as a share of GDP

Source: Author's analysis of Office of Management and Budget data.

As discussed back in Chapter 3, when it comes to the budget deficit, you want to be a **CDSH**: **c**yclical **d**ove, **s**tructural **h**awk. Not the most mellifluous acronym, I admit, but when the economy is humming along at full employment, you'd like growth to be spinning off revenues and workers bouncing off the safety net into the job market, so your spending on "automatic stabilizers," like Unemployment Insurance, falls. As you see in the figure that actually happened . . . once. In the full employment 1990s, the deficit flipped to surplus for a few years, driven almost exclusively by stronger economic growth (i.e., not tax increases or spending cuts).[171]

You see the inverse dynamic afoot in the Great Recession beginning in late 2007. Spending grew quickly relative to the economy and revenues fell. Both economic and policy forces were in play: GDP took a hit and spending went up sharply due to both anti-recessionary stimulus policies and the usual stabilizers. Taxes were cut significantly as well in order to boost household spending in the downturn.[172] The deficit grew to 10 percent of GDP in 2009 before falling back under 3 percent in 2014.

In fact, given current debt levels, under 3 percent is a good, working definition of "not-too-large."[173] That may sound arbitrary but it's not: deficits above that rate will tend to increase the debt burden (the burden from accumulated borrowing since the

---

[171] See Chapter 4, Baker and Bernstein, for an analysis of this point: http://www.cepr.net/index.php/publications/books/getting-back-to-full-employment-a-better-bargain-for-working-people

[172] Taxes can also decline in recessions when falling incomes put families in lower tax brackets, an interesting countercyclical feature of progressive tax systems.

[173] See Table 1 in this Ethan Pollack paper for a list of deficit/GDP ratios consistent with debt stabilization at different debt/GDP levels: http://www.epi.org/blog/debt-stabilization-does-not-require-single-number/

beginning of the nation) while deficits below that rate should decrease it. The reason is that at this level of deficit, you're generally raising enough to finance your operating costs, so you're only borrowing enough to service your debt burden, not to add to it. So, if you were to look at the debt-to-GDP ratio in 2015, for example, you'd find that it's pretty high in historical terms, lifted by the big deficits we needed to run to offset the downturn. But you'd also see that it's not growing because the deficit as a share of GDP is less than 3 percent.

So, we don't need to balance the budget to be fiscally healthy, but we do need our deficits to come down in good times, and it's okay for them to go up in bad ones. In strong, long recoveries, we'd like the deficit to be low enough to not just stabilize the debt (as a percentage of GDP) but to lower it as well, so while 3 percent is a good first target, getting below that is also important for at least two reasons. First, the larger the debt, the more our public finances are vulnerable to higher interest rates. A half-a-percentage-point rise in interest rates is a bigger headache with $10 trillion in debt as opposed to $5 trillion. Second, there's another recession out there somewhere, which means we'll need to run higher budget deficits again someday, which will add to the debt. And that's going to be a lot harder to sell with a debt burden of 75 percent of GDP than one of 40 percent of GDP.

But what's this about "well spent?" I certainly can make that judgment about my money, as can you about yours. But in this fiscal space, we're talking about a lot of different people's money, and one thing I can tell you about the "American people," as the politicians call us: we're no monolith. So how can we possibly answer the question I've set out here?

Actually, at least from 30,000 feet up, it's easy: the government should do the things the private market can't do, won't do, or at least won't do as efficiently as the public sector. Defense is an obvious function, but let's talk about policies closer to the reconnection agenda.

Social insurance: Like all advanced economies, we've decided to provide some degree of guaranteed pension and health care to the elderly (in our case, Social Security and Medicare), as well as health care to the poor and near poor (through Medicaid and the Children's Health Insurance Program, or CHIP). Once we make those decisions, the most efficient way to proceed is to pool risks, including solvency risk, across large and diverse populations, and finance the insurance programs through the tax system. There are no private firms who would do so on a nonprofit basis wherein everyone who's eligible must be covered, thus putting social insurance solidly in the "well-spent" category. In some countries, of course, not just the financing but the provision of health care is through the public sector, as with the UK's Health Service. But that's not how we roll—providers for those with public coverage are generally private (the health system for veterans is an exception). So our social insurance programs, at least on the health side, are really a public/private hybrid, which is worth remembering the next time people go off about how everything would be fine if we just "got the government out of the economy." More often than not, they don't mean social insurance, which means they're just blowing smoke. And if they do mean social insurance, then they *really* don't know what they're talking about.

Other safety net programs: As discussed above, other safety net programs are also a critical part of the reconnection agenda, but the only "firm" with the scope to set up and finance them is the federal government. How could a private firm set up and pay for nutritional support for low-income families, for example? Or Unemployment Insurance? What would motivate a large enough group of employers to set aside an insurance fund for UI benefits in the absence of government? It won't happen, which is why you see governments providing safety nets (which are in many cases significantly more robust than ours) in the economies of countries across the globe.

Environment: Since the environment is . . . um . . . kinda everywhere, private firms cannot be in charge of its maintenance. There's no pricing mechanism that would enable MyPvt Corp. to raise the necessary funds to fight climate change, for example. This is an old economics problem that derives from the "non-exclusivity" of certain public goods—if I eat that M&M, you can't. But air's not like that, so it's a classic public good.

Education: If this were not provided by the public sector, some people would surely buy it themselves, so why is it on the list? Because while some people might pay to educate their kids, others would not do so, and society writ large would be the worse for it. Absent public provision, the consumption of education services would be both sub-optimally low and too dependent on family income.

Infrastructure: Like education, it's not hard to imagine that gated communities could get together and pay for the roads behind their gates. But presumably at some point they'd want and need to venture out beyond those gates. There's been some talk of privatizing roads, but the public generally reacts negatively to the idea, perhaps because people with less means imagine themselves staring at a map, trying to plan a trip based on which roads they can afford to access. Also, private firms would be unlikely to pay for roads to rural or obscure destinations. Other types of infrastructure, like water systems or the electrical grid, are typically treated as public utilities, subsidized, and regulated by the public sector so everyone will have access to them.

Who knows what's coming?! Back when I worked for President Obama, shortly after he'd been elected, I asked him what surprised him most about the job so far. We had been dealing with a wrenching recession, credit market failure, and millions of home foreclosures; there were the usual rumblings in the Middle East and the disease SARS was posing a potential threat. But the President said none of that surprised him. What did? "Pirates!" he said. "That . . . I wasn't expecting."

My point is that when you're trying to figure out precisely where government should devote its resources, you need a residual, "who knows?" category.

I mentioned the words "public goods" above, and everything I listed belongs in that category. By definition, these things will not be privately provided, and we need an amply-funded public sector to meet the challenges they pose. Moreover, the less we provide these goods and services—if we ignore these functions—due to dysfunctional government or anti-government ideology, the worse off our economy and the people in it will end up—again, pretty much by definition. That is, the nature of public goods is such that if we skimp on social insurance, the maintenance of our bridges and public schools, and nutritional support for families facing hard times, no one's going to step up and make up the difference. We'll just have less retirement security, broken bridges, under-nourished kids (the impact of which we now know reverberates for years), decrepit, depressing school buildings sending kids an awfully negative message (the fact that this particular blight exists given all the claptrap about how much we care about education is a deep source of American hypocrisy, I'm sad to say, and one that just really gets to me[174]), and so on.

We're Likely to Need More, Not Less, Government in the Future

OK, that was all pretty much the windup. Here's the pitch. For a number of reasons, we're likely to need more, not less,

---

[174] Which is why I worked with some colleagues to craft the FAST! program (Fix America's Schools Today!), which actually was introduced in both houses of Congress . . . to no avail. https://www.govtrack.us/congress/bills/112/s1597

government going forward. Economist Larry Summers has made this case most forcefully.[175]

First, and this is the easiest part of the case to make: demographics. While accurately forecasting economic growth or productivity is somewhere between hard and impossible, we're actually good at forecasting the future demographics of the country because we roughly know how to extrapolate from the present. The aging baby boomers are the major factor here and because of them (/us), the share of elderly Americans is expected to rise from about 15 percent to about 20 percent over the next 20 years.[176] According to Summers, about a third of the federal budget is spent on those above age 65 already, and as their share of the population continues to grow, we will be forced to either devote more revenue to social insurance or do less for the elderly.

In fact, measured as a share of the economy, budget experts expect that only three components of the federal budget will rise over the next decade: Social Security, health programs, and interest on the debt. Our aging demographics are a big reason for the first two items on that list, which budgeteers tell us will

---

[175] http://www.washingtonpost.com/opinions/lawrence-summers-the-reality-of-trying-to-shrink-government/2012/08/19/0e786b40-ea00-11e1-a80b-9f898562d010_story.html

[176] http://www.ssa.gov/oact/tr/2014/V_A_demo.html#271410

require another 2 percentage points of GDP over the next decade.[177]

The next reason we'll likely need to devote resources to the public sector in the future is more nuanced: it's that the prices of much of what government buys are rising faster than the prices of what the private sector buys. Summers writes:

> Since the early 1980s the price of hospital care and higher education has risen fivefold relative to the price of cars and clothing, and more than a hundredfold relative to the price of televisions. Similarly, the complexity, and hence the cost, of everything from scientific research to regulating banks rises faster than overall inflation. These shifts reflect long-running trends in globalization and technology. If government is to continue providing the same level of these services, government spending as a share of the economy has to rise . . .

Economist Paul Van de Water has also looked into the future in this regard and, along with the demographic/health care and education points, he's noted the relatively new costs of homeland security, along with those of health care and income support of veterans engendered by recent wars in the Middle East.[178]

---

[177] See figure 4 here:
http://www.cbo.gov/sites/default/files/cbofiles/attachments/49973-UpdatedBudgetProjections.pdf
[178] http://www.cbpp.org/cms/index.cfm?fa=view&id=3385

Still, like they say: predictions are hard, especially about the future. There are some possible pressure valves that could perhaps bring down these projections. Interest rates keep coming in lower than expected, so it's possible that servicing the debt will be less costly than we think, but we can't count on that.[179] The most promising pressure valve is health care spending, which, as I document in the last chapter, has been increasing considerably less quickly than expected. However, these reductions have been factored into the predictions of the Congressional Budget Office and they still have health care spending rising as a share of GDP, as noted above. Of course, we could do less in these areas, and it is often suggested that the best way to deal with these future costs is to just bite the bullet and cut them.

That's a *dis*connection strategy, especially given the extent to which retirees depend on social insurance. Recall the statistic I cited earlier: Social Security benefits reduce elderly poverty rates from 44 percent to 9 percent, which tells you that a lot of people depend on them. In fact, for about two-thirds of the elderly, Social Security is their major income source; for 36 percent, old-age benefits account for at least 90 percent of their income. These shares are even larger for minorities and for women. This tells you two things re our discussion. First, the program is an economic lifeline, and second, while there's arguably room to cut

---

[179] Here's evidence that we keep overestimating future interest rates: http://www.nytimes.com/2015/02/24/upshot/we-keep-flunking-forecasts-on-interest-rates-distorting-the-budget-outlook.html

benefits for wealthy people, that's not where most of the money goes.

Cutting to the chase, we'll have to raise more revenue. How much more I cannot say given uncertainty regarding the future path of the variables noted above, especially health care costs, but at least while aging boomers are in the picture, infrastructure and climate change demand our attention, and inequality and poverty require safety net investments, most analysts (with my sensibilities) figure we're looking at shares of GDP well above the 18 percent average, and probably in the low- to mid-20s.

The key from a reconnection perspective is to raise those revenues progressively, though that doesn't mean taxing the very wealthy exclusively. We face a unique problem in this regard, as policy makers on both sides of the aisle have pretty much agreed that you can't raise taxes on the "middle class," and pretty much everybody thinks they're middle class.

Recall that during his second campaign, part of President Obama's platform was not to raise taxes on families earning below $250,000.[180] After he won, in the hurly-burly of one of those truly unfortunate "fiscal cliff" debates, that threshold rose to $450,000. And let me tell you, it was not only Republicans who were pushing for this higher threshold. Now consider this: only about 3 percent of households have incomes above $250,000, and

---

[180] I introduced some of this material here:
http://www.nytimes.com/roomfordebate/2015/02/04/can-tax-policy-distinguish-the-rich-from-the-middle-class/we-need-a-truly-progressive-tax-rate

less than 1 percent have more than $450,000. It's not realistic to believe we can ultimately meet our revenue needs solely on the top few percent.

That said, I of course haven't forgotten the data in Chapter 2 showing how so much of the growth in income and wealth in recent decades has accrued to those at the very top. Ideas like the one President Obama's floated in his 2016 budget—to tax capital gains on currently untaxed large inheritances—acknowledge this trend and raise serious revenues to boot ("step-up basis," as it's called, along with a proposal to raise the capital gains rate to Reagan-era levels, would raise $232 billion over the next decade[181]). And we can raise twice that much by simply lowering the rate at which wealthy taxpayers can use deductions and exemptions to write off part of their tax burden, from about 40 percent to 28 percent.

Another worthy idea, one that helps both on the revenue side and in terms of tamping down noisy, unproductive, high frequency trading, is a small financial transactions tax. Just three "basis points"—three one-hundredths of a percentage point, the equivalent of thirty cents on a $1,000 trade—is estimated to raise $350 billion in revenue over 10 years.[182] Critics worry that securities traders would just take their business elsewhere to avoid the tax, but the highly active London stock exchange has long had a small FTT, and Germany and others in Europe have been thinking about making the move for a while. Though I suspect

---

[181] https://www.jct.gov/publications.html?func=startdown&id=4739

[182] http://jaredbernsteinblog.com/you-down-with-fit-yeah-you-know-me/

that the magnitude of the tax is small enough and US trading platforms are so well-established that we could act alone without much risk, it would be better if the advanced economies held hands and jumped together on an FTT.

Most economists believe a transaction tax would lower the volume of trade in proportion to its size—wouldn't less trading diminish the dynamism and liquidity of our financial markets? Actually, especially with the algorithm-driven high frequency stuff, a small FTT would be more likely to reduce volatility, improve capital's patience (leave investments in place for a bit longer) and productive allocation, and maybe even reduce the inflated size of the financial sector, all while raising significant revenues. As the same Grandma said about direct job creation a few pages back—though admittedly, in this case she wasn't thinking about brokers' fees—"what's not to like?"

All those tax ideas tend to target individuals higher up the income scale, but while tax rates are and should stay lower on middle-class households—that's what we mean by progressivity—there should be no implicit "middle-class exemption" against ever facing higher tax rates, especially for households well above the median income (around $53,000 in 2013).

A final important tax system point is that we leave a tremendous amount of revenue uncollected every year, close to $400 billion—over 2 percent of GDP—according to some estimates. It's called the tax gap, and it's the difference between taxes owed and taxes paid. According to estimates by the Treasury Department, for each additional dollar we spend enforcing the tax code, we collect $6 of unpaid, yet owed, taxes. So . . . um . . . why don't we just collect the money, right?

In fact, the anti-tax crowd has been systematically whacking the IRS budget in order to preserve the tax gap and thus maintain and expand a big tax cut, albeit an illegal one.[183] In this regard, raising the budget for the IRS, a cause that tax and budget analysts Chuck Marr and Joel Friedman have consistently embraced, is an essential component of the reconnection agenda.[184]

Labor Standards

Throughout this text, I've stressed the importance of both job quantity and quality. They're related, of course, as the bargaining power that full employment (adequate job quantity) provides to working people enables them to push for higher pay (one dimension of better job quality). But there's a whole other source of job-quality-boosters by way of labor standards that have been established through the Fair Labor Standards Act from way back in the 1930s (sometimes enhanced and other times eroded thereafter), when it set the minimum wage at $0.25![185]

So for the final reconnection role for government in this chapter, I'll point out some of the key labor standards that need monitoring and updating. But before this very brief tour, let me quote some

---

[183] http://www.washingtonpost.com/posteverything/wp/2014/07/01/why-the-gop-really-wants-to-defund-irs/

[184] http://www.cbpp.org/cms/index.cfm?fa=view&id=4156

[185] About $4.15 in 2015 dollars.

relevant words from policy analyst and long-time labor lawyer/advocate Ross Eisenbrey, as he has long pressed policy makers to keep these standards up to date:

> Without institutionalizing rules that protect workers and mandate basic job quality, firms will be free, as they mostly are now, to cut their costs by lowering wages, denying overtime pay, skirting wage and hour laws, and using undocumented workers, part-timers, unpaid interns, and so-called independent contractors to avoid the regulations designed to protect the labor force. Working families cannot afford to wait for full employment to begin improving job quality and compensation, and, absent better policy, even full employment has been inadequate in the past to assure strong and broad wage gains.[186]

The caveat regarding full employment is important. Chapter 6 makes this point as well, recognizing that significant swaths of workers won't be reached or uplifted even by low unemployment rates. In this regard, full employment and labor standards are the belt and suspenders we need to keep our economic pants up (OK . . . sorry . . . a little late in the game to introduce new analogies . . . let's stick with the reconnection toolbox; plus, an empty toolbox, while not a pleasant image, is better than the image of our economic pants falling down).

---

[186] http://www.pathtofullemployment.org/wp-content/uploads/2014/04/eisenbrey.pdf

Overtime Pay: One of the most enduring labor standards is time-and-a-half pay for work beyond 40 hours per week. Of course, time-and-a-half applies to hourly wages; if your base wage is $14, the FLSA says you must be paid $21 when working OT. Clearly, this dis-incentivizes exploitative hours of work, helps to balance family life, and incents employers to create another job when OT looks too expensive.

But there is an important and little known wrinkle in the law that applies to salaried workers. Obviously, the law needed a mechanism to protect hourly workers from being designated as salaried just to avoid paying OT. Suppose someone working 40 hours a week at the current federal minimum wage (another FLSA labor standard, though one I turn to in the next chapter) of $7.25 could be paid a weekly salary of $290 ($7.25 * 40). Since they're no longer an hourly worker, wouldn't they be ineligible for time-and-a-half if they worked OT?

No, because the law includes a salary threshold below which you must be paid overtime even if your employer labels you a salaried as opposed to an hourly worker. The problem, and get ready because here comes a strong reconnection idea, is that the threshold is not adjusted for inflation, so even while it's occasionally been raised, it now covers too few salaried workers. That is, there are workers who are not paid hourly and who, based on their low pay, should be covered by overtime but are not because the salary threshold is too low.

To their credit, the Obama administration recognized this need to raise the salary threshold and, as I write in April 2015, is still considering where to put it (these folks measure 10 times, cut once). Based on an exhaustive review of all kinds of stuff with which I won't bore you, Eisenbrey and I argued that threshold, now $455 per week—still less than the poverty line for a family of four for a full-year worker—should go up to about $970, which is the 1975 threshold adjusted for inflation (our paper—see the footnote—explains why we think 1975 makes sense, including evidence that it covers the types of non-supervisory workers consistent with the spirit of the law).[187] Eisenbrey reports that this threshold would newly cover about *six million salaried workers*, which is why I view this as a critical reconnection tool.[188]

And I left out the best part! Since it's an administrative rule change, not a legislative matter, it won't be killed by our dysfunctional Congress. I challenge anyone to find a rule change or executive order (i.e., actions that do not require Congress) with the potential to lift the earnings of more lower- and middle-wage workers.

"Wage and Hour" Rules: You've probably heard of food safety inspectors, but I'll bet you've never heard of a "wage and hour inspector." Well, our labor department employs about 1,000 of 'em, to monitor and prevent legal violations that prevent workers getting paid what they're owed. These include "wage theft" (not

---

[187] http://www.epi.org/publication/inflation-adjusted-salary-test-bring-needed/
[188] http://www.epi.org/publication/where-should-the-overtime-salary-threshold-be-set-a-comparison-of-four-proposals-to-increase-overtime-coverage/

paying workers what they are contractually owed), misclassification (classifying regular employees as self-employed, thus making them ineligible for minimum wages, overtime, and other established protections), and nonpayment of overtime, all of which have led to significant wage losses for many lower-paid workers. Moreover, as far as we can tell, the decline in unionized workplaces and the diminished clout of workers in general, and lower-wage workers in particular, has led to increased incidence of these problems.[189]

At the same time, we've got many fewer wage and hour inspectors per worker. As Eisenbrey points out:

> When Congress enacted the FLSA in 1938, it funded one Wage and Hour Division (WHD) investigator for every 11,000 workers. By 2007, when there were only 731 WHD investigators for the entire nation, the ratio had fallen to 1 inspector for every 164,000 covered employees. Even today, with around 1,000 WHD investigators, the odds of any particular employer being inspected in any given year are trivial.

Yes, today's inspectors have computers and are of course more productive than those of yesteryear. But this kind of investigating often calls for "boots on the ground," so part of the reconnection agenda here is for more wage and hour inspectors.

---

[189] http://www.nytimes.com/2014/09/01/business/more-workers-are-claiming-wage-theft.html?_r=0

Level the Playing Field for Union Organizing: In a book where diminished worker bargaining power takes central stage, it's no surprise that enabling those who want to bargain collectively is an obvious goal. It is often suggested that unions, especially in the private sector, are shrinking as a share of the workforce because heavy industries where they had a larger footprint are shrinking. That's partially true, although I'd quickly point to the material in Chapter 5 on how global competition is tilted against our manufacturers as one reason that footprint has shrunk. But it's not just industrial composition in play here. Speaking of tilted playing fields, there's extensive evidence of both legal and structural changes that have undermined the ability of workers to engage in collective bargaining and driven the decline in unionization.

Employer practices and court rulings have blocked workers from forming unions. Eisenbrey cites examples where "courts have given employers the right to deliver captive-audience speeches (where employees are compelled to listen to anti-union propaganda without challenge) while denying unions access to employees." He also cites examples of cases where the National Labor Relations Act, which sets out the laws around collective bargaining arrangements and union elections, has inadequately enforced labor rights and fair elections, and administered wrist-slaps in cases of employer violations of the right to organize.

Back when I worked for the White House—when President Obama first took office—there was considerable energy to push the Employee Free Choice Act, legislation designed to address many of these shortcomings. But it never got very far due to stiff opposition on the Republican side and middling support from the Ds. That latter point is important. Simply put, one reason why unions have had such difficulty leveling the organizing playing field is that Republicans hate them more than Democrats love them. Vice President Biden is a notable exception, by the way. And while President Obama doesn't wake up every day trying to figure out how to get everyone in the union, I believe it's fair to describe him as truly unsatisfied with the tilt in the field (end of the day, the man is all about "the fair shake"—he feels like he got one and did pretty well with it, and it just violates his fundamental values when others don't get some of the same opportunities he got).

Part of the problem is that too many Ds are on the payrolls of some of the same anti-union firms and donors who support the union-busting, "right-to-work" industry (I discuss this crowd in the next chapter). It's also the case that unions are fighting for their survival on the ground and don't have the energy to lobby members of their behalf. In a way, though, the politics of this are pretty remarkable, in that anti-union Republicans seem to get what unions do—and are thus motivated to stop them—better than the Democrats who allegedly support unions. And what the unions do—even in their compromised condition today—is form by far the largest national institutional force dedicated to improving the bargaining power and living standards of working families. Anti-unionists understand that threat a lot better than many weak-kneed supposedly pro-union politicians.

Reversing the tilt requires policy interventions that allow crackdowns as opposed to the aforementioned wrist slaps on employers who illegally block organizing drives, allowing unions to organize subcontracted workers, significantly reducing waiting periods between union drives and elections, and providing union advocates the same access to potential members that employers currently enjoy.

Conclusion

As you see, unsurprisingly, the reconnection agenda has a central role for the federal government. That role involves the provision of public goods that help connect people to growth in ways that private sector firms would never adequately accommodate. I've cited social insurance, other safety net programs, infrastructure, climate change, labor standards, and more, and argued that, given our demographics alone, we're going to need to progressively raise more revenues.

If that sounds like a reach politically, I hear you. If it doesn't sound like a political reach, you must be living somewhere that doesn't get news from America. But I've got two answers for you on this point. First, as the next chapter explains, there's a fair bit of reconnection policy going on at the subnational level. Second, as the final chapter argues, there is a deep and untapped demand for a true reconnection agenda at the national level. And there's a big presidential campaign waiting in the wings. In that chapter, I dive into the political changes it will take to move these ideas toward fruition.

Chapter 9

The States of Things to Come—the Reconnection Agenda at the Subnational Level

As I stressed in the introduction, there is strong demand across the land for an agenda to reunite growth and prosperity, and I believe this latent demand can be tapped in the interest of a new, functional politics that supports and implements such an agenda.

As I also stressed, I could be wrong. It could be the case that the depth of political dysfunction is such that purposeful action at the federal level will simply remain impossible for years to come.

True, that's not exactly uplifting, but we are a nation of states and cities and communities, and while national politicians can spend years casting "symbolic" votes that do nothing other than signal to some narrow constituency that they're doing their bidding, subnational politicians have to, ya' know, do stuff. They can't blame Obamacare for their failure to remove the snow from the streets, at least not if they want to be there for the next snowfall.

Of course, ideology is alive and well at every level, and so great variation exists at the state level in terms of reconnection-type policies. From my perspective, this is a good thing. Yes, I'm all about the agenda I've been touting in prior chapters, but it's a big, diverse land with less pure reds and blues and at least fifty shades of cultural and political grays. There's room for a Massachusetts, with a minimum wage above the federal level, state EITC (wage subsidy for low-wage workers keyed off of the $60 billion/year federal program), and an Obamacare-style health care plan (signed into law, ironically, by Obama's vanquished opponent in the 2012 election, Gov. Mitt Romney). But there's also room for a Wyoming, with none of the above.

There are at least two good reasons to celebrate our geographical policy diversity. First, it's a hoary old adage in my biz, but it's still true: we can learn a great deal from the policy laboratories of the states. One of the more enlightening techniques of statistical policy analysis is to try to find states or cities that are economically and demographically similar, but in which one has a higher minimum wage than the other, more generous Unemployment Insurance benefits, etc. We can then compare outcomes on key variables of interest, arguably isolating the policy impact.

I can assure you beyond a doubt that this was the way we learned what we know about the impact of the minimum wage on employment, which, as discussed below, has been an essential factor in facilitating the spread across the states of this wage policy. Comparative research across states led many academics as well as average folks who didn't have a thumb on the scale either way to figure, "well, they did it there and the sky didn't fall. Let's try it here."

Second, policy variation across states allows for "Tiebout solutions." This is the idea thought up by this economist in the mid-1950s that people will tend to move to places that have the amenities that suit their preferences. I wouldn't push it as far as he did, but I've encountered lots of people who like living in places where taxes are low and services are low to boot. There's some evidence that people sort themselves into places that fit their profiles, though like many economic theories, there's not enough consideration of the "frictions" that block people from finding and being able to locate in the "right" place for them. Plus, there are important geographical clusters (Silicon Valley in CA, the Research Triangle in NC, Dysfunction Junction in DC) where people in certain fields may need to be regardless of whether such places are Tiebout solutions for them.

In other words, for good reasons, variation exists and the purpose of this chapter is to provide a brief survey of sub-national efforts to implement state- and city-level reconnection agendas. As you'll see, some pretty compelling examples exist in the areas of minimum wages, infrastructure investment, direct job creation, state safety net extensions (like the state EITC example noted above), and even the "ban the box" initiatives (fair chance hiring for those with criminal records) introduced in Chapter 6.

But while I'm all for state variation, there are, in-my-not-at-all-humble-opinion, a few really bad ideas that states should not pursue. I present a few examples at the end of the chapter.

Lifting the Wage Floor at the State Level

Way back in the introduction, I pointed out that higher minimum wages are one part of the reconnection agenda with which most Democrats, at least, are comfortable (I'm talking politicians; among people, even (narrow) Republican majorities support a higher minimum wage[190]). And yet, given the stiff opposition by a deep and well-funded lobby supported by industries that hire low-wage workers, in recent years federal action on a higher national minimum wage has not been forthcoming. Currently, the federal minimum is stuck at $7.25, which, adjusting for inflation, is more than 20 percent below where it was at its peak in 1968.

Thus, nudged by a dedicated and pretty relentless group of activists—the vanguard of the reconnection army!—as of early 2015, 29 states and DC have minimum wages above the Federal level, ranging from $7.50 in Arkansas, Maine, and New Mexico to $9.47 in Washington state ($9.50 in DC). Several cities have raised their own minimums as well, including San Francisco ($11.05), Oakland ($12.25), Chicago ($10 effective on July 1, 2015), and Santa Fe, New Mexico ($10.66). Seattle is famously going up to a national high of $15, but with a multi-year phase-in.

---

[190] See, for example: http://www.politico.com/story/2014/01/minimum-wage-increase-poll-101950.html

A number of states and cities have, unlike the federal policy, indexed the minimums to inflation.

Opponents representing low-wage employers (versus advocates who are often supported by unions) tend not to argue their true cause—holding down labor costs and thus boosting profitability—and instead try to make the argument that the policy doesn't help low-wage workers; it hurts them by pricing them out of the labor market. Probably the most prominent opponent is a group called the "Employment Policies Institute," a thumb-on-the-scale, pseudo-research organization run by public relations magnate Rick Berman, who in turn is supported by the restaurant industry, a large employer of minimum wage workers.[191]

Just to give you the flavor of what we're dealing with here, Berman, who also fights against measures to curb climate change (the guy's a real sweetheart), is one of these DC types who, according to the *New York Times*, told a bunch of industry execs to whom he was speaking that they "must be willing to exploit emotions like fear, greed and anger and turn them against the environmental groups. And major corporations secretly financing such a campaign should not worry about offending the general public because 'you can either win ugly or lose pretty,' [Berman] said."[192] He went on to advise the execs that if they want their anti-union, anti-environment, and anti-minimum wage videos to

[191] http://www.nytimes.com/2014/02/10/us/politics/fight-over-minimum-wage-illustrates-web-of-industry-ties.html
[192] http://www.nytimes.com/2014/10/31/us/politics/pr-executives-western-energy-alliance-speech-taped.html

go viral, they should use "kids or animals." Which is, I suppose, actually pretty good advice.

At any rate, groups like Berman's argue not that minimum wage increases will hurt their clients (low-wage employers), but that they will hurt the workers they're intended to help. They have, however, at least on an empirical basis, a heavy lift, as scads of research based on these economic experiments we can now conduct between states fails to support their claims. It's not that you can't find workers who've been hurt by a minimum wage increase. It's that their numbers pale in comparison to those who have been helped.

In economics terms, this means the "disemployment elasticity" must be close to zero. That simply means that for an X percent increase in the minimum wage, far less than X percent of workers lose jobs. Instead of getting bogged down in an exhaustive review of the literature on this, I have the benefit of being able to cite two recent meta-analyses of this question. These are extensive research exercises wherein analysts aggregate the results from hundreds of studies with thousands of findings, and, using statistical techniques, summarize the key findings that surface from the lit. What struck me in these cases regarding the minimum wage was that both meta-analyses independently reached almost exactly the same conclusion:

Belman and Wolfson: "Bearing in mind that the estimates for the United States reflect a historic experience of moderate increases in the minimum wage, it appears that if negative effects on employment are present, they are too small to be statistically detectable."[193]

Stanley and Doucouliagos: ". . . with 64 studies containing approximately 1,500 estimates, we have reason to believe that if there is some adverse employment effect from minimum-wage raises, it must be of a small and policy irrelevant magnitude."[194]

The Congressional Budget Office recently applied some of these estimates of disemployment effects to guesstimates about the impact of a proposed federal minimum wage increase from the current $7.25 level up to $10.10, phased in over a few years (as is typically the case—most proposals nowadays include a phase-in period). They estimated that about 24 million workers would get a raise and half-a-million could lose a job or have their hours reduced.[195] Some analysts argued that a more careful estimate based on some of the newer vintage studies evaluated by the meta-analysts would have lowered the job loss number by half,[196] but even so, we're talking about 49 beneficiaries to one job loser. And remember, there's a lot of churn in the low-wage labor market, so anyone who's temporarily displaced by an increase in

---

[193] http://www.upjohn.org/publications/upjohn-institute-press/what-does-minimum-wage-do

[194] https://www.hendrix.edu/news/news.aspx?id=64671

[195] http://www.cbo.gov/sites/default/files/44995-MinimumWage.pdf. The CBO estimated that 16.5 million workers would see direct pay raises and another 8 million would get an indirect wage bump. The thinking behind this latter group is that since employers already pay them more than the old minimum wage, some of them will get paid more than the new minimum. These are referred to as spillover effects.

[196] http://jaredbernsteinblog.com/the-minimum-wage-increase-and-the-cbos-job-loss-estimate/

the wage floor has a decent chance of getting a better job relatively soon.

End of the day, nothing's perfect, unintended consequences occur, and the goal of reconnection-oriented policy makers is to maximize the benefits and tamp down the costs. Which brings me back to some thoughts about why this state-level minimum wage bonanza we've seen in recent years is so interesting and, I'd argue, so positive.

There's a keyword in that Belman/Wolfson summary quoted above whose significance you might have missed: "moderate." That is, they correctly note that historically, increases in the minimum wage, whether at the federal or state level, have been small enough not to shock the system, which is surely why they haven't generated the job loss effects opponents go on about.

But there is, of course, a great deal of variation in wages and prices across states; what's moderate in one place could be high or low in another place. The median wage in Idaho in 2013 was about $14.90; in Maryland, it was about $19.85. Moreover, and unsurprisingly, prices follow wages. The correlation between wages and prices across states is about 0.8 (where zero is totally uncorrelated and 1 is perfectly correlated).[197] Prices in the New York City area are about 22 percent above the national average, while those in Jackson, TN are almost 20 percent below average.

---

[197] State hourly wage data were kindly provided by the Economic Policy Institute. Price data come from the BEA's "regional price parity" program: http://www.bea.gov/newsreleases/regional/rpp/rpp_newsrelease.htm

Housing is about twice as costly in Massachusetts as in Mississippi.

That means any given federal increase will have quite disparate impacts across states. The proposed federal increase to $10.10 noted above, for example, was estimated to lift the wages of 24 percent of Alabama's workforce compared to only 14 percent of Connecticut's.[198]

In this regard, one advantage of sub-national minimum wages is that they can and do reflect these differences. In 2014, the voters of Arkansas, bless their red hearts, voted to increase their minimum wage from $7.25 to $7.50 initially, going up to $8.50 in 2017. That may not sound like much to you Northeastern city slickers, but after Mississippi, Arkansas has the lowest price level in the country. Seattle, on the other hand, a city of above-average prices, recently announced a city minimum wage of $15, though with a long phase in period (e.g., for smaller businesses, the phase-in will be complete in 2021).

One of the most prominent minimum-wage analysts in the country, economist Arin Dube, agrees that this variation makes sense and goes further, suggesting that places considering higher minimum wages might want to set them at something like half the median wage of that area. I reviewed Dube's research and wondered "why median? Why half?" As I wrote at the time:

---

[198] http://www.nytimes.com/2014/06/28/upshot/a-minimum-wage-that-makes-more-sense.html?abt=0002&abg=1

While any such choice would have an element of arbitrariness to it, in the 1960s and 1970s, when policy makers regularly attended to the national minimum wage, its average relative to the median was 48 percent. That's one reason economic inequality didn't grow much in those years. Internationally, the average minimum-to-median among countries tracked by the O.E.C.D. is also about 50 percent. 'In contrast,' Mr. Dube writes, 'the U.S. minimum wage now stands at 38 percent of the median wage, the third lowest among O.E.C.D. countries after Estonia and the Czech Republic.'[199]

But does this all mean the federal minimum wage is no longer necessary? Definitely not, for two reasons. First, while Arkansas (and Nebraska and South Dakota) voted to raise their minimums, there are about 20 states that are still tied to the federal level. Though Arkansas kind of messed up my talking point on this, I used to say that the federal minimum wage was the southern minimum wage. For a number of southern and mid-western states, that may well still be true for years to come.

Second, as I stressed in the last chapter, updated *national* labor standards are a critical component of the reconnection agenda. In this case, the well-being of low-wage workers, many of whom are now adults, full-time workers, and parents, depends on a national wage floor that adjusts to increases in prices as well as overall

---

[199] http://www.nytimes.com/2014/06/28/upshot/a-minimum-wage-that-makes-more-sense.html?abt=0002&abg=1

growth in the economy over time.[200] Therefore, regular increases in the national minimum wage floor, or an increase of some magnitude that is then indexed to inflation or to the median wage, as Dube suggests, should be seen as precisely the type of glue or duct tape or whatever's the right adhesive that we want in the reconnection toolbox (hey, so I'm not Mr. Handyman . . . everybody's got their job to do).[201]

Other Reconnectors at the State Level

Minimum wages are the most fully developed and deployed aspect of the reconnection agenda at the state level, but there are many others. In what follows, I briefly review what's out there, chosen in large part because I think these are the ones that have the best chance to make a real difference in reconnecting growth and earnings at the sub-national level and to perhaps gain some traction at the national level.

Subsidized employment: Back in Chapter 6, I wrote about the importance of subsidized employment programs as a piece of the agenda, especially when it comes to reaching those who have difficulty finding work even in robust labor markets. I also spoke fondly of an actual, real-life program in this space—TANF (Temporary Assistance for Needy Families)subsidized jobs— implemented back in the days of the Great Recession, when the

---

[200] http://www.nytimes.com/2014/06/10/upshot/minimum-wage.html

[201] As of early 2015, Senate Democrats have a new proposal to raise the minimum wage to $12.00 by 2020 and then index it to the median wage, a proposal that neatly meets the reconnection criteria set out in the text.

federal government was providing states with the resources to temporarily pay for jobs of particularly disadvantaged job seekers.

If you ask me and others who unsuccessfully pulled to have it extended, the TANF jobs program ended before its time, in late 2010. You'd think that was the end of it, because, as poverty analyst Donna Pavetti points out, it was less a DC-directed program with all kinds of rules to follow than it was "a funding stream that states could use to provide subsidized employment" and other services to help the poor "weather the downturn."[202] Once the stream dried up, no more subsidized jobs.

Except, much to my surprise (and I followed this thing pretty closely), according to Pavetti:

> . . . states have shown new interest in funding and operating their own subsidized employment programs . . . In some states, these investments are the first investments states have ever made in subsidized employment programs, while in others, they represent major expansions of smaller initiatives. Three states— Nebraska, Minnesota, and California—are creating new or expanding existing subsidized employment programs targeted to TANF recipients. Colorado, Connecticut, and Rhode Island target their programs to broader groups of unemployed individuals.

---

[202] http://www.pathtofullemployment.org/wp-content/uploads/2014/04/pavetti.pdf

TABLE 5

Recent State-Funded Subsidized Employment Programs

State	Total Funding	Target Population
California	$134.1 million proposed for fiscal year 2015, up from $39.3 million allocated for fiscal year 2014	TANF recipients
Colorado	$2.4 million for two years	Non-custodial parents, veterans, and displaced workers 50 years or older; all must have incomes below 150 percent of the federal poverty line
Connecticut	Funding for two separate programs, one at $10 million and one at $3.6 million	Unemployed in high unemployment areas or large population center, family income less than or equal to 250 percent of the federal poverty line
Minnesota	$2.2 million per year for two years (starting in July 2014)	Long-term TANF recipients
Nebraska	$1 million per year for two years (starting in July 2014)	TANF recipients
Rhode Island	$1.25 million	Unemployed adults and college students; funds also to be used to establish non-trade apprenticeship program

Source: Pavetti's analysis of state budget documents, program announcements, and press releases

Table 5 provides a list of these state programs along with their costs and target populations. A few points are worth noting about the data therein. First, the price tags are relatively small, as was that of the national program; yes, some of these states have quite small populations, but still, whenever you're talking single-digit millions (or single-digit billions at the national level, as was the case during the Recovery Act when the national program cost $1.3 billion), you've got a great chance of giving something a try (as Table 5 shows, the California price tag is the highest). The relevant policy point here, as I stressed in Chapter 6, is that these jobs are relatively cheap to create.

And yes, that's partly because they don't pay much above the minimum wage and they're temporary. But the point is to give someone who needs it a push over the barriers to entry in the job market that have often blocked them for years. The reality is that there are people at whom employers won't give a second look unless they have to, say, due to very tight labor markets, or because the worker comes with an initial subsidy. And given a chance to prove themselves, research following up the TANF subsidized jobs found that many such workers surprised their employers, who kept them on after the subsidy ended.[203] A small Nevada program of this ilk, though funded by federal dollars, recently reported that 80 percent of its participants got subsidized

[203] http://www.offthechartsblog.org/new-evidence-that-subsidized-jobs-programs-work/

jobs, and 90 percent "were kept by employers after their trial period."[204]

I'd argue this meets both criteria noted above: it's a bona-fide reconnector and it could and should be scaled up to the national level.

Sectoral training and earn-while-you-learn apprenticeships: Chapter 6 also delved into these strategies, citing the work of Holzer and Lerman, who argue that that such programs are necessary if we're to get to full employment, especially as regards underemployed youth.[205] In fact, Georgia and Wisconsin have run effective youth apprenticeship programs since the early 1990s.

Holzer and Lerman also highlight the example of South Carolina, which has expanded its apprenticeship program and seen "sizable gains in jobs and training at modest costs." A state-run program called Apprenticeship Carolina (AC) provides employers with assistance in setting up apprenticeship slots at no cost. In addition to the $1,000 annual tax credit per apprenticeship that businesses can receive, they also benefit from AC representatives who handle their information and technical needs, their paperwork, and, importantly, the integration of classroom learning at local technical colleges with their apprenticeship programs.

---

[204] http://www.theatlantic.com/business/archive/2015/02/a-better-way-to-help-the-long-term-unemployed/385298/?utm_source=SFTwitter

[205] http://www.pathtofullemployment.org/wp-content/uploads/2014/04/holzerlerman.pdf

When the program began in 2007, AC had 90 participating employers.[206] As of this writing, around 700 employers serve about 5,700 active apprentices, and about 11,500 South Carolinians have benefited from the program, a number that's likely to grow.[207] And the program looks pretty efficient: its costs are low, its staff small, and it seems to be reconnecting its youth participants to employers and to the broader economy with a pretty nice bang-for-the-buck. Holzer and Lerman argue for scaling this function up to the national level and I think they're right.

Fair Chance Hiring: This key piece of the puzzle (hiring rules that give people with criminal records a chance to get a look from employers) is thus far very much a state- and city-level phenomenon. In early 2015, 15 states and about 100 cities had rules in place that bar mostly public employers, with some inroads into private-sector employers, from asking applicants about their criminal records until later stages of the job interview. As discussed previously, such measures have been shown to both increase hiring among the tens of millions with criminal records and protect employers in sensitive occupations from personnel risks (importantly, two of our largest low-wage employers, Walmart and Target, have agreed to "ban the box").[208]

[206] http://www.pbs.org/newshour/making-sense/how-to-close-the-youth-skills/
[207] http://www.apprenticeshipcarolina.com/index.html
[208] http://www.nytimes.com/2015/02/28/opinion/remove-unfair-barriers-to-employment.html?emc=edit_th_20150228&nl=todaysheadlines&nlid=57413760&_r=1

In various writings, policy analyst (and star shooting guard from our office basketball squad) Mike Mitchell has documented that— my words, not his—state policies got us into this incarceration mess, so absent federal intervention, which isn't coming any time soon, they're going to need to get us out of it.[209] For example, Proposition 47, passed in California in the November 2014 election, makes "targeted sentencing reductions by reclassifying certain offenses from felonies to misdemeanors, for both current and future offenders" and requires "the state to calculate the savings from the reforms each year and deposit them in a dedicated fund" so that they can be earmarked for investments in "mental health services, drug treatment . . . supporting at-risk youth in schools, [and] victim services."[210]

Infrastructure: Back when touting the use of fiscal policy as part of the reconnection agenda, I pointed out that investment in public infrastructure is both an important pubic good and a job creator in weak labor markets. As economist Josh Bivens has shown, infrastructure investment can provide both a short-term payoff, by boosting aggregate demand, and a long-term payoff, by promoting productivity growth and creating jobs that pay a decent wage.[211] Such work is also "non-tradable." You can't fix a Cleveland bridge in Guangzhou, China. I did not note, however, that most infrastructure spending, north of 75 percent if we're talking

---

[209] http://www.cbpp.org/cms/index.cfm?fa=view&id=4220

[210] http://www.offthechartsblog.org/california-votes-to-shrink-prison-population-and-reinvest-savings/

[211] http://www.epi.org/publication/short-long-term-impacts-infrastructure-investments/

transportation (including mass transit) and water systems, comes from state and local governments.[212] The problem is that they're perennially strapped.

Of course, state infrastructure has always been supported by federal bucks as well, but the problem in recent years, and it's one I speak to in more depth in the next chapter, is that the part of the federal budget that's been more squeezed than any other—non-defense discretionary appropriations—is where some of these bucks typically live (most federal infrastructure grants to states are on the mandatory side of the budget, but that's not been exactly flush either, especially the seriously underfunded Highway Trust Fund[213]). So some states have been sidling up to the idea of public-private partnerships (PPPs) in order to design, support, and operate infrastructure investments.

At some level, states and cities, which, as you recall, are distinguishable from the federal government in that they actually have to get things done, are saying "we don't have a reliable partner in DC . . . does anybody else want to dance?" The challenges are numerous. First, private investors must get a return, which typically means the project must generate a revenue stream, as in a toll road or a port that collects fees. Second, as you can imagine, there are all kinds of legal issues regarding default and regulatory risk (e.g., who bears the cost of a new regulatory

---

[212] http://www.cbo.gov/sites/default/files/cbofiles/attachments/49910-Infrastructure.pdf

[213] http://www.washingtonpost.com/posteverything/wp/2014/06/25/why-did-the-white-house-pass-up-an-opportunity-to-support-a-mostly-good-bipartisan-idea/

requirement on a public asset born of a PPP?). But examples are accumulating wherein PPPs are working in both water utilities and highways.[214]

On the other hand, there's a fairly short leap between PPPs and privatization of public services, the latter of which has the potential to both undermine state and local revenues by trading a revenue stream for a lump sum, and to compromise services. There is a rigorous debate over whether privatization of formerly public services actually saves money, and summarizing (trust me): it's no slam dunk. So while PPPs and such are worthy ideas, there is no infrastructure fairy dust that somehow builds and maintains infrastructure for free. The fiscal chokehold I speak about in the next chapter is a constraint on both infrastructure at all levels of government and the reconnection agenda.

One other state-level development worth noting here has to do with "green" infrastructure investment (investments in clean energy) often motivated by "renewable portfolio standards." These are simply state-based policies "that require or encourage electricity producers within a given jurisdiction to supply a certain minimum share of their electricity from designated renewable resources . . . including wind, solar, geothermal, biomass, and some types of hydroelectricity."[215] A majority of states—29 plus DC as of April 2015—have adopted renewable standards, while

---

[214] http://www.brookings.edu/research/reports2/2014/12/17-infrastructure-public-private-partnerships-sabol-puentes

[215] http://www.eia.gov/todayinenergy/detail.cfm?id=4850

eight others have voluntary renewable energy targets.[216] The boldest standards are in California, which requires 33 percent of the state's energy resources to be renewable by 2020, and Hawaii, where state legislators have just recommended making the target 100 percent by 2040. Hawaii currently "gets just over 21 percent of its power from renewable sources."[217]

It may sound gimmicky, but I gotta tell you, time and again I've seen government work a lot better when it has a tangible target. Given the long-term nature of this type of investment, it's too early to definitively evaluate the costs and benefits of RPS, but some prominent scientists reviewed and summarized the research in May of 2014 and their findings look promising. A few studies found that the benefits looked like they handily exceed the costs in a couple of states, and a larger body of research suggests that the "incremental costs" of RPS systems ("the additional cost of renewable electricity above and beyond what would have been incurred to procure electricity in the absence of the RPS") have generally been modest, appearing to top out below "2 percent of average retail rates for the large majority of states."[218] The benefits, on the other hand, which may include "air emissions reductions, health benefits, fuel diversity, electricity price stability, energy security, and economic development," are

---

[216] http://www.ncsl.org/research/energy/renewable-portfolio-standards.aspx
[217] http://thinkprogress.org/climate/2015/03/11/3631791/hawaii-ready-for-100-percent-renewable-energy/
[218] The 2% figure is for the most recent year available; a weighted average over the 2010-2012 period returned an incremental cost estimate of only 0.9% of retail sales. http://emp.lbl.gov/sites/all/files/lbnl-6589e.pdf

typically significant. In six studies on the emissions and health benefits of state RPS policies, "[e]stimates of benefits ranged from roughly tens to hundreds of millions of dollars on an annual basis depending on the state and scenario."[219]

While these initiatives create considerable economic activity for a critically important cause—reducing carbon emissions—there are questions as to how many jobs they create. Economist Robert Pollin has dug most deeply into this question, however, and his results look to be of a promising magnitude. For example, he argues that money spent on the creation of "green jobs" create more jobs-per-buck than jobs in the oil-extraction industry.[220] Also, Fred Block points out that when states take RPS seriously, as California is doing, there is significant spillover to key innovation sectors, like renewable energy storage (Block points out that there are more than 100 CA companies working on energy storage).[221] And taking these standards seriously in terms of jobs and wages means not just creating the supply of renewable energy through the requirements of the standard, but also creating demand through seeing that both state government and households are active consumers and that equipment design and production stays in state.

---

[219] http://emp.lbl.gov/sites/all/files/lbnl-6589e.pdf

[220] http://www.peri.umass.edu/green_recovery/

[221] http://prospect.org/article/markets-states-and-green-transition

And of course this should be scaled up nationally, but don't hold your breath . . . actually, unless you're in an RPS state, do hold your breath.

Worksharing: Another reconnecting development that's begun to appear in a few states in recent years is the increased use of something called "worksharing," an alternative to traditional Unemployment Insurance (UI). In a typical downturn, if you get laid off and you've got enough of a work history to qualify, you can get UI compensation to offset some, typically about half, of your earnings for a set number of weeks (usually 26 weeks, but that's extended in downturns).

There is, however, another alternative. Companies facing disruptions to demand can tap the same UI resources to use worksharing, wherein they reduce the hours worked of their broader workforce instead of laying a few people off. Under worksharing, a firm with 100 workers that needs to cut employment by 10 percent could instead cut each employee's hours by 10 percent, and use UI funds to partially compensate those with reduced hours for their lost earnings. Basically, instead of concentrating the impact of the negative demand shock on a few people, worksharing spreads a bit around to everyone.

The upside is of course fewer layoffs, less of an increase in unemployment (though "underemployment," people working fewer hours than they'd like, goes up), along with the retention of workers the firm might not want to lose. The downside is everybody gets dinged a bit.

The unique case of the German labor market over the recent downturn provides a great example of the use of this tool.[222] Their GDP fell just as much as ours did but their employment and jobless rates fell much less (see Figure 17). The difference has a lot to do with their pretty aggressive use of worksharing, or as they mellifluously call it, "kurzarbeit." By mid-2009, 1.4 million out of about 42 million German workers were benefiting from the program.

FIGURE 17

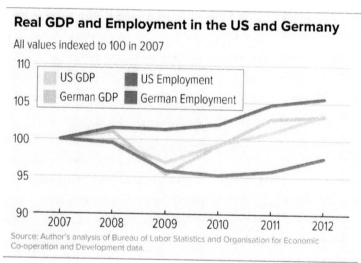

Real GDP and Employment in the US and Germany

All values indexed to 100 in 2007

Source: Author's analysis of Bureau of Labor Statistics and Organisation for Economic Co-operation and Development data.

Yet as economists Michael Strain and Kevin Hassett note, worksharing programs in the United States

> are little publicized and are under-utilized. Programs are available only in certain states (27 including the District

---

[222] http://jaredbernsteinblog.com/us-germany-and-yoyos-vs-witts/

of Columbia as of November 2013), and only 314,000 workers utilized the program during its peak in 2010— less than a quarter of the participants of Germany though the U.S. labor force is almost four times larger.[223]

Why don't more US employers use worksharing? Research by Kathrine Abraham and Susan Houseman suggest that what we have here is a classic information problem: "First and foremost is lack of information about the availability of this option in states with work-sharing programs . . . many employers are unaware that the programs even exist."[224] Following their work, however, the US Department of Labor awarded $38 million to 13 states (Arkansas, California, Connecticut, Illinois, Iowa, Massachusetts, Missouri, New Hampshire, New York, Pennsylvania, Rhode Island, Texas, and Wisconsin) for the development and/or expansion of worksharing programs, a nice example of federal/state complementarities at work.[225]

But based on the economic theory that the US ain't Germany— there's just less economic solidarity here than there—could worksharing work in America? Well, based on the equally trenchant economic theory that Rhode Island = the US, the answer would appear to be yes. For reasons that have never been entirely clear to me, RI Senator Jack Reed has always loved him some

[223] http://www.pathtofullemployment.org/wp-content/uploads/2014/04/hassett_strain.pdf
[224] http://www.brookings.edu/~/media/research/files/papers/2014/06/19_hamilton_polici es_addressing_poverty/work_sharing_abraham_houseman.pdf
[225] http://www.dol.gov/opa/media/press/eta/ETA20150155.htm

worksharing. As Strain and Hassett highlight, RI had a uniquely high rate of worksharing claims during the Great Recession, such that the state's labor department estimated that the program saved almost 10,000 jobs between 2009 and 2010, which is actually 2 percent of their employment in those years.[226]

I can boldly assert that simply making sure employers know more about the option, streamlining weekly claim-filing processes, improving websites, and integrating worksharing with state rapid-response systems should be in the reconnection toolbox.[227] To be clear, worksharing looks to be a very good way to deal with a market failure—inadequate labor demand—which, of course, is one of the main problems the reconnection agenda sets out to fix. Throughout the book, I've stressed the inadequacy of both the quantity and quality of jobs. Worksharing is a venerable policy in that it helps to distribute the burden of that problem more broadly, but it doesn't solve it.

Balancing work and family: Here's a prediction for you: a key plank in Hillary Clinton's platform in her presidential campaign will be policies that help families balance their work life with their family life. These policies include paid sick leave, maternal and paternal leave policies, worker-centered scheduling, help with child care for working parents, and tax policies that don't penalize second earners. I'm far from a political consultant, but I think

---

[226] http://www.pathtofullemployment.org/wp-content/uploads/2014/04/hassett_strain.pdf

[227] http://www.nelp.org/page/-/UI/2014/Lessons-Learned-Maximizing-Potential-Work-Sharing-in-US.pdf?nocdn=1

that's a smart plank, because it's at the intersection of good policy and good politics. It's also another useful tool for the toolbox, and here again, some states are in the forefront.

If you compare women's employment rates across countries, you see a pretty compelling and somewhat startling result. In almost every country except the US, the employment rates of women have gone up since 2000, while in the US they've fallen sharply, from about 74 percent to around 69 percent. Working age women in the UK, France, Germany, and Canada all used to have lower employment rates than us. Now they're all higher.

You may reasonably ask: why do work/family balance discussions quickly become about finding ways for women to juggle work and family more easily? It's an excellent question that speaks to both the highly unequal degree of a different kind of "worksharing" within the home, as well as the highly disproportionate share of single parents that are mothers (over 80 percent). But the fact is that in Europe, such balancing policies are much more in place and they're clearly implicated in these differential employment rates.

In 2014, the *New York Times* reported that "nearly a third of the relative decline in women's labor force participation in the United States, compared with European countries, can be explained by Europe's expansion of policies like paid parental leave, part-time work and child care and the lack of those policies in the United States . . . Had the United States had the same policies[, the] women's labor force participation rate would have been seven percentage points higher by 2010."[228] Note that the research from which that finding is drawn shows that the largest impacts would be among middle- and lower-wage women. That doesn't surprise me (or you either, I suspect) for two reasons. First, child care is just really damn expensive. Second, the flexibility of scheduling in the American workplace is basically upside-down from this perspective. Those with the least resources have the least flexibility and vice versa. A law partner or an economist with a family emergency can often leave work more freely than the guy running the fryer.

Though President Obama made a commitment to work-family balance policies in his 2014 State of the Union speech, and followed up with proposals for paid sick leave, an expanded child care tax credit, and a second earner deduction in his budget, you will not be shocked to learn that these ideas aren't going anywhere in Congress.[229] Moreover, the state action here is way behind the minimum wage and renewable standards. But three plucky—and quite blue—states have paid sick leave laws on the books: California, Massachusetts, and Connecticut (note also that the Obama plan smartly sets aside a few bucks to help states develop their own plans in this space).

---

[228] http://www.nytimes.com/2014/12/14/upshot/us-employment-women-not-working.html?abt=0002&abg=1; the finding cited comes from this study by Kahn and Blau: http://www.nber.org/papers/w18702

[229] https://medium.com/@WhiteHouse/president-obamas-state-of-the-union-address-remarks-as-prepared-for-delivery-55f98254449b2

In January 2012, Connecticut introduced a new law allowing employees at businesses with workforces of 50 or more (with the exception of manufacturing businesses and nationally chartered nonprofits) to earn up to five days of paid sick leave a year. Though businesses complain that this is effectively an increase in their labor costs (and if they weren't already offering sick leave, they've got a point since, at least initially, they bear the cost; they may well try to pass it on to workers over time through lower wages), a study of the law by the Center for Economic and Policy Research in March of 2014 noted that "most employers reported a modest effect or no effect of the law on their costs or business operations; and they typically found that the administrative burden was minimal. [Despite] strong business opposition to the law prior to its passage, a year and a half after its implementation, more than three-quarters of surveyed employers expressed support for the earned paid sick leave law."

But because of its large exemptions, the Connecticut law covers only between 12 percent and 24 percent of its workforce.[230] Not so in San Francisco, where the first citywide paid sick leave ordinance has much broader coverage. The San Francisco law grants up to nine days a year for employees at companies with 10 or more workers and five days for everyone else. As a 2011 review by the Institute for Women's Policy Research found, "most San Francisco employers reported that implementing the [ordinance] was not difficult and that it did not negatively affect their profitability." Though about one in seven employers

---

[230] http://www.cepr.net/documents/good-for-buisness-2014-02-21.pdf

reported negative effects, two-thirds of employers said they supported the law, and the study concluded that it "is functioning as intended," in no small part because of its greater benefits for low-wage and minority workers and its likely impact on public health ("Parents with paid sick days were more than 20 percent less likely to send a child with a contagious disease to school than parents who did not have paid sick days").[231]

If I'm right about Secretary Clinton, you'll soon be hearing a lot more about these ideas. If I'm wrong and these ideas don't become central issues in the 2016 presidential race, we still may see more states trying to help working parents trying to balance work and family. The reality of working parents is here to stay, but, as other advanced economies have long recognized, it's expensive and stressful to make that work while maintaining family balance. Thus, these ideas have a place in the reconnection toolbox (which is getting kinda full—we may need to bump the analogy up to a toolshed).

What Not To Do: Bad Ideas at the Sub-national Level

Above I cited the old cliché about states being the laboratory of democracy and, as such, fertile testing grounds for the reconnection agenda. But laboratories sometimes host mad scientists, and so I would be remiss to leave this chapter without some investigation into some potent disconnection agendas that have bubbled up from the states. Two strong candidates for what

---

[231] http://www.working-families.org/network/pdf/SF_Report_PaidSickDays.pdf

not to do are so-called "right-to-work" laws and Kansas-style trickle down economics.

I've stressed throughout this book that the decline in collective bargaining is one reason why productivity growth and pay have grown apart in recent decades. One reason for this is the adoption of "right-to-work" laws, now in place in half the states, with recent inroads into more heavily unionized Midwestern states like Indiana, Michigan, and Wisconsin.

Back in the Reagan years, some clever propagandists named a big-ass intercontinental missile "the peacekeeper." Well, the folks who came up with that benign name for a missile that held 10,300 kiloton warheads pale beside the geniuses who came up with "right-to-work" as the name for a law that undermines unions. In fact, RTW does not confer some new right or privilege on those in states that adopt it. To the contrary, it takes away an existing right: the ability of unions to require the beneficiaries of union contracts to pay for their negotiation and enforcement.[232]

RTW laws make it illegal for unions to negotiate contracts wherein everyone covered by those contracts has to contribute to their negotiation and enforcement. Of course, if they'd called it "right-to-freeload," to reap the benefits of union bargaining without paying for them, it wouldn't have fared as well. But that's what it does.

---

[232] Some of this material is adapted from here:
http://www.washingtonpost.com/posteverything/wp/2015/03/02/right-to-work-for-less-gov-scott-walker-wants-to-lower-worker-pay-in-wisconsin/

What it doesn't do, for good reason, is force people to join a union if they don't want to. RTW advocates argue that they're fighting against "forced unionism," but there have been no "closed shops" in America for more than 20 years. In fact, if you're a worker covered by a union contract in a non-RTW state and you object to the stuff the union spends its/your money on outside of negotiating and enforcing the contract that covers your bargaining unit (say, their political activities), you don't even have to pay full union dues. Most of what local unions do, by the way, is around the contract, so such fees amount to 80 percent to 90 percent of full dues, but when opponents claim that workers in non-RTW states "can be compelled to join a union and pay dues at a union shop whether they wish to or not" or that they "can even be forced to pay union dues for partisan political activities with which they don't agree," they're making stuff up.[233]

After cooking up such a fine misnomer, the RTW advocates went to work on the state economic numbers. It's an ancient DC lobbyist's tactic: hire some econo-chop-shop to make it look like your preferred policy unleashes reams of growth and jobs. The problem is not just that RTW doesn't have macroeconomic consequences (its impact is distributional, as I'll show in a moment), but RTW laws also do not systematically loom large when businesses make location decisions. According to location consultants, staying out of non-RTW states has never broken into

---

[233] http://www.washingtonexaminer.com/why-every-state-should-guarantee-the-right-to-work/article/2550668

the top 10 factors determining location.[234] What matters instead—and here we veer back into good state ideas—is infrastructure (see above!), quality of local education and other amenities, quality of the workforce, and access to markets.

As I write in early 2015, one could easily point out that Mississippi, a RTW state, had the highest state unemployment rate at the end of last year and the lowest job growth. You could just as easily point out that North Dakota, as a RTW state, had the lowest unemployment rate and highest job growth. In fact, that sounds uncomfortably like a DC pundits' debate.

Thankfully, journalist Brad Plumer reviewed the exhaustive research on the effect of RTW on state economies:

> There's a dizzying amount of research on the subject, but a few broad conclusions have emerged over the years: Right-to-work laws do weaken labor unions. The laws appear to tilt the balance of power so that workers reap fewer of the gains from growth. And it's still hard to find definitive evidence that right-to-work laws help (or harm) a state's overall economy. [235]

Economists Heidi Shierholz and Elise Gould do the rigorous statistical analysis to quantify Plumer's "appear to tilt" point, or, in our terms, "appear to inject a wedge between growth and

---

[234] http://www.prwatch.org/news/2015/03/12759/shooting-messenger-alec-allies-attack-academic-studies-right-work

[235] http://www.washingtonpost.com/blogs/wonkblog/wp/2012/12/10/how-right-to-work-laws-could-reshape-michigans-economy/

prosperity," which is why this RTW issue appears on these pages in the first place.[236] These two economists look at the difference in pay between RTW and non-RTW states and find that the "raw" difference, with no effort to control for the wide variety of wage determinants, is about 14 percent in favor of non-RTW states. But that makes no more sense than ignoring North Dakota's energy-extraction boom in celebrating its low unemployment rate.

When they add a full set of controls to their model, including workers' characteristics, state economic conditions, and state price differences, they still find a significant wage advantage in non-RTW states of about 3 percent, which, for full-time workers, amounts to $1,500 per year.

Look, there are no perfect institutions in America, and unions are no exception. But they exist for a critically important reason: to balance out the inherent power of employers over workers and thus to enforce a more equitable distribution of the fruits of growth. In this regard, it is not a coincidence that as unions have diminished in numbers and power, the earnings of the middle class have stagnated.

So if RTW is as bad as all this, why are we seeing even union-stronghold states adopting the law? Is it really just the corporate campaign and clever labeling?

I suspect that's the main factor driving the spread of RTW, but there's a fundamental argument RTW'ers employ that sounds

---

[236] http://s4.epi.org/files/page/-/old/briefingpapers/BriefingPaper299.pdf

pretty resonant to most people: why should anyone have to pay for something they don't want?

The answer, according to political scientist Gordon Lafer, is that unions are membership organizations that in this regard are no different from any other ones:

> There are many organizations that, like unions, require membership dues. For instance, an attorney who wants to appear in court must be a dues-paying member of the bar association. One may dislike the bar association, but must still pay dues if he or she wants to appear in court. Condominium or homeowners associations similarly require dues of their members. A homebuyer can't choose to live in a condominium development without paying the association fees. Yet the national corporate lobbies supporting RTW are not proposing a 'right to practice law' or a 'right to live where you want.' They are focused solely on restricting employees' organizations.[237]

A member of a bargaining unit that must, whether she likes it or not, pay for the costs engendered by the contract is no more "paying for something she doesn't want" than if she were paying her condo fee. You might not like the condo fee, but it's as much the cost of living there as the rent. This is really just another twist on the freeloading point made above. You don't want to be in a bargaining unit (or the legal bar, or the condo association), you

---

[237] http://www.epi.org/publication/right-to-work-is-the-wrong-answer-for-wisconsin/

must go work elsewhere. But unions can no more negotiate and enforce contracts without dues than the condo staff can mow the lawns and clean the pool without fees.

And that, of course, is the real point of RTW: to undermine unions and further diminish their bargaining clout on behalf of maintaining the disconnection. So don't go there, states.

The Kansas three-step: In 2012, the state of Kansas began a big, portentous fiscal "experiment," as Governor Sam Brownback called it, in trickle down economics. It had three basic parts:

- Big tax cuts;

- A shift from income taxes to consumption taxes;

- The ability to write off (i.e., pay no taxes on) a certain form of business income.

I've disparaged this idea for quite some time—you cut taxes, you get less revenue and not much else. But under the assumption (hard to believe, but just go with me) that Brownback doesn't follow my blog, he and the KS legislature doubled down on trickle down. As Mike Leachman explained in early 2015, here's the situation on the plains re how this is all working out:[238]

"Kansas' finances are a mess." Kansas' fiscal accounts, according to Leachman, reveal that "the tax cuts have proven even

---

[238] http://www.offthechartsblog.org/5-pieces-of-context-for-the-new-kansas-budget/

more expensive than originally imagined." They were expected to reduce revenues by around 10 percent, but that was of course before the supply-side fairy dust kicked in and made up all the losses and more by creating "tens of thousands of jobs," as Brownback predicted.[239] Back in the real world, Leachman reports that, "[t]o get through the past two years, the governor has nearly drained Kansas' operating reserves, leaving the state highly vulnerable to the next recession."

"Kansas' schools and other services have been weakened and face even more cuts. General state aid for schools per student is 15 percent below pre-recession levels. And with the state's financial picture so bleak, more cuts are likely on the way, though a court ruling that the state's school funding is so low it violates the state constitution may help."

Part of what Kansas did was to shift from taxing income to taxing consumer spending, i.e., they cut the income tax and raised the sales tax. Economists tend to like this idea because it incentivizes saving over spending.[240] But a moment's thought reveals that this assumption is far more applicable for families with enough income to save. For low-income families who must consume virtually all of their income, there's no way to escape this tax shift. Thus, step two of the Kansas three-step:

---

[239] http://www.nytimes.com/2014/06/29/upshot/kansas-tax-cut-leaves-brownback-with-less-money.html?ref=business&abt=0002&abg=1

[240] Economists also believe that relative to income taxes, consumption taxes generate fewer negative impacts on the supply of labor and capital; they argue such taxes are thus more pro-growth.

"Taxes are down for the wealthy but up for the poor. Kansas'
tax cuts didn't benefit everyone. Most of the benefits went to
high-income households. Kansas even *raised* taxes for low-
income families to offset part of the revenue loss; otherwise, the
cuts to schools and other services would likely have been even
bigger."

As a share of income, state taxes rose in KS by 1.3 percent for the
poorest families and fell 2.2 percent for the richest ones.[241] Much
of what you've read here—and seen documented in Chapter 2
(and Appendix A)—shows that we've already got enough income
inequality going on before the tax system kicks into place. Surely,
we don't need the tax system to make it worse! As economist
Alan Blinder puts it, if the income distribution was overseen by
football referees, Kansas would get a flag here for "unnecessary
roughness."

About those tens of thousands of jobs?

"The tax cuts haven't boosted Kansas' economy. Since the tax
cuts took effect two years ago, Kansas has seen private sector jobs
grow by 2.6 percent, notably slower than the 4.4 percent growth
nationally."

Step three provides a classic example of JB's rule #1 of tax
policy, especially in the tax-avoidance-prone US of A: if your tax
code favors a particular type of income, that type of income will

---

[241] http://www.washingtonpost.com/blogs/wonkblog/wp/2014/09/29/kansass-mid-
term-elections-are-a-referendum-on-supply-side-economics/

suddenly become very popular. Reporter Josh Barro (a different JB) explains how the JB rule played out in KS:

> Many small firms are structured as S-corporations, and federal law requires an S-corporation's owner/managers to pay themselves at least a 'reasonable' salary. But by converting to a limited liability company, or L.L.C., owners can set their salaries to zero and take all of their income from the company as profits, thus avoiding any Kansas tax.[242]

It gets worse. This break is supposed to help small businesses, but Barro reports that there's no size limit on small businesses in KS tax law. So big businesses can be small businesses. Welcome to trickle down world.

Much of the reconnection agenda is about ways to boost pretax earnings, strengthen the bargaining power of working people, and move the economy to full employment. In that regard, state fiscal policy may seem a bit far afield. But the problem in Kansas is somewhat akin to the inadequate financial market oversight analyzed in Chapter 7: there are things policy makers do to disconnect growth and prosperity, like the sales tax shift just discussed or RTW, that make it that much harder to reconnect.

In that spirit, while this is far from an exhaustive list of what not to do at the state level, I've picked on a couple of things that I think are germane to connections and disconnections from growth

---

[242] http://www.nytimes.com/2014/06/29/upshot/kansas-tax-cut-leaves-brownback-with-less-money.html?ref=business&abt=0002&abg=1

and prosperity. Other economically and fiscally healthful advice to states: don't overspend on incarceration (discussed in the context of fair chance hiring), and, in the words of state fiscal expert Nick Johnson, "don't lock fiscal policy into the state Constitution." This is a swipe at Taxpayer Bill of Rights, or TABOR, laws that lock in unrealistic levels of spending and revenues while requiring unpopular, supermajority votes to raise revenues (or simply banning such actions outright).[243] In the spirit of RTW, disconnection advocates in some states are trying to get ahead of us reconnectors by preemptively banning some of the very ideas noted above, including ban the box[244] and higher state minimum wages.[245] Needless to say, such actions are antithetical to the reconnection agenda.

Conclusion

The history of social policy in our nation, both progressive and regressive, shows that oftentimes ideas, both useful and damaging, bubble up from the states and cities. I'm all for the state labs, though we need to recognize that some of what they cook up will act more like a lock on the reconnection toolbox than a helpful policy tool. The goal then is to separate what works from what doesn't, scale up the former, and draw down the latter.

---

[243] http://www.cbpp.org/cms/index.cfm?fa=view&id=2521

[244] http://www.columbiatribune.com/business/street_talk/state-bill-seeks-to-outlaw-local-ban-the-box-laws/article_3b1f24bd-0e90-56be-b21a-0ec3d0764947.html

[245] http://www.huffingtonpost.com/2014/04/15/oklahoma-minimum-wage_n_5152496.html

But if you've followed some of these developments in recent years, you may know something pretty important and relevant and unsettling that happened in November 2014. It's just a microcosm and I don't want to over-interpret it, but it poses a challenge to a lot of what's in this book. Even with all that fiscal mess I just told you about going on in Kansas—and it was well known and publicized during the election, and by bipartisan sources (more than a few Republicans were unhappy with the cuts to education, for example)—Gov. Brownback was re-elected.

He won by a much narrower margin than in his first time out, and it's a deep red state. But as I stressed from the beginning of the book, my political eyes are wide open. I am, need I remind you, a denizen of DC with an office a few blocks from the Capitol, right at the corner of Dysfunction Junction. So trust me when I tell you that, like it or not, we've got to get into some politics.

Thus, in the next and final chapter, we explore the politics of the reconnection agenda and why even a hard-boiled, eyes-wide-open, econo-political operative like myself believes the agenda can come to fruition.

Chapter 10

Politics and the Reconnection Agenda

So, there you have it, the reconnection agenda, put forth in the hopes that its application, in whole or in parts, could help reconnect the economic prosperity of low- and middle-income families to that of the broader economy. Hopefully, these ideas are familiar by now: harnessing fiscal and monetary policy in the pursuit of full employment, a more level international playing field for our manufacturers, direct job creation measures to help those who even in strong economies are left behind, and financial market oversight to break the shampoo cycle.

You will note that none of these ideas are particularly radical or even outside the realm of common sense. To be fair, I say that as someone who has mucked about in the swamp of federal economic policy for 25 years, so I'm not 100 percent sure what common sense is anymore. But I'm not trying to be cute; I recognize that, particularly in these hyper-partisan times, every idea has its opponents.

That lesson was drummed into my psyche when I worked for the White House and first lady Michelle Obama was publicly touting her organic garden. She was immediately the target of stiff opposition from the fertilizer lobby.

In the same way one might have thought that nobody opposes organic gardens, no one overtly opposes full employment. Still, as noted in Chapter 4, if you depend on paychecks, you weight the unemployment/inflation tradeoff differently than if you depend on portfolios (recall: unemployment disproportionately hurts those who depend on paychecks; inflation erodes assets). No one wants financial markets to go boom every few years, but if you work for the financial lobby, you're a lot more motivated by your clients' interests than by breaking the shampoo cycle. Few will say they don't care about persistent, large trade deficits. But the inflow of cheap goods from abroad is central to the business model of some of our largest retailers.

So I'm no babe in the woods here, but that said, I purposely choose to elevate policy ideas that don't historically have either a bright red or a bright blue target on their back. True, I've mentioned the minimum wage in passing, and I pointed out that some of these ideas have some budgetary costs, though outside of public infrastructure, about which we really don't have a choice (assuming we want functioning roads and bridges and water systems, someone's got to pay for them), the budgetary costs are actually pretty minimal. The direct jobs program for which I advocated in Chapter 6, for example, could probably be scaled up for around $2 billion.

And yet, I realize you may be thinking: "great, I just dove way more deeply into economic policy than a sane person should, only to resurface into a political reality where none of this stuff could ever come to fruition."

Of course, I feel your pain, but there are numerous reasons why you shouldn't trust that "never come to fruition" part. In this final chapter of the reconnection agenda, I go through why and how a politics that is more open to these ideas not only could open up but is already poking its head up in 2015. Of course, deeply endowed whack-a-mole forces are taking shots at this nascent agenda, but here's the important thing to remember: there is a real demand for some version of these types of ideas, both among the people and their representatives.

Both Sides are Talking Reconnection . . . and Hold the Cynicism, Please.

Let me explain. As I write, politicians from both sides of the aisle are finding they cannot avoid talking about the economic problems described in Chapter 2. A look at the trends in real middle-class incomes (and particularly middle-class wages) explains why, especially amidst gains at the top of the income and wage scale. There's no better example than former Massachusetts governor and presidential candidate Mitt Romney, who briefly and publicly considered another presidential run. Recall that in his 2012 run for high office, Gov. Romney argued that income inequality reflects nothing more than "the bitter politics of envy" among the less well-off and should be discussed only in "quiet rooms."[246] Yet in his most recent incarnation, he was inveighing against the Obama White House for not doing enough to lower poverty, reduce inequality, and boost the middle class.[247] And he's not the only one, as other potential 2016 Republican presidential aspirants, including Paul Ryan, Marco Rubio, and Jeb Bush, have made similar noises.[248]

Now, one could easily go to the cynical place with all this newfound interest, as in the political cartoon on the next page, and there's of course ample room for such cynicism in today's politics.

But I wouldn't immediately go to the cynical place. First, while these concerns may come from Democratic HQ, as in the cartoon, back in Chapter 1 I argued that neither party had the policy market cornered on a viable reconnection agenda. Recall that a primary motivation for this book is my contention that the Ds' toolbox isn't exactly brimming with solutions to the fundamental disconnect. Second, I welcome anyone who wants to talk about these issues and I'd go further: if you're a politician claiming concern about middle-class economics and you're *not* talking about reconnecting growth and prosperity, I'd argue that you're missing the big picture and your constituents should look and listen elsewhere.

---

[246] http://nymag.com/daily/intelligencer/2012/01/romney-quiet-rooms.html

[247] http://www.washingtonpost.com/blogs/post-politics/wp/2015/01/16/romney-moving-toward-2016-run-outlines-vision-to-eradicate-poverty/

[248] http://www.washingtonpost.com/posteverything/wp/2015/01/20/the-president-lays-out-an-inequality-reduction-agenda-that-will-reverberate-well-beyond-tonight/

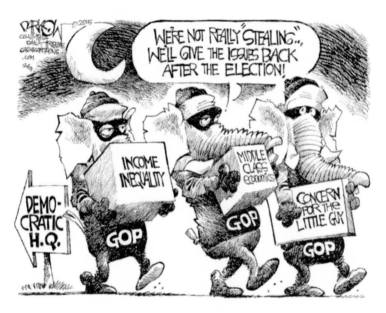

Source: Darkow, *Columbia Daily Tribune*, Feb 9.[249]

Third, there's a litmus test here, and it's a simple one. For years, I've carefully tracked the economic policy agenda of both major political parties, and the Republican agenda is easily summarized: more macroeconomic growth, boosted by lower taxes on businesses and investors, and less regulation.[250] Jeb Bush, for example, writing with co-author Kevin Marsh in 2011, outlined what they call "the economic grand strategy," or, in other words,

249

http://columbiatribune.mycapture.com/mycapture/enlarge_remote.asp?source=&remoteimageid=14320341

[250] As Dean Baker points out, the regulation point is nuanced, as conservatives often support regulation that benefits businesses, including patents and trade restrictions protecting privileged occupations, two areas of regulation that economists widely view as generating inefficiencies.

http://www.cepr.net/documents/cns_policies_2006_07.pdf

their version of the reconnection agenda. And what is this sweeping new idea? Wait for it . . . As they succinctly put it, "In a word: growth."[251]

Yes, that's an awfully underwhelming grand strategy betraying a pretty serious lack of imagination. By which I'm of course not saying anything against growth (I'm all for it, too!) but anyone who's been paying even the slightest bit of attention knows that when it comes to reconnection, while growth is necessary, it is far from sufficient.

The Limits of Growth as a Reconnection Agenda

Did I really just write that?! "Growth" is a limited strategy?! Revoke his econ-card!

This is a case where a picture's worth a thousand words, and Figure 18 (also Figure A8) shows the growing gap since the late 1970s between productivity growth and median compensation. Think about this in the context of the "grand strategy" of growth. How could "growth" possibly be a fully effective reconnection strategy when growth is increasingly eluding the majority of the workforce?[252]

---

[251] http://www.wsj.com/news/articles/SB1000142405311190400730457649811092947067

[252] Policy analyst Scott Winship has criticized this figure on the basis that it compares the pay of the 80 percent of the workforce that are non-managers to the overall productivity measure. But the point is that before the wedge of inequality took hold, the pay of these non-managerial workers closely tracked productivity. The fact that this is no longer the case is the central finding of such "wedge" graphics.

FIGURE 18

The "Wedge" Between Growth and Productivity

Cumulative Percent Change Since 1948

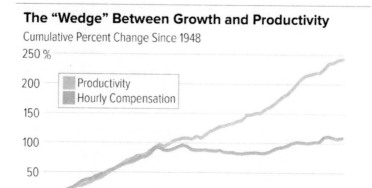

Note: Compensation is for blue-collar production workers and non-managers in services.
Source: Economic Policy Institute analysis of Bureau of Labor Statistics and Bureau of
Economic Analysis National Income and Product Accounts data.

THE RECONNECTION AGENDA | JARED BERNSTEIN

One can dismiss the "it's-all-about-growth" strategy as trickledown economics, a demonstrable failure, but let's look slightly deeper. The idea is that by lowering the tax and regulatory burden on the wealthy investor types, you'd free up investment capital that would flow into productive investments and drive the top line in the figure below up faster. But that idea ignores the heart of the problem: the diminished correlation between that productivity line and the middle-class compensation line, i.e., wage inequality.

Then there are the issues with the part of the argument on how tax cuts will spur growth. For example, there's little correlation

http://www.forbes.com/sites/scottwinship/2014/10/20/has-inequality-driven-a-wedge-between-productivity-and-compensation-growth/

between cuts in taxes on investment income and investment itself.[253] In fact, looking across countries, economists have found compelling evidence that cuts in top marginal tax rates correlate with higher levels of after-tax income inequality, a correlation I'd hazard is probably causal. But they've found no such correlation between cuts in top marginal tax rates and growth.[254]

In other words, there are two very big problems with the grand strategy of growth. The first is that not enough growth is reaching those on the wrong side of the inequality divide, and it is thus a failed candidate for a reconnection agenda. This problem is definitional: at its essence, growing inequality means that growth is less likely to reach most households. Second, even absent inequality, generating faster growth simply isn't as simple as the tricklers would like it to be. Further enriching the wealthy by loosening the regulatory ties that bind them actually does not lead to better growth outcomes.

So with that extensive throat clearing, here's the litmus test: if politicians are just tacking the words "poverty," "inequality," and "middle-class wages" onto their same old "growth agendas," then clearly they are conspiring with the thieves in the cartoon above. It's the old "if-your-only-tool-is-a-hammer-then-everything-looks-like-a-nail" problem. I totally get that "less government, lower taxes, less regulation" and all that sort of stuff may have a perfectly legitimate appeal to certain voters. What I'm saying here is that, given the newfound bipartisan concern for the fundamental

---

[253] http://www.cbpp.org/cms/index.cfm?fa=view&id=5260

[254] http://jaredbernsteinblog.com/optimal-research-on-optimal-taxation/

disconnect between growth and broadly shared prosperity, that agenda, grand strategy or not, is wholly inadequate.

The Political Challenges of the Rs . . . and the Ds

That's hopefully a useful litmus test, but other than bipartisan interest in the disconnect, what gives me hope that there's anything here that could lead to . . . um . . . ya' know . . . better actual policy outcomes?

Well, start from the fact that as you saw in the last chapter, better policy outcomes have actually been spotted in various hamlets across the land. As I stressed in that chapter, this is in no small part a function of the fact that governors and mayors have to do stuff. "They can't blame Obamacare for their failure to remove the snow from the streets," and that, as I argued, creates a whole different mindset, one that at least in part asks "what can my administration do to address the real problems people face?" And the point of the first part of this chapter is that we've actually made a real advance: at least rhetorically, both sides recognize the need for a reconnection agenda. When people named Romney and Rubio and Bush are talking about how the growing economy has left the middle class behind, even if they're just trying to bash the president, that's still actually a good start.

Now, I'm about to devolve into some political punditry, and I apologize in advance. But stay with me, because I think I can connect some dots here in a way that could be hopeful.

The conventional wisdom is that Rs face a particularly tricky path to the White House because any candidate conservative enough to gain the support of their base would be too far right to win the general election, and vice versa. The implication is that if a more moderate, Jeb-Bush-type could somehow squeak through the primary, he'd be sitting pretty for the general.

But that calculus ignores the above discussion, which I would argue was also the lesson, at least vis-à-vis economic policy, of the Obama v. Romney showdown in 2012. Sure, a Chamber-of-Commerce, business-oriented establishment Republican with a trickle down agenda will get lots of love from the business community, but in a climate of middle-class wage stagnation, they don't necessarily determine national election outcomes. Demonstrably, it doesn't work for Rs to avoid or ignore the disconnect between growth and prosperity, nor does it work to just tout macroeconomic growth. They need something more concrete that voters will recognize as part of a reconnection agenda with a chance of working. I'm not saying it's got to be everything I've been going on about in these pages, but I'm quite certain tax cuts for the rich ain't it.

Importantly, this doesn't default to the Ds either, at least not if they too are unable to convincingly articulate the policy glue that will reattach growth and middle-class well-being. Their mistake in this space, however, is not just an inadequate toolbox. It's an assumption that at the end of the day, they'll survive a general based solely on the allegiance of this new demographic invention called the "rising American electorate," or RAE: unmarried women, minorities, millennials, and immigrants—the largest and fastest-growing part of the voting public.[255]

But as the 2014 midterms revealed, the RAE don't necessarily show up. As long as overall growth fails to consistently reach them, simply pointing out that you've got their back compared to the other guy isn't much of a motivator. Their turnout may well hinge on whether they believe a candidate will try to implement a set of policies that convincingly relinks growth and their living standards. Simply touting growth is obviously inadequate. But not explaining and championing the policies that would channel growth toward those who hear about it but don't experience it won't work either.

Sorry, But People Don't Trust Government to Get Any of This Right.

Suppose policy makers did suggest a robust reconnection agenda? Why wouldn't we run right into the buzzsaw that government cannot be trusted to get anything right, from launching a website to keeping the lights on in Congress, without putting us through formerly unheard of budget adventures like "fiscal cliffs," "sequestrations," and "debt ceilings?" And these questions are not just rhetorical. The Gallup Poll's measure of how often do you "trust government in Washington to do what is right?" stands at a stark 19 percent, close to its all-time low. And let me reassure you

---

[255] http://www.democracycorps.com/National-Surveys/the-role-of-the-rising-american-electorate-in-the-2012-election/

that, given Congress's recent track record, I myself am not in the 19 percent (one wonders who is?).

So how then can I argue for a policy agenda to be implemented in no small part by the "government in Washington?" True, the politically independent Federal Reserve and sub-federal policy makers loom large in the reconnection agenda, but let's keep it real: it cannot come to fruition without a functional DC onboard.

There are two reasons why I can confidently argue for a major role for a functional federal government in a reconnection agenda, one simple, one less so.

The simple one is that there is no other institution that can do what needs to be done. By definition, private businesses will not provide public goods that are part of the agenda. Back in Chapter 8, I mentioned an infrastructure program to repair our stock of public schools called FAST! (Fix America's Schools Today!, with the "!" added to give it a kind of Broadway musical feel!). Obviously, no private firm will finance a national program to repair our public education infrastructure. Neither, of course, will private industry provide public education, or social insurance, or the fight against potential pandemics,[256] or a safety net for the poor, or countercyclical policies in recessions.

And here's the thing: though I fear the 81 percent who do not "trust the government to do what is right" recoil at this assertion, I'm sure I'm correct that we're going to need more, not less,

---

[256] http://www.nytimes.com/2015/02/21/opinion/finishing-off-ebola.html?ref=international

federal government in coming years. The intersection of our aging demographics and social insurance programs alone ensure this outcome, though I could easily add climate change and geopolitical security, not to mention inequality and poverty themselves.

And believe me, for all their rhetoric to the contrary, no politician really wants to meaningfully cut Medicare or Social Security, and for good reason (a reason that complements this theme): the federal government can more efficiently provide such insurance to retirees than can the private sector. Same with safety net measures like nutritional assistance and low-income wage supports like the Earned Income Tax Credit (which, for the record, has been beloved by conservatives since Reagan; most recently, Republican budget leader Paul Ryan argued for expanding the EITC[257]).

The Affordable Care Act enforced lower private administrative costs (more on that in a moment), but before it went into effect, such costs were estimated to be around 15-25 percent for small group coverage and well north of that for the individual market[258] (note: private—as opposed to public—administrative costs include profit margins). Administering Medicare, on the other

---

[257] See http://www.nytimes.com/2015/02/02/us/obama-budget-to-seek-to-stabilize-deficit-and-address-income-inequality.html?_r=0. Though critical of President Obama's budget in general, Rep. Ryan agreed with the President on the need to increase the earnings subsidy for low-income childless workers.

[258] From correspondence with health care expert Edwin Park, Center on Budget and Policy Priorities.

hand, costs about 2 percent of program expenditures,[259] and Medicaid, nutritional support, and the EITC all devote well over 95 percent of their expenditures to the services they provide, i.e., their administrative costs are less than 5 percent of program spending.[260] In other words, not only would the private sector not provide these services but, based on their profit margins if nothing else, they couldn't possibly provide services as cheaply.

Most recently, we observe government efficiencies (there, I said it!) at work in the sharp decline in the growth of health care spending, some of which relates to improved delivery mechanisms introduced with the Affordable Care Act, or Obamacare. There are many ways to make this case but there are two that seem particularly important. Back in 2010, before Obamacare was upon the land, the Congressional Budget Office estimated, as is its wont, the cost to the government of providing health care over the next decade. Five years later, with Obamacare firmly in the economy, the CBO's projection for health spending over the decade was $680 billion *lower*.[261]

Now, remember, Obamacare ain't free. In fact, it adds about $1 trillion to the government's 10-year tab to provide coverage for close to 30 million people, to help low- and middle-income families pay their insurance premiums, and to expand coverage through Medicaid (the law raises the needed revenue to finance its

---

[259] https://kaiserfamilyfoundation.files.wordpress.com/2013/01/7731-03.pdf;

[260] http://www.cbpp.org/cms/?fa=view&id=3655

[261] http://www.offthechartsblog.org/projected-health-spending-has-fallen-since-2010-even-with-health-reforms-coverage-expansions/

cost, and, in fact, is scored as reducing the deficit). And yet, even given those new commitments, health spending by the federal government is predicted to come in almost $700 billion below pre-ACA estimates.

The other germane point regarding these cost savings has to do with "crowd-out." I can tell you for a fact that this was a main motivator of the guy Obamacare is named after. The first time I met the man, during his brief Senate stint, he was deeply motivated to solve the problem that inefficient health care spending was crowding out our ability to invest in other priorities. The easiest way to see that crowd-out is to observe that that for years, health spending per person rose faster than GDP per person, which means health care spending grew as a share of GDP each year, from 5 percent in 1960 to 10 percent in 1982 to around 17 percent in 2010. But starting a few years ago, the real growth of per capita national health spending slowed to a yearly rate of about 1 measly percent, compared to an historical average since the 1960s of about 4.5 percent.[262] And just like the arithmetic says, once the growth of health spending comes in line with GDP growth, its share stops rising. Thus, health spending relative to GDP has been flat at about 17.5 percent for about three years running. If this trend sticks, and I think there's a decent chance that it will, it means there's a whole lot more fiscal oxygen in the

262

http://www.whitehouse.gov/sites/default/files/docs/recent_trends_in_health_care_costs_9.24.14.pdf room than we thought, and thus opens up the possibility for both a sustainable budget path and reconnection investments.

How much of the health spending slowdown has to do with government actually getting something right, i.e., the cost-savings in the ACA? Clearly not all; note that the favorable trend began before the act was implemented. But there's been extensive research on this question, and the consensus is that the health-care delivery mechanisms in Obamacare are part of what's driving trends I expect to persist.[263] These trends include incentives to reduce hospital readmissions, better use of IT, anti-fraud measures to reduce ripoffs of Medicare and Medicaid, and, probably most important, payment systems such as bundled payments ("fixed payments for a comprehensive set of hospital and/or post-acute services, including services associated with readmissions"[264]) that incent quality of care over quantity.

And please remember this: all of these positive outcomes have occurred in a climate of deeply intense political hostility, wherein one chamber of Congress has voted more than 50 times to repeal the policy. Imagine how much better the outcomes might be if everyone was pushing the wagon instead of trying to blow it up.

I know that discussion of Obamacare was a long diversion, but it is key to my theme. By dint of its size and scope, only the federal government can provide guaranteed health care to broad swaths of

---

[263] http://jaredbernsteinblog.com/are-health-costs-really-slowing-and-what-does-it-mean-if-they-are/

[264]

http://www.whitehouse.gov/sites/default/files/docs/erp2013/ERP2013_Chapter_5.pdf

the population while controlling its costs. You may well respond, "OK, but why would we want it to control costs of some goods and services and not others? Where do you draw the line?" And the answer is that in all advanced economies, including our own, health care is widely recognized as a non-market good. You don't believe me? Try this experiment: get really, really hungry and go to the supermarket and see if they'll feed you. Now, get really, really sick and go to the emergency room, where they will treat you, regardless of your insurance status. That's all you need to know to confirm that like it or not, we've taken health care "out of the market."

Of course, that doesn't answer the question of why health care and not another goods? At root, the answer is largely a moral one. I mentioned "advanced" economies above. In this context, that adjective means that in our society, we've collectively decided that we will combine our resources to help those facing a medical emergency. It is, again, definitional. It's a thing that advanced economies all do. Yes, there are some within our society who would rather not fulfill that or many other functions that define advanced economies, but they are still a minority.

And yet, that minority is having disproportionate influence on today's politics, a development that a larger political strategy must acknowledge.

The Strategy of Dysfunction

The second reason I've not given up faith in government's ability to help implement a reconnection agenda: dysfunctional government is not an accident. It is not ordained from above (or below). It is a focused and extremely effective political strategy by those who benefit tremendously from its success. Dysfunctional government is a tactic, and thus one that can be reversed.

Trust me when I tell you I've been observing and participating in DC politics from inside the petri dish long enough to recognize that something changed in and around 2010. Yes, as soon as Obama was elected, partisans were pledging to do what it would take to make him a one-termer, but that kind of politicking is not what I'm talking about. What I'm saying is more nuanced and has to do with the part of the political process you don't see: the arrival in DC of people who have a vested interest in dysfunction. I'm talking about folks whose platform was and is: *Washington is broken—send me there and I'll make sure it stays that way.*

Ask yourself who benefits from government shutdowns, threats to default on the national debt, the inability to pass adequate or lasting appropriations, pledges to lobbyists never to raise taxes, and endless, fruitless, time-wasting votes to repeal Obamacare. Clearly it is those whose incomes rise with tax cuts, deregulated industry, and eroded labor standards. Government dysfunction is thus both the natural outcome of and a complementary force to increased income inequality, concentrated wealth, and money in politics.

What's more, as emphasized in Chapter 7 on financial regulation, the dysfunctionistas embrace classical economic ideology to bolster their case. "Markets will self-regulate," so pay no attention to that bubble you see forming in [fill in decade-appropriate sector]. "Government doesn't create jobs," so ignore the 22 million existing government jobs (fed, state, and local) and the half-a-trillion from private contracts with the government each year. "Deficit spending crowds out more efficient private investment," so ignore the obviously damaging impacts from premature fiscal tightening (austerity) both here but much more so in Europe.

The reason the Gallup Poll says what is says about the level and trend in people's lack of trust in government—why I myself am with the majority—is not because government cannot function effectively. It is because the conservative strategy of breaking government so no one will believe it can do anything useful is working flawlessly.

Sounds Like Resistance is Futile, No?

Not only is resistance not futile, but as I've tried to stress in these pages, this playing of the dysfunction card is self-defeating. Its defeat may be, if not imminent, then closer than you think. Persistent government dysfunction can only work if, at the end of the day, we really do not need functioning government. But if the fundamental disconnect is as real and persistent as the research in Chapter 2 shows, then that proposition is false. And it's not just about reconnecting middle-class incomes and growth. It's also about reliable roads and bridges and airports and water systems, functioning credit markets, public schools and universities, and of course environmental threats.

Exhibit A of this contention is once again the content in the political cartoon featured earlier. Jeb Bush and Mitt Romney and so on have raised the issues of poverty, inequality, and middle-class income stagnation, thereby implying not only that the incumbent has failed to fix them, but also that they've got the ideas to do so. As I've stressed, thus far their idea is trickle down, which won't do it, and the electorate knows that.

If I'm right, we are thus ripe for a revealing and portentous debate in the run-up to the 2016 general election. President Obama ran and won twice by pointing to the fundamental disconnect and arguing that his policies would reconnect growth and prosperity. The data show very limited success but he gets a huge asterisk in the historical playbook. He took the helm when the economic ship was in the worst storm since the 1930s, and to his credit, he steadied it relatively quickly (of course, the Fed also played a key role). But before he could go much beyond stabilization, gridlock blocked his every move.

Who knows where the economy will be when people start paying attention to the next election, but chances are, and forecasts suggest, that it will look much like it does now, in early 2015, with a solid recovery underway that has still, after six years, not reached very far into the middle class. It is thus extremely unlikely that a successful candidate can argue, "steady as she goes." It is, as I've stressed, equally unlikely that a candidate can make a compelling argument for trickle down ideas—tax cuts for the wealthy, spending cuts for the poor, repealing Obamacare, obstructing the EPA, and maintaining the dysfunction.

So what's a candidate to do? Simple: *the only way to convincingly win the support of the American electorate in 2016 is to present a convincing reconnection agenda.*

Conclusion: Not All Reconnection Agendas are Created Equal

OK, I grant you that sounds like a self-serving setup—a bunch of chapters on this idea of a reconnection agenda, all leading up to the assertion that the next president will need such an agenda to get elected. But the fact that I believe this is the logic of today's politics does not mean I expect proposed reconnection platforms to mirror what you've read in these pages.

I obviously hope they do and believe they should. But some will and some won't.

I've already pointed out a litmus test—a growth-only agenda is inadequate—for judging if those who are new to this sort of thing are serious or are just temporarily borrowing ideas from Democratic HQ for the campaign. But there needs to be a litmus test for both sides, not just conservatives. What are the features of that reconnection agenda that might actually work?

Most importantly, the components of the agenda—the granular policies that form the glue of the reconnect—must target not just the secondary distribution of income, but the primary one as well. Let me explain.

I am virtually certain that the candidates who aspire to high office will run on some version of a middle-class tax cut. I don't love the idea, but I understand it and am sympathetic. A stroll through Chapter 2 could easily lead one to conclude that a tax cut would offset some of the impact of the inequality wedge that's diverted income growth from households in the bottom half of the income scale.

So what's not to love? First, as discussed in Chapter 8, we've got a long-term revenue shortfall, and one big reason is that tax policy is largely asymmetric; it is a ratchet that only goes down. Also, the actual middle class, as opposed to the imaginary one within which almost everyone thinks they reside, doesn't pay much in federal income taxes, so if you want to help them, you either have to cut the payroll tax, which has negative implications for Social Security's fiscal health, or extend the EITC much further up the income scale than even more moderate politics would allow.

But the bigger problem with this tax-cut-response to inequality is summarized by economist Larry Mishel: the problem isn't what the government takes out of your paycheck; it's what employers fail to put it.[265] We cannot fix a wage problem with tax policy. We can ameliorate it, and we should do so by ensuring the code remains progressive. But unless we get to the heart of the wage problem behind middle-class income stagnation, we'll find ourselves returning to the tax code every few years for another round of redistribution.

---

[265] http://www.nytimes.com/2015/02/23/opinion/even-better-than-a-tax-cut.html?_r=0

Good luck with that, by the way.

As I've stressed in these pages, the heart of the fundamental disconnect lies not in the tax code, but in the collapse of bargaining power—itself a function of the absence of full employment, persistent trade deficits, eroded labor standards, declining collective bargaining, and the shampoo cycle, to name a few factors—that used to enable workers to claim a legitimate share of the productivity growth they themselves were helping to produce.

These factors all erode what economists refer to as the "primary distribution of income," or market outcomes, as opposed to the "secondary," or after-tax, distribution. The causal factors behind wage inequality and stagnation largely play out in the primary distribution. Pressures from globalization, high unemployment, and booms and busts reduce the ability of middle-income workers to press for higher pay even as their firms' output, productivity, and profits are rising.

To be clear, that doesn't mean the tax code isn't messed up. It is, and it's part of the problem. There are no firm barriers between market outcomes and the secondary, post-tax distribution. In fact, there's convincing research that indicates that pre-tax executive compensation has risen to such ahistorical heights in part because it is taxed at such historically low levels.[266] Such exorbitant paychecks were less sought after when most of the marginal dollar was taxed away. So I stand solidly behind the ideas to

---

[266] http://eml.berkeley.edu/~saez/piketty-saez-stantchevaAEJ14.pdf

improve the secondary distribution stressed in Chapter 8, from a robust safety net (which we now see has important and positive implications for upward mobility) to a more progressive tax code. They are critical parts of the reconnection agenda.

But if that's all there is, then the agenda is insufficient. There is a critical theme to the underlying parts of the agenda I've tried to elevate in this book. The importance of full employment, and the monetary and fiscal policy involved; persistent trade deficits, and the role of dollar policy; the need for direct job creation and fair chance hiring practices; breaking the shampoo cycle; and so on—these ideas all strike at market outcomes. They purposely intervene in the allocation of growth prior to the knock-down, drag-out arguments we have about taxes and transfers.

That's intentional, because I believe it is both substantively and strategically mistaken to embrace the more typical center-left Democrat's view that, just as their right-wing counterparts say, market outcomes are sacred (though as a footnote above points out, the view is more accurately summarized as "they're only sacred when we say they're sacred"). In this paradigm, the difference between Ds and Rs is actually quite marginal: they both salute market outcomes, but Ds will redistribute some of the fruits of those outcomes to the least advantaged, while Rs will complain (with little to no evidence) that doing so worsens market outcomes in the next round.

So the litmus test for Ds is this: are you willing to go after market outcomes? To change the way wages, incomes, and wealth are distributed in the primary distribution? If not—if you're all about just waiting for taxes and transfers to do all the reconnecting—then your agenda is insufficient.

This is asking a lot from our politicians and policy makers. It's asking them and their staffs to become learned in the technical aspects of the policies espoused throughout. It's asking them to expose "government is broken; let's keep it that way" as the damaging, absolutely unsustainable tactic that it is. It's asking them to call out those who borrow reconnection themes solely for the election. And it's asking them to get out of their comfort zone that says, "we would never mess with markets!" and recognize the necessity of targeting both primary and secondary distributions.

That's a lot to ask, but if we want to see growth once again reach those who keep hearing about it as opposed to benefitting from it, I humbly submit that those are the right questions.

OK, end of political analysis—don't say I didn't warn you. Like any economist, for better or worse, I've thought about this problem in terms of demand and supply. I believe the electorate will demand a reconnection agenda. The risk, as I see it, is that there are lots of different such agendas that will be on offer, and informed consumers need to be able to separate the wheat from the chaff.

As this is a "living book"—one to which I'll feel free to add to and subtract from as events progress—stay tuned to my various outlets, especially my "On The Economy" blog,[267] for ongoing, play-by-play analysis of the evolving policy debate. I deeply appreciate the effort my readers have devoted to the reconnection agenda thus far, and believe me, I hesitate to ask for another few minutes of your attention. But democracy—the real, participatory version, the one where we recognize that we're in this together, whether we like it or not—requires such vigilance.

So, I'll see you online and anywhere else our paths might cross as we continue to track and promote the progress of the reconnection agenda.

---

[267] www.jaredbernsteinblog.com

Appendix A: Growth Without Prosperity Figures and Tables

FIGURE A1

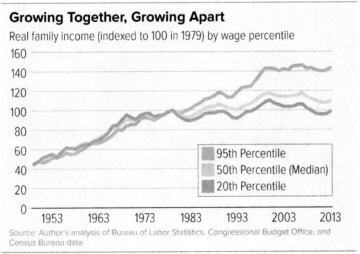

Growing Together, Growing Apart

Real family income (indexed to 100 in 1979) by wage percentile

- 95th Percentile
- 50th Percentile (Median)
- 20th Percentile

Source: Author's analysis of Bureau of Labor Statistics, Congressional Budget Office, and Census Bureau data.

THE RECONNECTION AGENDA | JARED BERNSTEIN

FIGURE A2

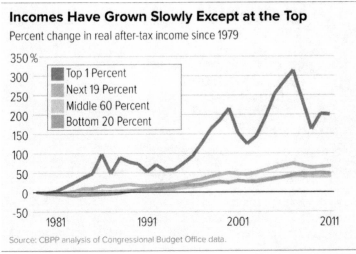

Incomes Have Grown Slowly Except at the Top

Percent change in real after-tax income since 1979

- Top 1 Percent
- Next 19 Percent
- Middle 60 Percent
- Bottom 20 Percent

Source: CBPP analysis of Congressional Budget Office data.

THE RECONNECTION AGENDA | JARED BERNSTEIN

Change in Income Shares by Quintile

Percentage point change between 1979 and 2011

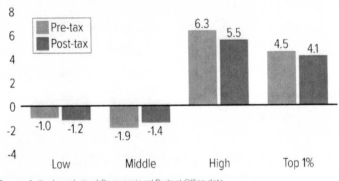

Source: Author's analysis of Congressional Budget Office data.

Real Annual Earnings

Percent of 1979 value in 2012 dollars

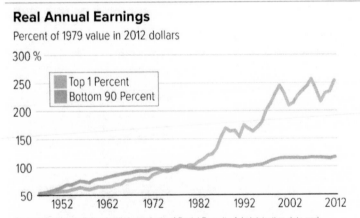

Source: Economic Policy Institute analysis of Social Security Administration data and Kopczuk, Saez, and Song, "Earnings Inequality and Mobility in the United States: Evidence from Social Security Data Since 1937," February 2010.

TABLE A1

Real Annual Earnings

	1947	1979	2012	Change, '47-'79	Change, '79-'12
Top 1 Percent	$131,072	$255,760	$648,541	95%	154%
Bottom 90 Percent	$14,392	$27,110	$31,741	88%	17%
Ratio	9.1	9.4	20.4		

Source: Economic Policy Institute and author's analysis of Social Security Administration data and Kopczuk, Saez, and Song, "Earnings Inequality and Mobility in the United States: Evidence from Social Security Data Since 1937," February 2010.

FIGURE A5

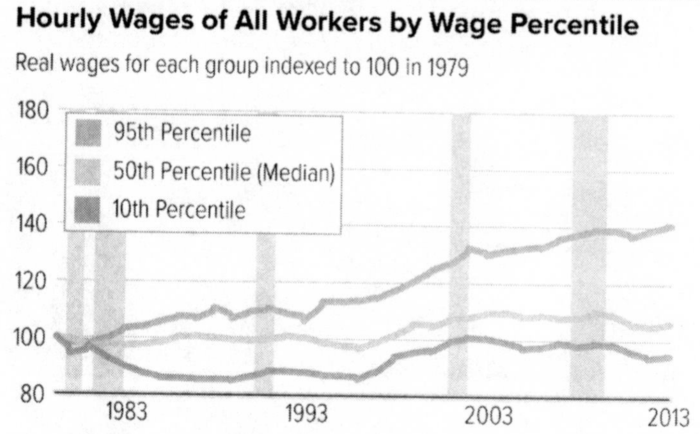
Hourly Wages of All Workers by Wage Percentile
Real wages for each group indexed to 100 in 1979
180
160
140
120
100
80
95th Percentile
50th Percentile (Median)
10th Percentile
1983
1993
2003
2013

Source: Economic Policy Institute analysis of Current Population Survey Outgoing Rotation Group microdata.

THE RECONNECTION AGENDA | JARED BERNSTEIN

Hourly Wages of Men by Wage Percentile

Real wages for each group indexed to 100 in 1979

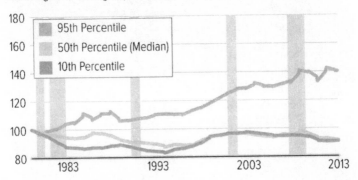

Source: Economic Policy Institute analysis of Current Population Survey Outgoing Rotation Group microdata.

Hourly Wages of Women by Wage Percentile

Real wages for each group indexed to 100 in 1979

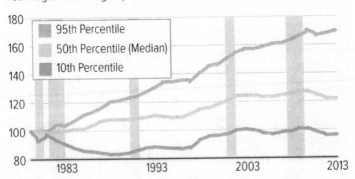

Source: Economic Policy Institute analysis of Current Population Survey Outgoing Rotation Group microdata.

The "Wedge" Between Growth and Productivity

Cumulative Percent Change Since 1948

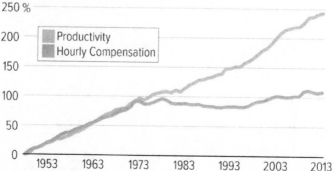

Note: Compensation is for blue-collar production workers and non-managers in services.
Source: Economic Policy Institute analysis of Bureau of Labor Statistics and Bureau of
Economic Analysis National Income and Product Accounts data.

Income Concentration at the Top Has Risen Sharply

Share of total before-tax income flowing to the highest income families
(including capital gains)

Source: Saez's analysis of IRS data.

Wealth Concentration at the Top Has Risen Sharply

Share of total wealth held by the wealthiest families

Legend:
- Top 1 Percent
- Top 0.5 Percent

Source: Saez and Zucman, "Wealth Inequality in the United States since 1913: Evidence from Capitalized Income Tax Data," October 2014.

Residential Segregation Has Increased

Proportion of families living in different neighborhood types, metropolitan areas with population > 500,000

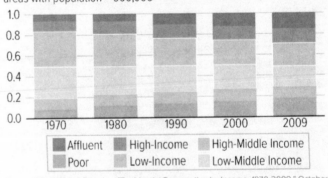

Legend:
- Affluent
- High-Income
- High-Middle Income
- Poor
- Low-Income
- Low-Middle Income

Source: Bischoff and Reardon, "Residential Segregation by Income, 1970-2009," October 2013.

Education Debt Has Increased for Most Americans

Ratio of mean education debt to mean income (for families with education debt) by net worth group

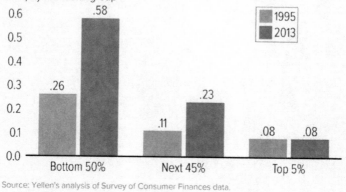

Source: Yellen's analysis of Survey of Consumer Finances data.

Spending on Enrichment Opportunities for Children

Average spending on books, computers, high-quality child care, summer camps, and other goods and experiences

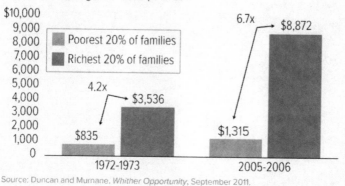

Source: Duncan and Murnane, *Whither Opportunity*, September 2011.

Mobility and the Middle Class

Commuting zones in which the middle class is larger have greater expected upward mobility for low-income children

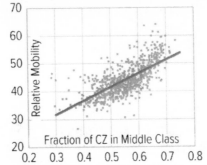

Source: Bradbury and Triest, "Inequality of Opportunity and Aggregate Economic Performance," October 2014.

Union Strength and Inequality Negatively Correlated

Share of workers represented by a union and share of income going to the top 10 percent

Source: Economic Policy Institute and author's analysis of Historical Statistics of the United States, unionstats.com, Piketty and Saez 2003, and The World Top Incomes Database.

The Trade Deficit and Manufacturing Compensation

Higher trade deficits as a percent of GDP (left axis) are associated with stagnant earnings for blue-collar workers in manufacturing (right axis)

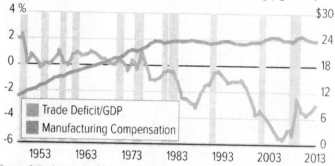

Source: Author's analysis of Bureau of Labor Statistics and Bureau of Economic Analysis National Income and Product Accounts data.

Wages and Unemployment

Median real hourly wage effects of doubling the unemployment rate

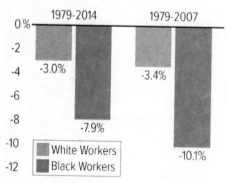

Source: Wilson, "The Impact of Full Employment on African American Employment and Wages," March 2015.

Appendix B: Figures from *Explaining the Housing Bubble* by Adam Levitin and Susan Wachter

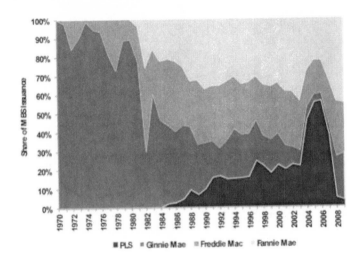

PLS ■ Ginnie Mae ■ Freddie Mac ■ Fannie Mae

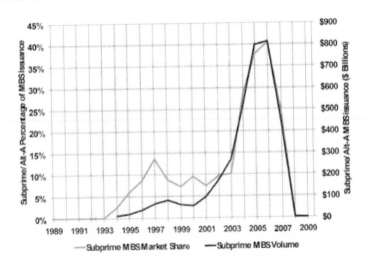

Subprime MBS Market Share ———Subprime MBS Volume

FIGURE B3

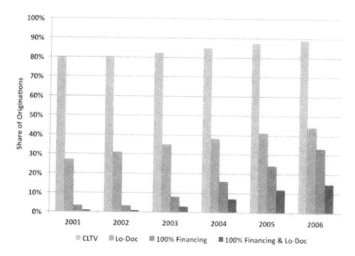

FIGURE B4

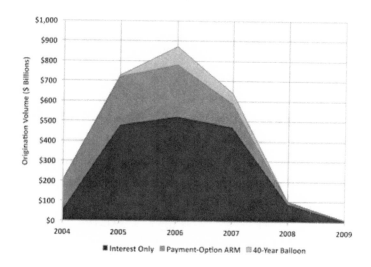

Appendix C: Summary of Policy Recommendations

Throughout *The Reconnection Agenda* I make numerous policy recommendations intended to promote full employment, reduce the likelihood and likely severity of future recessions, boost the bargaining power of middle- and low-wage workers, help increase our manufacturers' competitiveness, break the bubble/bust cycle, and ultimately reconnect growth and broadly shared prosperity. In this appendix, I collect these ideas and note where they appear in the text.

Improving fiscal and monetary policy:

- Recognize the limits of the "NAIRU" or "FEUR" (the lowest unemployment rate consistent with stable inflation) as a guidepost (Chapter 3 and Chapter 4).

- Use broader measures to assess labor market slack, including "wage targeting" (Chapter 3 and Chapter 4).

- Consider "risk asymmetries" in the Fed's dual mandate, as full employment is a more pressing goal than price stability (Chapter 3 and Chapter 4).

- Use quantitative triggers to activate (and deactivate) countercyclical fiscal policies (Chapter 4).

- Recognize that when monetary policy is stuck at zero, fiscal policy is more important and more effective (Chapter 4).

- Use fiscal policy to invest in public infrastructure, including green infrastructure (Chapter 4 and Chapter 9).

- Recognize that revenues higher than historical averages will likely be required to meet the challenges of changing demographics, environmental concerns, debt service, and infrastructure/public goods (Chapter 8).

- Repeal "step-up basis," a tax break for wealthy inheritors (Chapter 8).

- Reduce the rate at which high-income taxpayers can take deductions (Chapter 8).

- Impose a small excise tax on financial market transactions (Chapter 8).

- Increase IRS funding to help close the "tax gap," or the difference between what's owed and what's paid (Chapter 8).

Taking action against countries that manage their currencies to subsidize exports and tax imports (Chapter 5):

- tax their exports to us,

- revoke their trade privileges,

- and/or allow for reciprocal currency interventions.

Protecting the safety net, strengthening labor standards, and expanding access to economic opportunities in both the short- and long-run:

- Reintroduce subsidized jobs programs for those facing steep labor market barriers (Chapter 6 and Chapter 9).

- Enact fair chance hiring practices, including "ban the box," and reform the criminal justice system (Chapter 6, Chapter 8, and Chapter 9).

- Support sectoral training, apprenticeships, and earn-while-you-learn programs (Chapter 6 and Chapter 9).

- Make key provisions of the Earned Income Tax Credit permanent and expand the credit for low-income, childless workers (Chapter 8).

- Implement universal pre-K, with subsidies that phase out as incomes rise (Chapter 8).

- Raise the overtime salary threshold (beneath which all workers get overtime pay) from $455/week to $970/week and index it to inflation (Chapter 8).

- Add wage and hour inspectors at the Dept. of Labor to push back on wage theft and other labor law violations (Chapter 8).

- Level the playing field for union elections to bolster collective bargaining (Chapter 8).

- Increase the national minimum wage to $12/hour by 2020, as per a new Senate plan (Chapter 9).

- Facilitate the spread of "worksharing," an alternative to Unemployment Insurance that minimizes layoffs (Chapter 9).

- Promote policies to help balance work and family, including paid sick leave, child care assistance for low- and middle-income parents, worker-centered scheduling, and more (Chapter 9).

- At the state level, avoid anti-union, so-called "right-to-work" laws and Kansas-style trickle down tax cuts (Chapter 9).

Providing better oversight of financial markets (Chapter 7):

- mandate adequate capital buffers,

- enforce a strong Volcker Rule against proprietary trading in FDIC-insured banks,

- strengthen the Consumer Financial Protection Bureau,

- and encourage "macro-prudential" regulation by the Federal Reserve (not to be conflated with monetary policy).

About the Author

Jared Bernstein has been a Senior Fellow at the Center on Budget and Policy Priorities since May 2011. From 2009 to 2011, Bernstein was the Chief Economist to Vice President Joe Biden and a member of President Obama's economics team. In addition to hosting *On The Economy* at jaredbernsteinblog.com, Bernstein has written several books and is a regular contributor to the *Washington Post* and the *New York Times*. He is a commentator on MSNBC and CNBC and tweets often at @econjared.

FEB 1 0 2023

CPSIA information can be obtained at www.ICGtesting.com
Printed in the USA
LVOW11s2207300316

481459LV00001B/37/P

9 781511 769389